Religious and Ethnic Communities
in
Later Roman Palestine

edited by

Hayim Lapin

University Press of Maryland

LIBRARY OF CONGRESS CATALOGING-IN-PUBLICATION

Religious and ethnic communities in later Roman Palestine / edited by
  Hayim Lapin
      p. cm. — (Studies and texts in Jewish history and culture ; 5)
    Includes bibliographical references and index.
    ISBN 1-883053-31-5
      1. Palestine—History—70-638.   2. Palestine—Religion—
    History—To 1500.   3. Palestine—Antiquities.   4. Judaism—
    History—Talmudic period, 10-425.   5. Christianity—Palestine—
    History—To 1500.
    I. Lapin, Hayim.   II. Series.
    DS123.5.R45 1998
    956.94'02—dc21   98-29098
                                                                    CIP

STUDIES AND TEXTS

IN

JEWISH HISTORY AND CULTURE

The Joseph and Rebecca Meyerhoff Center
for Jewish Studies
University of Maryland

V

General Editor: Bernard D. Cooperman

CONTENTS

PREFACE

ABBREVIATIONS

IV. PALESTINIAN CONTROVERSIES AND
THEIR LITERARY CONTEXT

INDEX

PREFACE

The essays published in this volume were originally presented as part of a symposium on "Religious and Ethnic Communities in Later Roman Palestine," held at the University of Maryland, College Park, on March 10, 1996. That conference was sponsored by the Joseph and Rebecca Meyerhoff Center for Jewish Studies and the Department of Classics at the University, without whose support neither the conference nor the present volume would have been possible. Thanks are also due to Professors Bernard D. Cooperman (general editor of the Studies and Texts series and former Director of the Meyerhoff Center), Marsha Rozenblit (Director of the Center in 1995–96), and James F. Harris (then Chair of the Department of History, now Dean of the College of Arts and Humanities) for their encouragement. Much of the editing was done while I was a recipient of an Iwry Summer Fellowship from the Meyerhoff Center (Summer 1996), a Memorial Foundation for Jewish Culture Fellowship (1996–7), and an NEH Fellowship at the Albright Institute for Archaeological Research in Jerusalem (1996–1997).

The work of editing this volume has given me the opportunity to engage with, and to learn much from, the work of the contributors to this volume. This, by itself, has made the project worth doing, and each of them has my thanks. In addition, a version of the introduction was presented to the Constructs group at the Society of Biblical Literature Annual Meeting (1997), and I am grateful for the criticism and comments that that session afforded, particularly from B. Malina and J. Flanagan. Others who read versions of that essay include G. W. Bowersock, D. Boyarin, J. F. Brooks, A. Eckstein, K. G. Holum, D. Krueger, S. Rubenstein, and D. Satran. These readers greatly improved my contribution; errors that remain are, of course, my own. Finally, Maxine Grossman took time out of her own busy schedule of writing and teaching to become, in many respects, a partner to this project.

ABBREVIATIONS

ADAJ	*Annual of the Department of Antiquities of Jordan*
AJA	*American Journal of Archaeology*
ANRW	*Aufstieg und Niedergang der römischen Welt.* Ed. H. Temporini, W. Haase. Berlin: W. de Gruyter, 1972–.
BA	*Biblical Archaeologist*
BAR	*Biblical Archaeology Review*
BASOR	*Bulletin of the American Schools of Oriental Research*
CBQ	*Catholic Biblical Quarterly*
CCSL	*Corpus Christianorum: Series Latina.* Turnhout: Brepols, 1953–.
CIJ	J. B. Frey. *Corpus inscriptionum iudaicarum.* Paris, 1936, 1952.
CRAI	*Compte rendus de l'Académie des inscriptions et belles-lettres*
CSCO	*Corpus scriptorum christianorum orientalum.* Louvain, 1903–.
CSEL	*Corpus scriptorum ecclesiasticorum latinorum.* Vienna, 1866–.
CSHB	*Corpus scriptorum historiae byzantinae.* Ed. W. Dindorf. Bonn: 1828–97.
DaM	*Damaszener Mitteillungen*
DJD	*Discoveries in the Judaean Desert.* Oxford: Clarendon, 1955–.
DOP	*Dumbarton Oaks Papers*
EI	*Eretz Israel*
EJ	*Encyclopaedia Judaica.* Ed. C. Roth. Jerusalem: Keter, 1972.

ESI	*Excavations and Surveys in Israel*
GCS	*Griechischen christlichen Schriftsteller.* Berlin: Akademie Verlag, 1897–.
HA	*Ḥadashot Arkheologiyot*
HTR	*Harvard Theological Review*
IEJ	*Israel Exploration Journal*
INJ	*Israel Numismatic Journal*
JE	*Jewish Encyclopaedia.* Ed. I Singer, C. Adler. New York: Funk and Wagnalls, 1901–6.
JJS	*Journal of Jewish Studies*
JQR	*Jewish Quarterly Review*
JRS	*Journal of Roman Studies*
JSJ	*Journal for the Study of Judaism in the Persian, Hellenistic and Roman Period*
JSQ	*Jewish Studies Quarterly*
JTS	*Journal of Theological Studies*
Leš	*Lešonénu*
LSJM	Liddell, H. G. and Scott, R. eds. *A Greek English Lexicon.* Rev. ed. with supplement, H. S. Jones, R. McKenzie. Oxford: Clarendon, 1968.
MDAIR	*Mitteilungen des deutschen archäologischen Instituts (Röm. Abt.)*
NEAEHL	*New Encyclopedia of Archaeological Excavations in the Holy Land.* Ed. E. Stern. Jerusalem: IES and Carta, 1993.
NTS	*New Testament Studies*
ODB	*Oxford Dictionary of Byzantium.* Ed. A. P. Kazhdan, *et alii.* New York: Oxford University Press, 1991.
PEQ	*Palestine Exploration Quarterly*
PG	*Patrologia graeca.* Ed. J. Migne. Paris, 1857–66.
PL	*Patrologia latina.* Ed. J. Migne. Paris, 1878–90.
QDAP	*Quarterly of the Department of Antiquities of Palestine*

RB	*Revue biblique*
SCI	*Scripta classica israelica*
USQR	*Union Seminary Quarterly Review*
VigChr	*Vigiliae christianae*
VT	*Vetus Testamentum*
ZAW	*Zeitschrift für die alttestamentliche Wissenschaft*
ZDMG	*Zeitschrift der deutschen morganländischen Gesellschaft*
ZKG	*Zeitschrift für Kirchengeschichte*

INTRODUCTION:
LOCATING ETHNICITY AND RELIGIOUS COMMUNITY IN LATER ROMAN PALESTINE

Hayim Lapin

University of Maryland

BY ACCIDENTS OF HISTORY, ancient and modern, we know a great deal about Palestine in antiquity. Because it is here that the rabbinic movement first emerged and flourished, the literary remains of this movement have much to say about Palestine, its history, and its peoples. Because it is here that the historical Jesus lived and worked, and here that the bulk of the Hebrew biblical (Old Testament) tradition is centered, Palestine played an important role in the imagination of late antique Christians, including the large numbers who came on pilgrimage or who immigrated to Palestine.[1] Because of latter day Christian fascination with the Holy Land and because of Jewish, Zionist, Israeli, and now Palestinian, interests in a usable national past, coupled with modern developments in "Orientalism," archaeology, and historiography, Palestine as a region is exceptionally well surveyed and excavated, and its populations well studied (or at least its Jewish and Christian populations; its "pagan" and post-Hasmonaean Samaritan populations are rather less so). The resulting body of material is deeply problematic—arising, for example, out of ancient communal conflicts or chauvinisms for which we tend to have only one side of an argument, or gathered and interpreted in a way that is frequently inseparable from contemporary questions of identity—but unquestionably rich. From

---

[1] R. L. Wilken, *The Land Called Holy: Palestine in Christian History and Thought* (New Haven: Yale, 1992).

1

the point of view of the study of religion or ethnicity, Palestine's riches are particularly attractive in that they can be exploited to uncover diversity and change, a characteristic utilized in one way or another by all the essays in this volume.

All of the following papers address, in their different ways, the question of religious and ethnic communities in Palestine between the second and seventh century. G. W. Bowersock's essay served as the keynote address of the conference on which this volume is based, and it plays the same important role here. Placing Palestine within a larger geographical and chronological context (the Near East between the second and the seventh century), Bowersock pays particular attention to the ways that Palestinian Jews adapted themselves to the norms of Graeco-Roman culture, while retaining an ethnic identity as Jews. At the same time, by stressing the specifically near eastern context, Bowersock's analysis emphasizes the disjuncture between the internal historical "rhythms" (p. 33) of Palestine (and presumably the Near East more broadly), and those of the rest of the Graeco-Roman world.

Leah Di Segni, Steven Fine, Jodi Magness and Gideon Avni, and Anthony Saldarini between them study differing aspects of the history of Palestine's religious and ethnic communities. Di Segni's essay is a contribution to the history of the Samaritans in Palestine—a major gap in studies of the history of late antique Palestine. After pointing out some of the difficulties of writing the history of Samaritans (and some of the presuppositions of scholars who write that history), Di Segni addresses in particular the problem of what is generally seen as a Samaritan revolt of 484 C.E., which, against the more general tendency, she treats as an episode of localized rioting rather than a full-fledged revolt. (Note that both Holum and Bowersock address the question of Samaritan revolts as well, and all three have rather different views.)

In his paper on "chancel" screens in Palestinian synagogues, Steven Fine contributes to the history of late antique synagogue architecture and its relationship to that of churches. The discussion is based on a genizah text that Fine understands as referring to reed mats serving as a partition for the *bêmâ*. Fine argues that the provenience of the text is

Palestine and that the partition is the functional equivalent of the screens or screen posts discovered in the remains of late antique synagogues and not best viewed as an echo of the Jerusalem temple *sôrēg*, and he attempts to locate the use of these screens in synagogues (a borrowing from ecclesiastical architecture) in the sanctity of the Torah scroll and all things connected with it.

The discussion by Jodi Magness and Gidon Avni of the lamps from burial caves near Beth Guvrin (Eleutheropolis) might have been grouped, on the basis of the location of the caves, with the essays in this volume dealing with urban environment. However, their own comparison of the burial practices with those of the village site of Beth Shearim (whatever else might account for the extensive necropolis there), and their focus on the material evidence that might reveal the traces of Christianization, suggest placement in a discussion of religious or ethnic community more broadly. On the basis of their correlation of the typological and chronological analyses of the pottery lamps from the burial caves with the incidence of "Jewish" or "Christian" symbols, the authors suggest a transition in the use of the caves from Jewish to Christian, a chronological framework in which this may have taken place, and some questions about the nature of this transition that are either left unanswered or raised more acutely by their analysis.

Anthony Saldarini's paper is the only essay in this volume that explicitly addresses definitions of ethnicity and community. Saldarini provides a fairly extensive discussion of both "primordialist" and "instrumentalist" analyses of ethnicity, and of the Roman and Palestinian setting for understanding the development of Jewish, Christian, and "Jewish Christian" groups, beginning in the first century. In addition, Saldarini proposes "a context for the instructional, apologetic, and polemical literature of early Jews and Christians in Israel and its neighborhood" (p. 142) by first examining "Jewish" documents from Nahal Hever and Wadi Murabba'at for the evidence these may shed on levels of interactions between Jews and others in Roman Palestine. Finally, Saldarini examines the Mishnah, the Gospel of Matthew, and the so-called "Ascents of James" portion of the Pseudo-Clementine *Recogni-*

tions as examples of Palestinian Jewish and "Jewish Christian" reformist movements against this context.

The papers of Holum, Rutgers, Tsafrir, and Weiss all deal with specifically urban settings although in different ways and asking different questions. Kenneth Holum examines the fate of Caesarea's Jewish and Samaritan populations ("proper" ethnic communities in Holum's terms, citing F. Barth). Holum explores the evidence for economic and social life of these communities both in the city proper and in its *territorium*, with attention to structures of patronage and protection that facilitated communal life. Finally Holum discusses the connection between the suppression of ethnic minorities and the demographic and economic decline of the city in late antiquity, with special attention to the Samaritan population (although he argues that much the same may have been the case for Jews).

Defining "Jewishness" at Sepphoris is the subject of the paper by Leonard Rutgers. Rutgers addresses this question through an examination of the material remains of a single house at Sepphoris, and the fill in the cisterns and baths deemed ritual baths in that house. Rutgers argues that the architecture and material culture of this particular house are consistent with that of contemporaneous Jerusalemite houses. However, rather than treating this as evidence of an imported Judaean culture he focuses instead on evidence that tends to locate this Sepphorian material culture in a wider regional context, and on the notion, borrowed from E. P. Sanders, of a "Common Judaism"—the conventional practices of the bulk of the population identified as Jewish—as a way of describing (and describing change in) the life of Jews in later Roman Palestine.

Yoram Tsafrir's paper discusses the treatment of pagan cult places in the process of the Christianization of Palestine and its general environs. In the first part of his paper, Tsafrir reviews the varieties of treatment, from the demolition of buildings, to their appropriation for specifically Christian purposes (usually after an extended time of disuse), to the reuse for secular uses of parts of existing temples. The second part describes the results of excavation of five cult sites at

Scythopolis. In at least one of these cases, according to the author, the desecration of the temple can be dated to approximately 400 C.E.. This is to be connected to the legal prohibitions on pagan cult worship at the end of the fourth century under Theodosius I, and confirms, for Tsafrir, that it is precisely then, and in response to imperial policy, that formal pagan practices came to an end in Scythopolis (and elsewhere).

Zeev Weiss discusses aspects of the public architecture of Tiberias and Sepphoris, which he treats as "Jewish cities," in order to explore the way in which Palestinian Jews adapted themselves to the wider Graeco-Roman culture. The presence of not only a standardized street plan but also baths, theaters, and an attested stadium, as well as mosaics utilizing standard mythological motifs, in cities where Jews made up the bulk of the population, suggests, Weiss argues, that it is likely to have been Jews who paid for and used these buildings. At the same time Weiss suggests some features of public urban culture in these two cities, notably the absence of statuary and of temples, that may mark these two "Jewish" cities out as distinctive.

Finally, Christine Hayes's contribution is a cautionary tale for the study of the religion and ethnicity of Jews in Roman Palestine: stories involving mînîm (or ṣĕdôqîm, translated by Hayes as "Sadducees") or Romans, and featuring Palestinian rabbis, may tell us fairly little about Palestine. Hayes's discussion is based on a passage of the Babylonian Talmud, and to the extent that she allows herself to comment specifically on the social context of the passage she examines, she locates that in Mesopotamia as well. Indeed, the burden of Hayes's essay is to argue that such stories may not tell us anything about the relationship of rabbis with non-rabbinic interlocutors or opponents at all, but rather serve as a complex and fraught framework through which rabbis might present themselves to themselves. Moreover, in both the body of her paper and in her extensive notes Hayes makes clear how much the transmission history of the materials incorporated into the Babli and the literary and redactional tendencies of that corpus as a whole have shaped what appear to be historiographical narratives. This is a lesson worth remembering, inasmuch as it may well undermine much of the historiographical enterprise for late antique Jewry, particularly for those of us who make use of Rabbinic sources.

Given the array of peoples and religions, and the extent and variability of change, in the region of Palestine from the first or second century to the seventh, one is inclined to attempt to be comprehensive in introducing a volume such as this. Yet, even were I capable of such encyclopedic virtuosity, the essays that follow demonstrate that the various disciplines and subdisciplines that contribute to a richer understanding of the social and cultural history of Palestine are themselves engaged in rethinking their projects. Instead, I will attempt to draw attention to the question of the study of religion and ethnicity in Palestine more generally.[2]

By way of introduction, let me begin by discussing the second part of the title, "later Roman Palestine," which sets the geographical and chronological range of this volume. The expression is deceptively simple. The territorial extent and regional subdivisions of "Palestine" (a term originally attaching, presumably, to the Philistine-inhabited coastal area) shifted repeatedly over the period covered by the following essays (roughly the late first—when *Palaestina* was not yet officially part of the territorial name—to the seventh century C.E.).[3] "Later Roman" is no less vexing. It is not only that—as Bowersock points out—the conventional terms (Roman, Byzantine, late antique) have referents that may or may not be applicable to Palestine (Bowersock, for instance, argues that they are not), but also that there is no agreement about which term to use or how one uses it. Does the "Byzantine" period begin, for example, with the reign of Constantine in the East (still the common dating among historians and archaeologists of Palestine), or in 363 (see Rutgers below,

---

[2]   See also the contribution of A. J. Saldarini in this volume, and the literature cited there.

[3]   See the brief discussion by Y. Tsafrir, "Boundaries and Geographical Limits," in Y. Tsafrir, L. Di Segni, J. Green, eds. *Tabula Imperii Romani: Iudaea-Palaestina* (Jerusalem: Israel Academy of Arts and Sciences, 1994), 13–19.

following D. Groh[4]), or later still (following Magness[5])? And in making use of such a label are we referring to an archaeological phase or to a political, social, religious, or institutional shift of some kind that separates the new "Byzantine" society from what came before? Moreover, using a unitary periodization implies that all the communities of "later Roman Palestine" experienced history at the same "pace" and in the same way. The reign of Constantine, to take one example, could be celebrated by Eusebius in Caesarea as the proper fulfillment of Christian cosmology.[6] No doubt, the vast majority of non-Christians in Palestine saw things differently.

Ultimately, the expression "later Roman Palestine" was chosen precisely because it does open these ambiguities, and allows a somewhat more inclusive range of topics. To my own mind, "later Roman" emphasizes continuities of institutionalized imperial authority—whether that was centralized in Rome or Constantinople—operating in the region throughout the period under discussion, while acknowledging long term change and, occasionally, upheaval. Bowersock asserts that "[t]he rhythms of Palestine were clearly not those of the rest of the

---

[4] D. E. Groh, "Jews and Christians in Late Roman Palestine: Towards a New Chronology," *BA* 51 (1988), 83–84; see also: E. M. Meyers, "The Byzantine Towns of the Galilee," in R. H. Hohlfelder, ed., *City, Town, and Countryside in the Early Byzantine Period*, (East European Monographs no. 120: Boulder: Columbia University Press, 1982), 117–19, 131. The burden of Groh's essay is to stress local, rather than imperial and political, criteria for chronology (previous histories "did not prepare us to see how little provincials cared or were affected by the crosscurrents of Mediterranean power," Groh, "New Chronology," 81). In practice, however, even the choice of 363 (because of an earthquake attributed to that year), is not without consideration of such "crosscurrents": "This date takes in sites abandoned, sites affected by the Gallus revolt, sites affected (if any) by Julian's failure in 361 to 363 to rebuild the Temple in Jerusalem, as well as sites damaged by the earthquake of 363" (p. 84).

[5] J. Magness, *Jerusalem Ceramic Chronology circa 200-800 C.E.* (Sheffield: Sheffield Academic Press, 1993).

[6] Eus. *Oratio de laudibus Constantini* 5.1–4.

Graeco-Roman world,"[7] choosing instead to locate those rhythms in the Near East. While there are certainly reasons to stress the peculiarities of Palestine and of its Jewish population in antiquity as well as Palestine's embeddedness in the ancient Near East, my own preference would be to emphasize the connectedness of Palestine with the wider Graeco-Roman world. One might cite as examples patterns of urbanization (which provided the locus for the development of both Christianity and the Rabbinic movement in Palestine) and the pressures upon the bouleutic class; a *koinē* of language (Greek) and of architectural and artistic conventions that is important even in the development of "native" or "provincial" culture (e.g., the building of synagogues); and, as I shall argue below, the importance of imperial power for creating ethnic and religious identity. Indeed, constructing a history of Palestine is unthinkable without viewing it also as a constituent part of that Graeco-Roman world. In the history of Palestine, and particularly in the history of its rabbinic Jews, we have a modality of Roman provincial culture that is worth studying as such.

The first part of the title, "religious and ethnic communities," will serve as the primary focus for the remainder of this introduction. Taking as my point of departure an example of Jewish "magic" that strikingly calls into question what is "Jewish" and what is "non-Jewish," I wish to propose a view of ethnicity and of religious adherence that— even when communities make exclusive claims on their members— recognizes the embeddedness of communities, and, indeed the very construction of their identities, in a wider world. What this means is that we will have to take seriously both the ways in which the religious and ethnic communities remain in contact with and influenced by each other and the ways that they maintain boundaries between themselves and other groups. An essential aspect of this "embeddedness," and one that is rather easily taken for granted precisely because of its ubiquitousness, is the role of power, or its relative absence, in shaping communities and identity.

---

[7]   Below, p. 33.

I begin, then, with the following prayer in Greek from a magical handbook, probably from Palestine in late antiquity.[8]

I reverence you, O East-rising Helios, good sailor, guardian of trust, apex (?), of good faith,[9] who of old was the setter of the mighty[10] wheel, holy orderer, ruler of the pole,[11] lord, well-lighting guide (?),[12] master (*tyrannos*), soldier.[13]

Invocations of the sun god are quite common in magical texts from late antiquity.[14] Nor are the terminology or conceptualizations for Helios in this particular passage exceptional.[15] Moreover, this short invocation,

---

[8] M. Margaliot, ed., *Sepher Ha-Razim* (Jerusalem: American Academy of Jewish Research, 1966), 4.61–63 (hereafter *SHR*; citations are to "firmament" and line number). Margaliot thanks Morton Smith for the assistance with the reconstruction; Smith himself published an English translation of the text in M. Smith, "Helios in Palestine," *Eretz Israel* [*Orlinsky Volume*] 16 (1982), 210* (reprinted in *idem, Studies in the Cult of Yahweh,* ed. S. J. D. Cohen [*Religions in the Greco Roman World* 130: Leiden: Brill, 1996], 1, 261) that presupposes some alternative readings; see also M. A. Morgan, *Sepher Ha-Razim* (*Texts and Translations* 25: Chico: Scholars Press, 1983), 71, n. 21 who presents still a third transcription. The alternative readings given in the following notes take all three versions into account, but are not intended to reflect an exhaustive treatment. See also P. S. Alexander, "Incantations and Books of Magic," in E. Schürer, *The History of the Jewish People in the Age of Jesus Christ,* rev. ed. G. Vermes, *et al.* (Edinburgh: T. and T. Clark, 1973–87), 3, 347–49.

[9] *Eupistos*; alternatively: *hypsistos,* "Most High."

[10] *Obrimos*; alternatively: *ouranios*: "heavenly."

[11] *Polokratōr.* Margaliot, *SHR,* p. 12, suggests *polypraktōr* (which he translates "engaged in many things") as an alternative. Given the preserved Hebrew consonantal text (*pyly pᵓnṭwr,* see variants at *SHR,* p. 138: *pyly pntwr, plyps plykntws*), the reading is far from secure.

[12] *Pompos euphōtos* (?).

[13] *Stratiōtēs.* Margaliot had read *astrothētēs*; the Hebrew text reads: *ᵓsṭrṭywṭws,* which favors the former.

[14] See, e.g., *PGM* I 195–222, IV 436–61 (with parallels elsewhere: see *PGM,* vol. 2, 239), 639–56, 1169–226; XIII 254–59.

[15] For instance, the image of the Sun as mariner, perhaps an appropriation of

to be said upon the appearance of the god, neatly corresponds to the
broader magical technology for handling divine visions.[16] The adept
undergoes purification (*SHR* 4.42–47) and adjures the angels to reveal
knowledge (4.47–57). Immediately, the god appears with thunder and a
flash of light (4.58–60), at which point the adept is to fall prostrate and
utter the above-quoted lines (4.60–63), followed by an appeal for revelation (4.63–65). The adept may then arise and ask questions (4.66–67),
after which the god is to be released (4.68–72).

What is exceptional is that this text is transcribed in Hebrew characters in *Sēper hā-rāzîm*, a Hebrew text that places magical "recipes" in
the context of an organized scheme of the seven firmaments or heavens
and the angels who reside there, culminating in the seventh heaven
(*SHR* 7), with biblicizing praise of the one God who rules all the world.
Admittedly, the Greek text is reconstructed from a string of text whose
medieval manuscript tradition is quite garbled.[17] Yet at least the broad
outlines appear secure enough that, even if individual expressions must
at best be guessed at, we have here a Greek prayer to a Greek god incorporated into a Jewish magic book. Moreover, this Greek invocation of
Helios cited in a ritual "to see the sun at night" (*SHR* 4.43) fits the
context too well to presuppose that the composer of the text did not
know its meaning or import. The same is true of a similarly reconstructed Greek text calling upon Lord Bouel (1.232–5), a divine being
with a Hebrew or Aramaic name (*bwʾl*) who is the chief officer of one of
the camps of angels in the first heaven (1.9, 209, 228–29).

Egyptian Re mythology (see, e.g., *PGM* I 346, IV 993–94), and the use of *tyrannos*
(*PGM* XIII 605), "ruler of the pole" (*polokratōr*) (*PGM* IV 676–77), or "apex (?)" or
"head man" (*koruphaios*) (see *LSJM*, *s.v.*, II. 3, as an epithet of Zeus) as descriptions
of gods all have parallels elsewhere.

[16]   See R. Lesses, "Speaking with Angels: Jewish and Greco-Egyptian Revelatory
Adjurations," *HTR* 89 (1996), 41–60; for the basic rubric cf. *PGM* XIII 1–343
(which does not include a release of the god).

[17]   See variants at *SHR*, p. 138.

Shortly before the invocation of Helios, within the same ritual, comes the following prayer demonstrating skillful use of Scripture in Hebrew (*SHR* 4.47–57):

> I adjure you, O angels who fly in the air of the firmament, by the one who sees and is not seen, by the king who reveals all secrets and sees all hidden things; by the god who knows what is in the darkness—and he overturns the darkness of death into morning, and he illuminates the night as day (cf. Amos 5:8), and all hidden things are revealed before him like the Sun, and nothing is too great[18] for him (Jer. 32:17), in the name of the holy king who travels on the wings of the wind (Ps. 104:3) … that I may see the Sun in its glory … and let none of the secrets be too great for me …, and that he may speak to me as a man speaks to his fellow (Ex. 33:11)….

What is of note here is not merely knowledge of passages from the Hebrew Bible. This passage also demonstrates a clever facility with Scripture and its implications. In referring to God as one who "overturns the darkness of death into morning and … illuminates the night as day" our author pointedly inverts the words of Amos 5:8, which depict Yahweh in his most threatening aspect, as one "who overturns morning into darkness of death and darkens day into night." "Nothing is too great for him" is a clear echo of Jeremiah 32:17, where such power is attributed to Yahweh as creator of Heaven and Earth (see also 32:27 and Gen. 18:14). The phrase recurs in the first person indicating the adept's own elevation as a result of the ritual, just as the allusion to Exodus 33:11 puts the ritual actor on the same level as Moses who spoke to Yahweh "mouth to mouth … in a vision and not in riddles, and he gazes upon the form of Yahweh" (Num. 12:8), and than whom, according to Deuteronomy 34:11, no prophet was greater.

The author makes strong claims for the adjuration, but the techniques of reading and of textual play are familiar from Hebrew and Aramaic Palestinian literature from late antiquity, and the source used,

---

[18] Perhaps, following the Septuagint (Jer. 39:17 [LXX]), we should translate "nothing is hidden from you," a reading that may also be presupposed in the citation of the verse in *Gen. Rab.* 9:3 (ed. Theodor, Albeck, pp. 68–69). See also *Tg. Onq.* and *Ps. J.* to Gen. 18:14.

the Hebrew Bible, marks the context of this passage as characteristically "Jewish." Thus within the depiction of one ritual we have elements that—had they appeared in another context—might have been construed simply as "Jewish," and others that might have been conventionally seen simply as a Graeco-Roman "pagan" magical ritual for inducing a vision of Helios. As a result, any attempt to locate *Sēper hā-rāzîm* within the religious, ethnic or cultural world of Palestine in late antiquity will have to struggle with the question of how, in this case, we identify what is Jewish or "pagan" at all.

In effect, there are two strategies for addressing questions of religious, cultural or ethnic differentiation or connection. One can focus on known communities, attempt to identify them both in their own terms and as contemporary outsiders might have seen them, and try to uncover the essential unities that link various communities that share the same name. Alternatively, and this is the view that I would like to propose here, one can treat ethnicity, religion, and community as cultural constructs that are constantly being redefined.

On the first view, which takes religious and ethnic communities as essentially knowable, problematic examples such as the individual or community presupposed by *Sēper hā-rāzîm* are then conceptualized as "syncretism," a kind of epiphenomenal mixing together of "pure" elements from heterogeneous sources. The new syncretism either becomes, over time, its own coherent community and tradition (this is a common description, for instance, of the rise of gentile Christianity), or remains at the margins (as does "magic" almost by definition, since religious practices taking place outside of recognized and dominant religious institutional frameworks are frequently labelled "magical"). This has generally been the approach taken by historians of religious and ethnic communities in the ancient world—especially those studying Judaism, Christianity, and Palestine. Its greatest utility is in focusing attention on the history and continuity of existing communities under changing historical circumstances. Yet it is these same circumstances that also call easy identifications of ethnic or religious communities into question.

Clearly, there were ethnic groups in imperial and late antique Palestine: Jews and Samaritans have continued as self-identified communities down to the present. Clearly, too, there were religious groups including, again, Jews and Samaritans, but also including Christians and the practitioners of a variety of "pagan" cults both native or local and imported. At least some of these groups produced literary and epigraphic remains that project an explicit communal identity.[19] At the same time, the period covered by the essays in this volume was one of enormous change: demographic growth in raw numbers, if the numbers of settlements discerned by survey and excavation are indicative; but also demographic shifts, such as the contraction and concentration of Jewish settlement to the Galilee and southern Judaea, a period of geographical expansion for Samaritans in the third century, and the rise of gentile Christianity through both conversion and immigration.[20] This was also a period in which ethnic groups in or near the region might disappear as distinctive corporate entities (e.g., the Idumaeans, or as Bowersock points out below, the Nabataeans) or emerge (e.g., the

---

[19] To that extent, at least, the term "communities" is justified; although Saldarini is quite correct to insist (p. 126) that, in general, that term carries with it a great deal of baggage, not all of it helpful.

[20] Population: see M. Broshi, "The Population of Western Palestine," *BASOR* 236 (1979), 1–10; the data consolidated by Z. Safrai, *Economy of Roman Palestine* (London: Routledge, 1994), 438–39; and Y. Tsafrir, "Some Notes on the Settlement and Demography of Palestine in the Byzantine Period: The Archaeological Evidence," in J. D. Seger, ed. *Retrieving the Past: Essays on Archaeological Research and Methodology in Honor of Gus W. Van Beek* (Winona Lake: Eisenbrauns, 1996), 269–83. (See also Y. Portugali, "The Settlement Pattern in the Western Jezreel Valley from the 6th Century B.C.E to the Arab Conquest," in A. Kasher, A. Oppenheimer, U. Rappaport, eds., *Man and Land in Eretz-Israel in Antiquity* [Jerusalem: Yad Izhak ben Zvi, 1986], 7–19, on differential patterns of growth or decline among sites of various size.) Samaritan expansion: A. D. Crown, "The Byzantine and Moslem Period," in *idem*, ed. *The Samaritans* (Tübingen: Mohr, 1989), 58–62. Jewish demographic contraction, Christian expansion: M. Avi-Yonah, *The Jews of Palestine* (Oxford: Blackwell, 1976), 18–20; 220–21 (based on literary sources). I have not yet seen the study by C. Dauphin, cited by Bowersock, n. 29, although a published version has been announced.

migration and sedentarization of Ghassanids in the Golan in the sixth century[21]). Similarly, religious communities too could disappear (e.g., the "Jewish Christians" discussed by Saldarini, or various "pagan" groups, through suppression or conversion) or be substantially altered (as in the case of the emergence of rabbinic Judaism, or in the case of imperial sponsorship for Christianity).

Given the tremendous changes in the ethnic and religious makeup of Palestinian society—on some level the subject of all the papers in this volume—is it not begging the question of what a Jew, or a Christian, or a Samaritan, or a "Hellene" was in late antiquity to assume that we know enough in advance to begin with such categories as already known? It seems to me that the kinds of problems acutely posed by such texts as *Sēper hā-rāzîm* require an alternative strategy for dealing with the questions of religious and ethnic difference in later Roman Palestine, one that takes seriously both the possibility of cultural choices and the construction and maintenance of boundaries of difference, of otherness, and, not infrequently, of hostility. In exploring such a strategy I would like to make four specific points.

I would like to argue, first, that the cultural world that the individuals and the communities of later Roman Palestine inhabited on a daily basis was wider than the horizons of their everyday life. Religious, theological, or "cultural" materials in general, like other commodities, could circulate both widely and locally. Because of its broad geographical and chronological spread, magical technique, as exemplified in such texts as *Sēper hā-rāzîm*, is merely a particularly baroque example of a shared cultural world in which, at least for educated readers and writers of texts, cultural materials originally produced in disparate places in the empire could be brought to bear on one another more or less freely. However, the logic that makes a Nilometer theme a suitable subject for

---

[21]   See C. Dauphin, "Jewish and Christian Communities in the Roman and Byzantine *Gaulanitis*: A Study of Evidence from Agricultural Surveys," *PEQ* 114 (1982), 132; see the critical evaluation of her approach by Z. U. Ma'oz, "Comments on Jewish and Christian Communities in Byzantine Palestine," *PEQ* 117 (1985), 59–68.

mosaics in late antique Palestine, at Sepphoris, at Beth Shean, and in the church at Tabgha (Heptapegeon), is another, if less threatening, one.[22]

Second, the discussion of "Graeco-Roman" magic in a "Jewish" context requires that we look at how cultural commodities are appropriated for use. The ritual practices that students of religion in antiquity have usually dubbed "magic" regularly confound customary categories of religion or culture. Thus, for instance, three amulets (probably from the sixth century) were found in the apse of a synagogue in southern Israel; one of these refers to Abrasax.[23] I do not think we should view this as "merely" an example of "cultural borrowing" by people for whom such amulets are "foreign." Yet even if one were to take such a stance, it would still be necessary to ask—even if answers are impossible—how Palestinian Jews who (it would seem) deposited such things in the synagogue understood what they were doing. Is it perhaps the fact that synagogues in late antique Palestine might be seen as holy places that accounts for their presence there?[24] It is also worth noting that one of these amulets refrains from naming either possessing demons

---

[22]   Sepphoris, reported in E. Netzer, Z. Weiss, "Sepphoris (Şippori), 1991–1992," *IEJ* 43 (1993), 191–93, and since discussed elsewhere; see E. Netzer, Z. Weiss, "New Evidence for Late-Roman and Byzantine Sepphoris," in J. H. Humphrey, ed., *The Roman and Byzantine Near East* (Ann Arbor: Journal of Roman Archaeology Supplementary Series 14, 1995), 165–76, esp. 166–71. Beth Shean, L. Roth-Gerson, *The Greek Inscriptions from the Synagogues in Eretz-Israel* [Hebrew] (Jerusalem: Yad Izhak ben Zvi, 1987), no. 7 and the literature cited there. The dedicatory inscription that accompanies the mosaic has led some commentators, including Roth-Gerson, to conclude that this inscription stems from a synagogue. If so, the question of how to deal with appropriate "Jewishness" arises yet again. For the depiction at Tabgha see A. M. Schneider, *The Church of the Multiplying of the Loaves and Fishes* (London: Coldwell, 1937), plates B and 13.

[23]   J. Naveh, S. Shaked, *Amulets and Magic Bowls*, rev. ed. (Jerusalem: Magnes, 1987), nos. 11–13; for the date see pp. 60–61. Abrasax (sometimes thought to be of Jewish/Semitic origin) appears, among amulets with a Palestinian provenance, also in no. 2 (Golan), and in J. Naveh, S. Shaked, *Magic Spells and Formulae* (Jerusalem: Magness, 1993), no. 19 (Galilee).

[24]   For inscriptions referring in Greek or Aramaic to "the holy place," see Roth-Gerson, *Greek Inscriptions*, 3, 16, 21, 23; J. Naveh, *On Stone and Mosaic* [Hebrew]

(it refers to them only generally) or protecting angels, and the effective part of the amulet seems to be the invocation of Exodus 15:26: "Every illness that I have put upon the Egyptians I shall not put upon you, for I am the Lord who heals you."[25] It seems possible that this should be seen as a kind of "purged" amulet, reflecting a Jewish piety less receptive to magical names, vocabulary, and rhetoric[26] than that of the others with which it was found, or than that of the author of *Sēper hā-rāzîm*. Even in the case of the invocation of Helios in *Sēper hā-rāzîm*, the overlapping interests in angelology and heavenly topography with late antique Jewish *Hēkalôt* mysticism, and the fact that the text survived in numerous manuscripts from the middle ages, suggest that this reconstructed magical text may not have been authored or universally received as marginal, much less transgressive of appropriate boundaries.[27] So we must still ask how such an adoption of—from our point of view— "pagan" rites, practices, and prayers might have been received (and explicit rejection is, in this sense, a kind of reception) by a multiplicity of groups or individuals in Palestine who nevertheless shared the label

---

(Jerusalem: Maariv, 1978), 26, 46, 60, 64, 65 (restored), and possibly 16 (Kfar Hananiah; the polykandelon). See S. Fine, *Synagogue and Sanctity: The Late Antique Palestinian Synagogue as a "Holy Place"* (Diss.: Hebrew University, 1993), especially 134–82.

[25]   Naveh, Shaked, *Amulets*, no. 13.19–20 (only part of the verse can be safely restored; the editors add the second half of the verse, "for I am the Lord who heals you" in lines 21–2 but no letters are visible).

[26]   Although not, for all that, necessarily conforming to Rabbinic legal expectations: see *m. Sanh.* 10:1; *t. Sanh.* 12:10; *y. Sanh.* 11:1 (28a–b), prohibiting the apotropaic use of Ex. 15:26.

[27]   See M. Smith, "How Magic Was Changed by the Triumph of Christianity," *Graeco-Arabica: Papers of the First International Congress on Greek and Arabic Studies*, ed. V. Christides, M. Papathomopoulos (Athens: Association for Greek and Arabic Studies, 1983), 2, 55–56, rept. *idem*, 1996, 2, 212, for the argument for the popularity of the text. For the relationship of aspects of magic with the *Hēkalôt* tradition see Alexander, "Incantations," 361; Lesses, 1996; Naveh, Shaked, *Magic Spells*, 20–22; P. Schäfer, "Jewish Magic Literature in Late Antiquity and Early Middle Ages," *JJS* 41 (1990), 74–91, esp. 76–81

"Jew." Yet even if we could dismiss *Sēper hā-rāzîm* itself as idiosyncratic, my argument is that all of the individuals in later Roman Palestine, and the communities to which they belonged, engaged by the very fact of their existence in selective appropriation or rejection of cultural commodities to which they had access. It is in this sense that we should see such phenomena as the mosaic representations of Helios and the zodiac in late antique Palestine. If Magness and Avni are correct in identifying certain symbols in the "Menorah Cave" (summarized below, pp. 104–5, 107) as Christian, one might well ask how it came to pass that the citation of Psalms or the use of inscriptions with the theme of "light" might be a peculiarly Christian marker.[28] The correlation between the *heis theos* formula and Samaritan provenance in Palestine—despite the evidence for the appropriating of "pagan" elements as well among Samaritans—suggests that we should similarly ask how Samaritans would have understood the formula.[29]

Third, I would like to propose that we view communities in later Roman Palestine and the individuals who constituted them not as static and essentially known entities, but rather as social formations that were continuously engaged in self-recreation. Once again, the invocation of Helios is a useful point of departure precisely because it presupposes an

---

[28] The passage from *SHR* discussed above, the Helios mosaics, and the varied use of the motif of light in Palestinian rabbinic texts in specifically Jewish contexts (e.g., *Gen. Rab.* 3:4 [ed. Theodor, Albeck, p 20], in which the Temple in particular is the locus of the creation of light) all suggest that Christians had no monopoly on light imagery; and Jewish texts in this period are clearly capable of citing Scripture. It should be noted, however, that according to a standard index of rabbinic verse citations, Ps. 119:105 is not widely cited (A. Heiman, *Torah Hakethubah Vehamessurah*, 2 ed. A B. Hyman [Jerusalem: Dvir, 1979], 3, 89), but at least one late antique midrashic passage associates this verse with Torah (*Cant. Rab.* 1, to Cant. 1:2).

[29] L. Di Segni, "Εἷς θεός in Palestinian Inscriptions," *SCI* 13 (1994), 94–115. Admittedly, knowledge of Samaritan culture in late antiquity is limited: see the contributions by B. Hall and A. D. Crown in A. D. Crown, *Samaritans*, 32–81. See also the suggestion by R. Pummer, "Samaritan Amulets from the Roman-Byzantine Period and their Wearers," *RB* 94 (1987), 251–63, that "Samaritan" amulets were made by Samaritans for non-Samaritan wearers.

author and a reading community that could accommodate it, even as it may also presuppose opponents. It is worth noting that much the same must also be said of the development of early rabbinic literature, with its more or less novel claims about law and rabbinic authority. The boundaries between what (or who) could be accommodated, moreover, were themselves changing. In the first century the presence of zoomorphic depictions in a palace of Herod Antipas is given as sufficient justification for its destruction (Josephus, *Vita* 65–67). In the Mishnah, a rabbi (traditionally dated to the late first or early second century) is said to dismiss the significance of a statue of Aphrodite in a bath house as mere decoration (*m. ʿAb. Zar.* 3:4), and the presence of depictions of zoomorphic and anthropomorphic figures in Palestinian synagogues, indeed of Helios himself, makes it clear that those who paid for synagogues could accommodate such things.

The question of how boundaries are continuously drawn and redrawn is crucial here, and it is best addressed first by a brief discussion of the descriptive terminology used to discuss the communities of later Roman Palestine. To begin with, "religious" and "ethnic" are problematic terms as they are applied to Palestine because they have significant areas in which they overlap and areas in which they fail to. If by "ethnicity" we mean, to take one common sort of definition, a group seen by both insiders and outsiders as sharing a common origin, history, and culture, of which religion can, as in our case, play a determinative part,[30] we may conventionally describe Jews and Samaritans as ethnic groups. "Gentiles" or "pagans," however, describe in negative terms: these are people who are neither Jews nor Samaritans. And for "gentile" Christians in Palestine, and, as the fourth century rolled on, surely for "pagans" as well, the significance of ethnic origin may not have been nearly as

---

[30]   For a discussion of ethnicity see, for example, F. Barth, ed., *Ethnic Groups and Boundaries* (Boston: Little, Brown, 1969) (especially Barth's introduction, the classic discussion of instrumentalist ethnicity), and S. Jones, *The Archaeology of Ethnicity* (London: Routledge, 1997), for a summary of recent research. See also the bibliography cited by Saldarini, below.

salient as religious adherence. Moreover, if the term Christian is empty of ethnic valence, "pagan" is doubly empty: it refers to non-Samaritans and non-Jews by ethnicity, and non-Samaritans, non-Jews, and non-Christians by religion. The messiness of ethnic and religious terminology is extended by the use in Greek of "Hellene" for "pagan," as when Sozomen (*Hist. Eccl.* 2.4.3) uses the term to refer collectively to non-Jews and non-Christians among the local inhabitants, Palestinians, Phoenicians, and Arabs (2.4.2) who frequented the shrine at Mambre. One of the contradictions of these overlapping conceptualizations is that the imperial government treated Jews as an *ethnos*, even as the terms by which they are described might focus on their "religion" (with varying degrees of approbation).[31] In laws of Christian emperors— quite possibly confirming in this respect widespread Jewish assumptions about the connections between their "ethnicity" and "religion" as well—we get the peculiar result that one can describe conversion *from* status as a Jew or Samaritan *to* Christianity (e.g., *Cod. Theod.* 16.8.5 [336], 28 [426]) in a way that one might not speak of Phoenicians or Arabs converting from Phoenicianness or Arabness.

The salience of "ethnicity" as a category of description, then, should not be taken for granted. I have already pointed out that ethnic groups might and did both arise and disappear during the period covered by the essays in this volume. Ethnic groups are born, develop, change, or die in at least two dimensions: diachronically, so that past experiences shape the state of individuals or communities in any given present, but also synchronically, so that present identity and present relations with other groups are negotiated through the articulation and maintenance of boundaries from within and from without and through the construction of past experiences into histories.[32] Similarly, religious groups are constantly engaged in a kind of self-redefinition, particularly in the case

---

[31]   See G. W. Bowersock's contribution to this volume, below.

[32]   See G. M. Sider, *Lumbee Indian Histories: Race, Ethnicity and Indian Identity in the Southern United States* (Cambridge: Cambridge University, 1993).

of Judaism or Christianity, which, unlike other forms of Graeco-Roman piety, could make exclusive claims on the identity of the adherent.

In this sense ethnicity (as well as religion) is a constantly re-articulated label by which groups come to be known to themselves and to others rather than reflecting some sort of racial, ethical, religious, or cultural essence.[33] Furthermore, even for as circumscribed an academic field as "Palestinian Jewry" ethnicity was likely to be experienced differently in, say, Caesarea where Jews had to coexist with Christians, Samaritans and "pagans,"[34] and in the Galilee where, Epiphanius could claim, although with evident exaggeration, no Greeks, Samaritans, or Christians lived (*Panarion* 30.11.9–10).

Recognizing the possibility of differential experiences of "sameness" is another important corrective to our all too easy identification of ethnicity, particularly of the "Jew" or the "Jewish," in antiquity.[35] We should expect fractures also along the lines of gender and class. At the very least, the literary sources at our disposal allow us to get some sense of the investment in certain kinds of social structures on the part of the same people—overwhelmingly men—responsible for articulating terms of communal identity or boundaries. One rabbinic text, for instance, while accepting the practice of long absences by male scholars from wife and family—although underscoring the dire effects of total dissociation from them—in pursuit of study with a male master, constructs a model of masculinity and an ideal of male textual community as much as it

---

[33] For an attempt to think through the problem of the "real" referent of Jewish ethnicity, see D. Boyarin, *A Radical Jew: Paul and the Politics of Identity* (*Contraversions* 1: Berkeley: University of California Press, 1994), 236–46.

[34] See the contribution of K. G. Holum in this volume.

[35] Cf., for instance, S. Mitchell, *Ancient Anatolia: Land, Men, and Gods* (Oxford: Clarendon, 1993), 2, 31–37, who presupposes, in what is an excellent discussion, the clear distinction between Jews and pagans (although he acknowledges overlap in cultic terminology and religious values), but sees paganism in Anatolia—both indigenous and Graeco-Roman—as part of an "almost infinitely flexible" system that "bound together the experience of almost all the inhabitants of the ancient world" (p. 30).

constructs "wifeliness" as the patient waiting for men, and excludes them from such community (*Gen. Rab.* 95 [Vatican ms.], ed. Theodor, Albeck, 1232; *Lev. Rab.* 21:8, ed. Margaliot, 484–87).[36] The text that Fine studies, with its apparent designation of women as enablers of study (below, p. 70 and n. 12), and its displacement of reward to some future or heavenly synagogue, similarly has implications for a specifically gendered "Jewishness." I have suggested elsewhere that rabbinic civil law, at least in its formulation in the Mishnah, reflects the concerns and interests of landed, town-dwelling men, even as it promotes an ostensibly egalitarian ethos.[37] To the extent that rabbinic discourse is not merely marginalized "talk" but is played out in the ideological and material lives of Palestinian subjects, study of rabbinic texts may afford insights not only into a "classical" Judaism, but into some of its fractures as well. Yet, it is a comment on the study of the history of identity in the fields represented here that none of the papers in the present volume addresses these issues head on, although they lurk beneath the surface in Fine's examination of synagogue topography and the place of women in it, or in Rutgers's and Weiss's discussions of "Jewishness" on the basis of material remains of Sepphoris and its elites.

One significance of this view of ethnic and religious groupings as projects of naming is that it forces us to take seriously the porousness and flexibility of boundaries: if they are always in a state of rearticulation, there is no necessary reason to assume they are isomorphic. As it turns out, we have better evidence for receptiveness to cultural forms

---

[36] See D. Boyarin, *Carnal Israel: Reading Sex in Talmudic Culture* (New Historicism: Studies in Cultural Poetics 25: Berkeley: University of California Press, 1993), 134–66, esp. 156–58. I differ from Boyarin here in drawing greater attention to the fact that the practice of Simeon b. Yohai, who did keep in touch with his family, is not questioned here. See also M. Satlow, "'Try to Be a Man: The Rabbinic Construction of Masculinity," *HTR* 89 (1996), 19–40. On gender in rabbinic culture, see now M. Peskowitz, *Spinning Fantasies: Rabbis, Gender, and History* (Berkeley: University of California Press, 1997).

[37] H. Lapin, *Early Rabbinic Civil Law and the Social History of Roman Galilee* (BJS 307: Atlanta: Scholars, 1995).

than for receptiveness to individuals who flirt with or transgress the boundaries. Thus, the synagogues of Palestine in late antiquity could incorporate what was "originally" a "pagan" set of motifs (Helios and the zodiac), as well as borrowed elements from Christian sacred architecture.[38] Samaritans, in turn, appear to have adopted elements of Jewish iconography in utilizing depictions of a monumental doorway (which Y. Magen understands as a Torah ark) in synagogue art.[39] The shrine of Mambre, converted into a Christian shrine under Constantine, was still, at the time of Sozomen's writing in the fifth century, a place frequented at the same festival time by Jews and "pagans" as well (Sozomen, *Hist. Eccl.* 2.4). Thus the shrine at Mambre served as a place whose valorization by one group did not result in its rejection or exclusive appropriation by others. Forms of piety could, then, be multicommunal (if not necessarily inclusive), while over time even localized communal sites of ritual practice could be shaped by contact with other groups.

As for individuals, Epiphanius's account (of dubious veracity) of the conversion of Joseph suggests, reasonably enough, that prominent Palestinian Jews might suffer severe popular reprisals for conversion to Christianity (*Panarion* 30.4.1, 12.1), but also that a deathly ill patriarch might call a Christian bishop in for baptism (30.4.5–7, 6.1–6). In fact, Epiphanius points to a number of cases of "crypto-Christian" interest among Jews, and these tend to involve the (magical?) invocation of Christ over the sick (30.9.1–10.1, 10.3–7). The account also presupposes that to Epiphanius's own personal knowledge a well-organized ecclesiastical community (Arians in Scythopolis) might make life difficult for individual "heretics" (in this case, "orthodox" Christians) (30.5.5–9).

---

[38]   Y. Tsafrir, "The Byzantine Setting and its Influence on Ancient Synagogues," in *The Synagogue in Late Antiquity* (New York: ASOR, Jewish Theological Seminary, 1987), 149–57. On chancel screens see J. R. Branham, "Sacred Space Under Erasure in Ancient Synagogues and Early Churches," in *Art Bulletin* 74 (1992), 375–92; and the contribution of S. Fine in this volume.

[39]   Y. Magen "Samaritan Synagogues" [Hebrew], *Qadmoniot* 25 (1993), 66–90, with criticism and response *Qadmoniot* 26 (1993), 6–8.

Communal self re-fashioning is the result over the long term of repeated choices, incorporations, and rejections among the variety of cultural elements that enter the communal horizon on every level of individual or collective life. I have suggested elsewhere that Palestinian rabbinic culture, for all its receptiveness to ideas current in the late antique world, promoted a closed, insular, Hebrew- or Aramaic-speaking world, governed by "Jewish" law, in which the primary institutions are rabbinic houses of study where rabbinic Torah is expounded.[40] Although one may argue persuasively that rabbis in Palestine were aware enough to playfully utilize the subjects of trinitarian controversies in their texts,[41] explicit references to Christianity are notable for their absence, much as "heretical" groups or individuals are largely reduced to the undifferentiated category *mîn*.[42] Jewish synagogues themselves, as has been noted above, come to respond to Christian public buildings—at the same time articulating and investing heavily in particularly Jewish sacred spaces—and it may turn out that Samaritan synagogues (which are not dated before the fourth century) reflect the same phenomenon. At any rate, Magen hypothesizes that there is a shift in later Samaritan synagogues towards preference for Semitic inscriptions in the Samaritan script, which may reflect a new reassertion in public spheres of corporate identity.[43]

Fourth, and finally, the appropriation and deployment of cultural commodities is not innocent, but rather takes place, consciously or not,

---

[40]   See H. Lapin, *Early Rabbinic Civil Law*, 239–41; *idem*, "Jewish and Christian Academies in Roman Palestine," *Caesarea Maritima: A Retrospective after 2,000 Years*, K. G. Holum, A. Raban, eds. (Leiden: Brill, 1996), 496–512.

[41]   B. L. Visotzky, "Trinitarian Testimonies," *USQR* 42 (1988), 73–85, rept. in *idem, Fathers of the World: Essays in Rabbinic and Patristic Literatures* (WUNT 80: Tübingen: Mohr, 1995), 61–74.

[42]   See n. 30 in the contribution of C. E. Hayes below, and the literature cited there.

[43]   For the dating of the synagogue see Magen, "Samaritan Synagogues," *passim*. For the question of Samaritan script see Magen, "Samaritan Synagogues," 89. On the problem of the exclusiveness of Samaritan script see the literature cited by L. Di Segni in this volume, n. 5.

against the background of a differential distribution of political and
social power.[44] The implication of power is clearest in the intervention
of imperial force in local religious or ethnic affairs, as in the following
few examples. It is Romans who destroyed the Jewish temple in Jerusalem in 70 C.E., and Romans who prevented its rebuilding; and in the
360s it was again an emperor, Julian, who may have authorized Jews to
rebuild their temple.[45] The emergence of Constantine (and Helena) as
patron and promoter of Christianity stands behind the "discovery" of
the Holy Sepulchre under a temple to Venus and the behind construction of a showpiece church on the site (Euseb., *V. Const.* 3.16–39) and of
others at the Mount of Olives and at Bethlehem (3.41–43), as well as the
construction of a church at the shrine at Mambre that a variety of religious groups frequented (3.51–53; Sozom., *Hist. Eccl.* 2.4).[46] The building of the Theotokos church on Mount Gerizim is described by
Procopius as a punitive measure following a clash between Samaritans
and Christians in 484 during the reign of Zeno (Proc., *Aed.* 7.5–7). (I
leave aside the question of whether this episode involved a full fledged
revolt, for which see the contributions of L. Di Segni and K. G. Holum
below.) Nor is such intervention necessarily restricted to the suppression of non-Christians, as the use of imperial troops to seat the Chalce-
donian bishop of Jerusalem, Juvenal, shows.[47]

All of these are examples, to which others could be added, of limited
undertakings involving commitments of financial and human resources.

---

[44]   See, for a discussion of implication of power in the ability of people to "make
their own history," T. Asad, *Genealogies of Religion* (Baltimore: Johns Hopkins,
1993) 1–24.

[45]   Avi-Yonah, 1976, 191–204; M. Stern, *Greek and Latin Authors on Jews and
Judaism* (Israel Academy of Arts and Sciences: Jerusalem: Magnes, 1976–1984), 2,
506–11; G. W. Bowersock, *Julian the Apostate* (Cambridge: Harvard, 1978), 89–91,
120–22.

[46]   See J. E. Taylor, *Christians and the Holy Places* (Oxford: Clarendon, 1993), 86–
156, for fuller discussion and bibliography. See also the contribution of Tsafrir in
this volume.

[47]   E. Honigman, "Juvenal of Jerusalem," *DOP* 5 (1950), 247–57.

What is far more important, but less clearly visible, is the way in which these events are merely focused points in a set of relationships and terms of discourse carried out over an extended period of time. Those relationships and that discourse were, of course, neither simply binary nor monolithic. The Christianity that was being imposed in the empire itself had parties and conflicts; the ability of the imperial government to oversee the lives of people on a day-to-day basis was nothing like that of modern states; and the same emperors themselves might respond at different times to different pressures or concerns.[48] Moreover, the religious and ethnic communities about which the essays in this book speak were continuously redefining themselves, less in view of governmental and ecclesiastical statements of proper relationships, than in the lived experience of people living in groups with porous and flexible boundaries between them. Nevertheless, because of the nature of our sources boundaries are, again, most clearly discernible at the level of the imperial government. With respect to Jews, power is expressed on the level of discourse not only in the sermons and writings of Christian preachers, but also in the fact that the compilers of the imperial law codes set aside specific titles for dealing with "Jewish" issues (*Cod. Theod.* 16.8, 9; *Cod. Just.* 1.9, 10). The point is not merely the increase in laws having to do with Jews with the reign of Constantine and later, but that Jews, along with Samaritans, heretics, and pagans, were constructed as distinctive categories of Roman subjects about whom certain kinds of statements could be made.

The differential relationships between rulers and ruled or between a Christian ecclesiastical and governmental elite and Jews and Samaritans, and the implications of those differential relationships for the ability of the various groups to "construct" the others, was in fact productive of religious and ethnic change, if not religious and ethnic iden-

---

[48]   Witness the concession of the emperor Theodosius I to Ambrose of Milan over the matter of a synagogue at Callinicum (in present day Syria) in 388 (Ambrose, *Epistulae*, 40, 41), and his reassertion of the rights of synagogues to protection from destruction in 393 (*Cod. Theod.* 16.8.9).

tities in the first place.[49] The disequilibrium of power does not merely result in the squashing of weaker players (although, in the long term it might, as in the case of "pagans"; Tsafrir's study has examined the public side of this process). It can also, precisely by circumscribing religious and ethnic communities such as Jews or Samaritans both discursively (i.e., in the way communities are talked about and viewed) and institutionally, paradoxically open up opportunities for self-identification, for "autonomous" development, and for resistance. Thus, for instance, the institution of the patriarchate emerged as a site of productive contradiction. It is the persistence on the part of the imperial government of treating Jews as an *ethnos*, increasingly, in the Christian empire, with special restrictions, that opened "space" for communal autonomy under patriarchal direction. Apparently during the fourth century, the patriarchs in Palestine officially attained an unprecedented degree of authority over Jewish communities far removed from Palestine.[50] At the same time, the rank attained by the patriarchs in the imperial administration and the contents of the letters of Libanius to the patriarch(s), reflect the attainment and cultivation on the part of the patriarchs of a "Roman" aristocratic character.[51] Moreover, if patriarchs of the fourth century continued to act as patrons of the rabbinic movement (it is precisely by the mid-fourth century that Palestinian rabbinic literature, although finally redacted in the fifth century and later, breaks off; and the fourth-century patriarchate remains a subject of some

---

[49]   This is the most important contribution of Sider, *Lumbee Histories*, for the present purposes.

[50]   See, e.g., *Cod. Theod.* 16.8.8 (392), confirming the jurisdictional authority of partriarchal appointees; 16.8.17 (404), reestablishing the right of the Patriarch to exact funds from Jewish communities (in the West) after its abrogation in 16.8.14 (399).

[51]   See Stern, *Greek and Latin Authors*, 2, 589–99. For the history of the patriarchs see the brief discussion in Lapin, *Early Rabbinic Civil Law*, 14–19 and notes thereto and the contribution of Bowersock to this volume. See now, M. Jacobs, *Die Institutionen des jüdischen Patriarchen* (*Texte und Studien zum Antiken Judentum* 52: Tübingen: Mohr, 1995).

debate), it is the Roman-constructed, aristocratic institution that sponsored the rise to power of a "nativist" revitalization movement.

It is on the level of the lived experience of the communities of later Roman Palestine that boundaries between communities and individuals are rearticulated. Alas, it is precisely about this level that we are worst informed. The account of Epiphanius of the experiences of Joseph of Tiberias (Epiph., *Panarion*, 30.4–12), problematic though it may be, brings together a number of themes—still at a rather elite level—in a narrative about the breaching of boundaries: the authority of patriarchs and their apostles in the communities of the diaspora; the building of churches in the Galilee, and especially one on the site of a Hadrianeion in Tiberias (the replacement in Tiberias of the representation of imperial ideology of a former age with its current, Christian manifestation); the possibility of contact between well-placed Jews and Christians in fourth-century Palestine (discussed above); the zeal of converts; the ability of a Jewish convert to Christianity to leverage imperial backing for an attempt to promote both the emperor-sponsored cult, and a reproach to the Jews, and, finally, communal resistance (in Epiphanius's account, through ineffectual magic).

Epiphanius's narrative is one about the triumph of Christianity, marked by the systemic disequilibrium of power in Galilee. Yet clearly, resistance, too, was possible since Jewish and Samaritan communities survived to the Muslim conquests and beyond. Such resistance could take the form of outright violence, as in the case of the Samaritan revolts, whatever the scale at which these should be understood. More frequently, resistance may be carried out more quietly: in the building of synagogues—in the case of Capernaum not far from a smaller and less impressive church,[52] or, for Jews, in dating formulae of inscriptions

---

[52]   Taylor, *Christians and the Holy Places*, 268–94, esp. 290–93. Admittedly, the late date for the Capernaum synagogue is still debated: see, e.g., Y. Tsafrir, "The Synagogues of Capernaum and Meroth and the dating of the Galilean Synagogue," in Humphrey, ed., *Roman and Byzantine Near East*, 151–61. In a forthcoming article J. Magness argues for a date not earlier than the late-fifth century for this

to the year in the sabbatical cycle or to the destruction of the Jerusalem temple.[53] Resistance, finally, can be illustrated in one last example of cultural borrowing: in commenting on Genesis 22:6 ("and Abraham took the wood for the burnt offering and put them on Isaac his son"), *Genesis Rabbah* states: "like one carrying his cross (*ṣĕlûb*) on his shoulder" (56:3, ed. Theodor-Albeck, 598). Whenever the originator of this saying may have lived (the saying is presented anonymously), an editor in late antique Palestine cannot possibly have missed it as an allusion to the crucifixion. Through contact Jews, too, could come on one level to speak of Isaac as a type of Christ; yet that acknowledgment quietly displaces Christ, and, in context, reasserts the centrality of Abraham and of Isaac to Israel's own salvific history.

Ultimately, it may well be that the story of the religious and ethnic communities in later Roman Palestine is one of increasing distance and even enmity, which could play itself out in local support for or hostility toward invading Persian, Byzantine, or Arab armies. The inclusion of an invocation to Helios in *Sēper hā-rāzîm* ought to remind us, however, that pristine, insular, and internally undifferentiated communities are a myth of ancient rhetoric and modern scholarly categories. The burden of this essay has been to suggest that it is precisely through the constant processes of contact, borrowing, and incorporation of cultural materials, that communities come to constitute themselves.

---

synagogue: J. Magness, "The Question of the Synagogue: The Problem of Typology," in J. Neusner, A. J. Avery-Peck, eds., *Judaism in Late Antiquity III: Where We Stand, Part III* (Leiden: Brill, forthcoming).

[53] Naveh, *Stone and Mosaic,* 13, 76; *CIJ* II 1208; E. L. Sukenik, "Jewish Tomb Stones from Zoar" [Hebrew], *Kedem* 2 (1945), nos. 2, 3 (no. 1 corresponds to *CIJ* II 1208); J. Naveh, *On Sherd and Papyrus* [Hebrew] (Jerusalem: Magnes, 1992), 203–6 (figs. 142, 143).

I.

FRAMING THE QUESTION

THE GREEK MOSES:
CONFUSION OF ETHNIC AND CULTURAL COMPONENTS IN LATER ROMAN AND EARLY BYZANTINE PALESTINE

Glen W. Bowersock

Institute for Advanced Study

THE NEAR EAST cannot easily be described in terms of distinct geographical regions. Nature has determined that its constituent parts are all fatally dependent upon one another, and the fortunes of one side of the Jordan valley inevitably impinge upon the fortunes of the other. This was as true of Canaan and Edom as it was of Judaea and Nabataea, and as it was (and is) of the Golan and Syria. The name of Palestine reflects this geographical interdependence. For centuries in antiquity it embraced the territory that lay between the Jordan and the sea, but from the fourth century of the common era onwards it was applied to much of Transjordan as well. Imprecision and interaction inhere in the geography and economy as well as in the nomenclature of the region, and this is undoubtedly why its culture has proved so fertile and its history so momentous. The shifting boundaries of Palestine symbolize the ethnic and cultural confusion of the peoples who inhabited it. Religions grew and flourished there in a profusion almost unexampled in the history of the world. Palestine was a special place because it was many places at the same time. To the eyes of an historian of the Roman Empire, no other place from Britain to the Euphrates, from the Danube to the Sahara was quite like it.

Apamea in Syria, lying to the northeast of Palestine on the other side of Mount Hermon, was a great intellectual center in Roman times. Philosophers of middle and late Platonism had their roots there from the second century to the fourth, and with the rise of Christianity Neoplatonism at Apamea championed Hellenism in the double sense it had in those days—the culture of the Greeks and the practice of polytheism. One of the important mediators of Roman Platonism in the second century was Numenius of Apamea, and he, faithful to the special character of near easterners of the age, was a great connoisseur of the culture of the Jews. He knew them from personal acquaintance because there was a substantial Jewish community in Apamea. So when he declared that the philosopher Plato, to whom he dedicated his life, was nothing more than Moses speaking Greek, he was proclaiming the common bond that linked a powerful intellectual tradition that had grown up in Palestine with the heritage of Greece.[1] And he proclaimed it in Syria.

The high esteem with which this distinguished polytheist philosopher regarded the great exponent of monotheism posed no problems for him. His comparison may well reflect his reading of Plato's *Laws* with reference to the biblical lawgiver. But the parallel could have been much broader, since he believed that the Jewish God was the father of all the gods.[2] Plato's quasi-monotheistic use of *ho theos* would be consistent with such an opinion. Besides, Numenius ranked the Jews as one of just four alien peoples of unimpeachably high reputation, recognizing only the Indian Brahmans, the Persian *magi*, and the Egyptians as their fellows in wisdom.[3] It was left to the Christians later to assert that Plato had actually stolen his ideas from Moses.[4] Yet even this absurdity was a desperate effort to claim Moses for themselves while they discredited the Greek philosopher to whom several of the earlier Christian apologists (Origen, for example) had been conspicuously indebted.

---

[1]   Numenius' quip is cited five times in extant ancient texts, and they are most conveniently surveyed in M. Stern, *Greek and Latin Authors on Jews and Judaism*, (Jerusalem: Israel Academy of Arts and Science, 1980) 2, 209–10, nos. 363 a–e. The earliest quotation occurs in Clement of Alexandria, *Stromateis* (erroneously called *Stromata* by Stern), 1.22, 150:4.

[2]   Ioann. Lydus, *de Mens.* 4.53 (Stern 2, 214, no. 367).

[3]   Euseb., *Praepar. Evang.* 9.7.1 (Stern 2, 211, no. 364a).

[4]   Cf. Suda, s.v. *Noumenios*.

In his lapidary utterance Numenius has given us in the Greek Moses a kind of icon for the situation we find in Palestine, an icon borne across geographical and cultural boundaries to signal the benign interaction of Hellenism and Judaism. It was the work of a Syrian who was ethnically neither Greek nor Jew. Ethnicities, like geographical boundaries, appear to dissolve, and religions function not alongside of cultures but within them. Such fluidity, openness, and interdependence do not necessarily threaten the identity of communities, although they could be perceived as doing so. Hellenism in the Hasmonaean period and the Roman presence in the Second Temple period did inspire fear and hostility. Bar Kokhba was able to exploit this sentiment again among the Jews in the reign of Hadrian. But then amazingly it seems to have died out without any loss of Jewish identity. The end of hostility to Rome witnessed a stupendous efflorescence of Jewish thought and scholarship in Palestine at a time when Roman power was at its strongest. Even more amazingly that efflorescence went right on, oblivious of major catastrophes, including the collapse of the imperial economy in the third century, the unprecedented capture of a Roman emperor by a Persian king-of-kings, and the rise of a Palmyrene state that was able to capture and occupy Egypt before the Romans were able to crush it.[5]

The rhythms of Palestine were clearly not those of the rest of the Graeco-Roman world. That is why it is just as difficult to discuss historical periods in Palestinian history after the Second Temple as it is be sure of meaningful boundaries on the ground. Avi-Yonah's classic work on the Jews of Palestine spanned the vast period from the Bar Kokhba war in the second century to the Arab conquest in the seventh.[6] By contrast Günter Stemberger's *Juden und Christen im Heiligen Land* was restricted to the time between Constantine and Theodosius.[7] Peter

---

[5]   Cf. G. W. Bowersock, "Polytheism and Monotheism in Arabia and the Three Palestines," *DOP* (forthcoming).

[6]   M. Avi-Yonah, *The Jews of Palestine, A Political History from the Bar Kokhba War to the Arab Conquest* (Oxford: Blackwell, 1976).

[7]   G. Stemberger, *Juden und Christen im heiligen Land: Palästina unter Konstantin und Theodosius* (Munich: Beck, 1987).

Schäfer's recent *History of the Jews in Antiquity* covers a whole millennium, from Alexander the Great to the Arab Conquest.[8] The large compass is unwieldy, the small one meaningless. There is an unmistakable continuity in Palestine from the end of the Bar Kokhba war to the Persian invasion in the early seventh century. Avi-Yonah had it almost right. A continuity of this kind is not to be seen in any other part of the Mediterranean world in the same centuries, with the possible exception of North Africa between the first and the fifth centuries.

It is ultimately a trivial matter how we designate the *longue durée* in Palestine, but it is important to avoid misconceptions. Designations of chronological frames such as Late (or Later) Roman, Early Byzantine, and Late Antique carry baggage that one would sooner avoid. The first two imperceptibly imply something about the locus of power—Rome or Constantinople—and the third, as it has been brilliantly interpreted by Peter Brown, implies a new and vibrant spiritual world beginning in the fourth century. None of these implications is appropriate for Palestine.

Rome had virtually nothing to do with the Near East from the fourth century onwards, and therefore a historian of the ancient world cannot comfortably listen to a discussion of fifth-century Scythopolis under the heading "Late Roman." Constantine's conversion affected the region only gradually as churches arose and pilgrims arrived. The growth of Christianity there could hardly be characterized as Byzantine except in a purely temporal sense. Furthermore, the rearrangement of provincial boundaries by the early Byzantine administration only confirmed what the previous centuries had already witnessed in fact: that was the integral role of Transjordan in Palestine. As for late antiquity, the term is currently so bound up with the idea of rebirth and revitalization from the fourth to the seventh centuries that an historian can only rub his eyes when a reading a book titled *The Rabbinic Class of Roman Palestine in Late Antiquity*.[9] Much of this valuable work is devoted to the third

---

[8]   P. Schäfer, *The History of the Jews in Antiquity* (Luxembourg: Harwood, 1995).

[9]   L. I. Levine, *The Rabbinic Class of Roman Palestine in Late Antiquity* (Jerusalem and New York: Yad Izhak ben Zvi and JTS, 1989).

century, and, besides, for most secular historians Palestine is no longer
Roman in Late Antiquity.

What is distinctive about Palestine is the unimportance of the age of
the imperial Tetrarchs. The upheavals that rocked the Roman government and ultimately fragmented it into four and subsequently two great
bureaucracies barely touched Palestine. The brief and glorious ascendancy of Palmyra in the third century looked dangerous to the emperor
Aurelian, but in the Near East it was only another manifestation of the
region's self-sufficiency and interdependence. The army of Zenobia
attacked the Roman military establishment at Bostra, but it proceeded
thence across southern Palestine into Egypt without a sign of opposition or resistance. The Arabs of Palmyra, like Numenius in Apamea,
were part of a Hellenized Semitic world in which each of the constituent
communities lost nothing of its peculiar character.[10] Palestine was a
part of their greater cultural community, and they went through it on
their way to Egypt as if they belonged there.

This world may be dated, as Avi-Yonah recognized, from the Bar
Kokhba war or perhaps, more accurately, from the foundation of Aelia
Capitolina. That was the last radical transformation of Palestine, with
its expulsion of the Jews from Jerusalem, until the Persians invaded the
city, and after them the Muslims. The strong and secure nexus that
served to bind together the imperial government with the Jewish
community of Palestine and the Hellenic population (in the cultural
and not necessarily in the ethnic sense) is nowhere better illustrated
than in the history of the patriarchate from Judah the *nāśîʾ* in the later
second century to Libanius and Theodosius in the later fourth and early
fifth centuries. It was frequently observed that the patriarch ruled like
king over his people. He governed an amalgam of communities that
constituted a nation.[11]

---

[10]   See, for a recent assessment, Ernest Will, *Les Palmyréniens: La Venise des sables*
(Paris: A. Colin, 1992).

[11]   L. I. Levine, "The Jewish Patriarch (Nasi) in Third Century Palestine," *ANRW*
II.19.2 (1979), 649–88; M. Jacobs, *Die Institution des jüdischen Patriarchen* (Tübingen: Mohr, 1995).

But it was a most unusual nation, since fundamentally the religion of the Jews was a part of their ethnicity. Although apostates and converts could certainly be found, Judaism was an ethnic religion. Christianity was not, nor were any of the polytheist cults. Hellenism was never a religion, even if Neoplatonism came close to being one. Hellenism was the culture of the eastern polytheists, but identifying people as Hellenes never served to reveal where or how they worshipped. There was a dissonance, therefore, in the relation between the Jewish *ethnos* and all the other *ethnē* of the Mediterranean. This dissonance, although always potentially subversive, was the firm basis for the security of the Jews for hundreds of years after Bar Kokhba. Knowing that they were not only different but seen to be different, the Jews were able to participate actively in the culture of their region without excessively compromising their principles.

The mass of Jews can never have attained the standards of conduct and contemplation mandated by the rabbis, but they manifestly practiced their religion without a guilty conscience. Archaeology has documented this amply in recent years. But Lieberman was able to write as early as 1942:

> The cultural influence of Hellenism on the people was even larger and deeper than could be inferred from the facts recorded in rabbinic literature. The middle class of the Jewish people lived together with heathens and Christians in the big cities of Palestine; they traded together and they worked together. The people could not help admiring the beautiful and the useful; they could not fail to be attracted by the external brilliance and the superficial beauty of Gentile life.[12]

The role of the patriarch proves that what Lieberman wrote was just as true of more than the Jewish middle class. The House of Hillel traced its ancestry to David and enjoyed a power and wealth associated with the greatest aristocrats and potentates of the age. All this occurred with the permission and support of the ruling authorities and the pagan elite. The patriarchate has been much examined over the years, but it is worth

---

[12]   S. Lieberman, *Greek in Jewish Palestine* (New York: Feldheim, 1942), 91.

looking at it again in the context of later Roman Palestine. If Plato was
the Greek Moses for a Hellene in Syria, the patriarch was the Jewish
emperor for a Christian in Egypt. In a famous passage in his letter to
Africanus, Origen wrote that the ethnarch of the Jews was, with the
agreement of the Roman emperor (*sunkhōrountos Kaisaros*), no different from a king of his people (*ethnous*).[13] It is generally acknowledged
that Origen is referring here to the Jewish patriarch, whose virtually
imperial authority is generously documented in rabbinic sources and
whose favor at Rome is implied in a much discussed allusion to an
emperor Antoninus. The patriarch was obviously perceived by the Jews,
by the Christians, and by the Romans alike as a kind of client king. He
functioned in several cultural spheres at the same time. He was a leader
and lawgiver for his people, and he was a local aristocrat who, like many
urban notables throughout the Roman empire, ensured through personal contact the benevolence of the external ruler. He was a man of
great learning and wisdom, and in this aspect he closely resembled the
powerful intellectuals who dominated the Greek cultural scene of the
second, third, and fourth centuries. These were the sophists and philosophers, whom Philostratus placed together with kings as close associates of the miracle-worker Apollonius of Tyana. The immensely rich
and powerful sophist Herodes Atticus in Athens was once described by
a contemporary as a king (*basileus*) of eloquence, and the sophist Polemo
in Asia Minor traveled with a vast entourage worthy of an emperor as he
rode in his chariot equipped with silver bridles.[14] His biographer
reports that he conversed with cities as his inferiors, with emperors as
not his superiors, and with gods as his equals.

Yet the fusion of cultural elements in the role of the Jewish patriarch
in no way eclipsed his ethnic identity. It actually strengthened it. It
conferred upon him an international recognition and authority. The
recent suggestion by Martin Goodman, in the volume edited by Lee

---

[13]   Origen, *Epist. ad Africanum* 20.14.

[14]   Philostr., *Vit Soph.*, ed. G. Olearius (Leipzig, 1709), 586 (Hadrian of Tyre on
Herodes); 532 (Polemon); 535 (Polemon).

Levine on *The Galilee on Late Antiquity*, that the emperor simply toler-
ated the patriarch's doing what he did because his authority was limited
to purely religious matters is wide of the mark because it misses altogether the cultural fusion within the ethnic context.[15] Origen does not
say that the emperor "allowed" the patriarch to exercise his power but
rather that he explicitly authorized it. The participle *sunkhōrountos*
means that the emperor consciously granted the power. Goodman's
translation from Origen (he does not cite the Greek) tellingly fails to
include any rendering at all of the genitive absolute that contains this
important word together with the precise naming of the emperor.

Furthermore, Origen's use of the word *ethnos* cannot be weakened
to refer only to religion, nor can the word ethnarch, which was well
known for exercise of political authority in the Herodian dynasty, be
restricted to religious jurisdiction. Origen was perfectly well acquainted
with the word patriarch from the Septuagint and the New Testament,
and he saw fit to use it more than fifty times, usually for the biblical
patriarchs although once, interestingly, for a member of the House of
Hillel.[16] He avoided the term in naming the *nāśî*ᵓ precisely because he
wanted to designate a holder of real political power. In suggesting that
the Roman authorities saw no harm in leaving merely religious leadership in the hands of the patriarch, Goodman presupposes, as he argued
in the *Journal of Roman Studies* in 1989, that the Romans drew a distinction between ethnic Jews as inhabitants of the Empire and religious
Jews.[17] They did not.

In support of this contention, a digression at this point on Jewishness in the Roman state might be useful. The pagan sources leave no
doubt that the Romans had only one criterion for determining who was

---

[15]   M. Goodman, "The Roman State and the Jewish Patriarch in the Third
Century," in L. I. Levine, *The Galilee in Late Antiquity* (New York: Harvard and
JTSA, 1992), 127–39.

[16]   Origen, *Select. in Psalm.* 6, of a Iullus.

[17]   M. Goodman, "Nerva, the *Fiscus Iudaicus* and Jewish Identity," *JRS* 79 (1989),
40–44.

a Jew, and that was circumcision. Anyone acquainted with the legal history of circumcision in this period and the evidence for epispasm will know that. Goodman had the eccentric idea that the notorious tax on Jews was imposed from Nerva onwards only upon those who volunteered to declare themselves as Jews and that it was therefore confined to the publicly religious. This has only to be stated to be refuted. Goodman even goes so far as to assert that the special exemption from Hadrian's ban on circumcision that Antoninus Pius introduced for the sons of Jews was cunningly designed to stop an accretion of male proselytes.[18] But he acknowledges that this did not happen, and it is highly likely that although Pius' ruling would have technically precluded the circumcision of adult male proselytes, it would undoubtedly have accommodated the circumcision of their sons. In any case, it is evident that the Jews were indeed an *ethnos* in Roman terms, and that their religion was seen as a part of their ethnicity and not separable from it. After Pius had permitted *Iudaei* to circumcise their sons, he went on to state that the ban on circumcision should continue to be applied to those *non eiusdem religionis*. It could hardly be clearer that Pius believed the Jews to have a religion by virtue of being Jews, whether they practiced that religion or not. Although the first Christians, being manifestly Jews, were undoubtedly circumcised, they gave up the ritual and thereby removed themselves from the Jewish nation. Apostate Jews attempted to achieve the same status by epispasm.

To return to the patriarchate, the complex nature of the ethnicity of the Jewish *nāśîʾ* in the cultural context of the Roman world became even more eloquently documented in the correspondence between the Greek rhetorician Libanius and the patriarchs of the fourth century. Libanius felt free to communicate in sophisticated Greek and to allude to Odysseus, Achilles, and Telephus, as well as to more obscure figures, all of whom he expected the patriarch to recognize.[19] It is more than likely

---

[18]   Modestinus, *Dig.* 48.8.11: *Circumcidere Iudaeis filios suos tantum rescripto divi Pii permittitur: in non eiusdem religionis qui hoc fecerit, castrantis poena irrogatur.*

[19]   Lib., *Epist.* 1098, 1105 (Stern, 2, 595–97, nos. 502 and 503).

that Libanius, for his part, would have understood allusions to the history and legends of the Jews that might have appeared in the letters he received from the patriarch. Numenius' enthusiasm may have been greater than most, but we should not assume that others brought up in the traditions of Greek *paideia* were altogether ignorant of the principal traditions of the Jews. The author of the treatise *On the Sublime* could quote from the Book of Genesis,[20] and a Greek pupil of the eminent sophist Herodes Atticus could cite the Septuagint text of Deuteronomy on a funerary inscription.[21] In the third century the martyr Pionios, thoroughly trained in pagan classical sources, was nonetheless able to harangue the Jews at Smyrna with a succession of pertinent examples from their own culture.[22] The widely assumed ignorance of things Jewish among the Greeks is not well founded for the eastern provinces.

It may be argued that all the male members of the House of Hillel, not merely the *nāśî᾽* himself, bore the title of patriarch. This possibility is briefly raised by Martin Jacobs in his new and substantial book on the institution of the Jewish patriarch (*Die Institution des jüdischen Patriarchen*), but he does not explore the matter.[23] The problem for him, as for many authors of doctoral theses, is that he examines each piece of evidence meticulously one at a time and consequently has trouble seeing the issues that emerge from a synchronic study of several texts together. Libanius addresses one of his letters to "the patriarchs" in the plural, and the consistent use of the plural throughout the letter proves that the epigraph in the manuscripts is not a textual error.[24] The problem has

---

[20]   Longin., *De Subl.* 9.9 (Stern, 1, 364, no. 148).

[21]   L. Robert, "Malédictions funéraires grecques," *CRAI* (1978), 241–89, particularly pp. 244–49 ("Malédictions chez des disciples d'Hérode" and "Un rhéteur judaïsant"), reprinted in *Opera Minora Selecta* (Amsterdam: Hakkert, 1969–90) 5, 697–745, esp. 701–5.

[22]   L. Robert, *Le Martyre de Pionios*, ed. G. W. Bowersock and C. P. Jones (Washington: Dumbarton Oaks, 1994), 58–59 and 82–89.

[23]   M. Jacobs, *Patriarchen*, 267–68.

[24]   Lib., *Epist.* 1097 (Stern, 2, 594–95, no. 501).

never been seriously considered, but if one compares the repeated use of the plural *patriarchae* in the various imperial utterances in the Theodosian Code, and the rare use of the singular,[25] it might be prudent to assume that although the *nāśîʾ* was a patriarch (and obviously the most important one), not every patriarch was or could be the *nāśîʾ*. If this is the case, we can see why Origen chose to use the word ethnarch, and why the Hillel he names as patriarch is unknown to the tradition as a *nāśîʾ* at the time. Eusebius in the next century railed at the Jewish patriarchs, but no one seems to have noticed why. It is not, as has been claimed, that Eusebius simply thought them foolish, but that he scorned them as mere youths, striplings who were undeveloped in body and mind. This would be incomprehensible with reference to the *nāśîʾ*, but not to his young sons.

A Latin document from the late fourth century not only supports this supposition but provides additional proof of the confusion of ethnic and cultural features that characterizes the age. Like Numenius, this document exaggerates but tells us something by doing so. As we have seen, the startling notion that Plato was nothing more than Moses speaking in Greek nonetheless serves to illustrate the crossing of ethnic and cultural boundaries at the time it was put forward. Similarly the author of the imperial biographies known collectively as the *Historia Augusta* fabricated a letter from Hadrian to Julius Servianus that tells nothing about Hadrian but much about the epoch when the author was writing.[26] The subject is the Egyptians, and what is said in the letter, particularly about the substantial Samaritan community in Egypt, would be inconceivable in the Hadrianic period. But as a comment on the late fourth century the letter mirrors, in its distorted way, a recognizable

---

[25] In *Cod. Theod.* 16.8: the prevalence of plurals here is noted by Jacobs, *Patriarchen*, 267–68.

[26] *S.H.A, Quad. Tyrann.* 8.1–10 (Stern, 2, 636–37, no. 527). See the article by W. Schmid, "Die Koexistenz von Sarapiskult und Christentum im Hadrianbrief bei Vopiscus," *Bonner Historia-Augusta-Colloquium 1964–5* (Bonn: Habelt, 1966) 153–84, and above all R. Syme, "*Ipse Ille Patriarcha*," in *Emperors and Biography: Studies in the Historia Augusta* (Oxford: Clarendon Press, 1971), 17–29.

world: "Those who worship Serapis are, in fact, Christians, and those who call themselves bishops of Christ are, in fact, devotees of Serapis. There is no chief of the Jewish synagogue, no Samaritan, no Christian presbyter, who is not an astrologer, a soothsayer, or a trainer of athletes. Even the great patriarch himself (*ipse ille patriarcha*), when he comes to Egypt, is forced by some to worship Serapis, by others to worship Christ."

The ease with which Christians, Jews, and Samaritans accommodated themselves to the cults and cultural practices of polytheism is robustly parodied here, but the joke would make no sense without an underlying reality. Almost everyone now accepts that the patriarch to whom the writer refers is the Jewish patriarch, since the remarks about his coming to Egypt and being forced to worship either Serapis or Christ would make no sense for the Christian patriarch of Alexandria. But if he is indeed the Jewish patriarch, the Latin phrase that refers to him deserves special scrutiny, *ipse ille patriarcha*. Why *ille*? This, we may suppose, is the *nāśîʾ* as opposed to other patriarchs. Latin *ille* in such phrases indicates a reference to the most eminent or famous bearer of the name. If there had been only one person who could be called patriarch, it would have been quite sufficient to name the patriarch himself, *ipse patriarcha*. The *Historia Augusta* is thus a witness here not only to the instability of boundaries but to the structure of a celebrated institution.

Ethnic Jews were subject to their patriarch, but they lived out their lives in local communities. Their relations to the scholarly rabbinate were distant, but their synagogues stood close to the Christian churches and the polytheist shrines that constituted the centers of other local communities. The decorations of dwellings and even of places of worship among the adherents of the various religions of Palestine could draw without apology or embarrassment upon a common stock of Hellenic motifs, like the stories of Dionysus and Heracles that grace the mosaic discovered at Sepphoris in the late 1980s.[27] The shared myths that the

---

27   E. Meyers *et al.*, "Artistry in Stone: the Mosaics of Ancient Sepphoris," *BA* 50, (1987), 223–31. See also G. W. Bowersock, *Hellenism in Late Antiquity* (Ann Arbor and Cambridge, 1990), 49.

various communities knew and enjoyed in no way compromised the ethnic or religious identity of their members. Libanius had not insulted the patriarch when he introduced the story of Telephus and Achilles into his letter. The sixth-century mosaic at Scythopolis with a medallion containing a bust of Tyche with her walled crown betrays nothing about the identity of the inhabitant of the room, who can only have rejoiced in a familiar image that evoked many centuries of urban life. The Jews who dwelled in a house in the western suburb of the city cannot have been repelled or unsettled by the scene of Ulysses and the Sirens that they saw every day.[28]

In evoking the religious communities of Palestine we must remind ourselves again, as we did at the beginning, of the size and connectedness of this vast region. There is an understandable tendency to concentrate on the north, and on the Galilee in particular. Many Jews moved there in the second century, and so much of importance in the creation of Jewish tradition was accomplished there. Sites like Tiberias, Scythopolis, and Sepphoris properly occupy our attention for their historical role and their surviving antiquities. Comparatively less attention is accorded to the Christian communities that grew up in southern Palestine. The extraordinary increase in the number of late antique churches in the Negev and in Transjordan needs to be remembered. Jewish communities proliferated as well in many areas outside of the Galilee. Unfortunately the ease with which adherents of monotheist religions used polytheist motifs and myths make it difficult to count or evaluate the pagan communities. But if we simply concentrate on Jews and Christians the vigor of religious communities outside of the Galilee is striking, even surprising.

In the area around Tel Aviv archaeological remains for the fifth century reveal nearly thirty Jewish communities and a comparable number

---

[28]   For these images at Scythopolis, see the discussion in Y. Tsafrir and G. Foerster, "From Scythopolis to Baysan—Changing Concepts of Urbanism," in G. R. D. King, Averil Cameron, eds., *The Byzantine and Early Islamic Near East 2: Land Use and Settlement Pattern* (Princeton: Darwin, 1994), 95–115, esp. 102.

of Christian ones. The territory around Ashkelon shows ten synagogues in the same period, by comparison with fourteen churches. The region of Jericho, not conspicuously populous, nonetheless had five identifiable Jewish communities and only nine Christian ones. The Haifa region was densely populated with Jews in the fifth century, showing thirty-seven communities in contrast to a mere nineteen Christian congregations. Even the land around Jerusalem, which was, as is well known, predominantly Christian with more than sixty communities, still had eight synagogues in the fifth century. The Beersheva region, far better known to Byzantine sources than rabbinic ones, had two Jewish communities and only six Christian.

The distribution of religious communities naturally changed over time, drawing more and more Jews to the Galilee and wiping out the communities elsewhere—but not wholly. In the seventh century, on the eve of the Persian and Arab conquests, the Tiberias area boasted at least thirty-five Jewish communities, substantially more than two centuries earlier. But then the same area had more Christians too: thirteen congregations had grown to thirty. On the other hand, the coastal land near Haifa and Tel-Aviv had become seriously depopulated. The thirty Jewish communities documented around Tel-Aviv in the fifth century had disappeared altogether by the seventh, and the thirty-seven around Haifa had been reduced to thirteen. The Christians in both areas predominated.

These interesting figures, taken selectively from the massive tabulation of the archaeological records of the Mandate and Israeli governments prepared by Claudine Dauphin,[29] illustrate the slow but powerful demographic changes that took place across Palestine in the final centuries of the post-Hadrianic peace. They demonstrate the huge number of small communities and suggest the tenacity of many of them. Above all, they show that if we observe the Jews flourishing in the Galilee we must not forget to observe them working and praying elsewhere in Palestine,

---

[29]   Claudine Dauphin, *La Palestine Byzantine du IVe siècle au VIIe siècle ap. J.-C. — Le peuplement*, Thèse pour le Doctorat d'État (Paris, 1994), 3 vols. in 8 parts.

alongside Christians and a declining but sometimes noisy population of polytheists. Nor must we forget those Christians who worshipped by the Sea of Galilee, and those pagans who made their way past Jews and Christians in the busy streets of Caesarea in the sixth century to mount the steps of the temple of Hadrian.

Inevitably trouble occurred from time to time, as when Constantine ordered the destruction of a great cult center by the sacred oak at Mambre, which had attracted pagans as well as Jews and Christians in great throngs.[30] At Gaza, Eudocia's enormous church was built on the site of the shrine of Marnas in a vain effort to suppress that city's vibrant and often tumultuous pagan community, which the bishop Porphyrius found himself wholly unable to restrain.[31] The two celebrated Samaritan disturbances, whatever be thought of their extent or severity, should probably be seen as fundamentally internecine conflicts of the non-Christian monotheists.[32] Occasionally violence was imported into Palestine by fanatics from the outside, like the murderous monks from Mesopotamia in the early fifth century.[33] But overall, violence was infrequent. The ethnic and cultural communities with their broad range of religious observances and their local roots were integral parts of a larger Palestinian world. These communities did not exist with walls around them to keep them from associating with each other. Quite the contrary. Among educated persons bilingualism was common, and trilingualism not unknown. The communities enriched each other, and sometimes converted each other.

The most widespread conversions were undeniably of polytheists to Christianity. The nature of the conversion is usually impossible to document, but in the case of one ethnic group we have some instructive

---

[30] *Euseb., V. Const.* 3.52–53; Sozom., *Hist. Eccl.* 2.4.

[31] *Vit. Porph.* 39–51, 75, 84.

[32] For details and a somewhat different perspective on these revolts see the paper of Leah Di Segni in the present volume. On the nature of the revolts, see also Bowersock *DOP* (forthcoming).

[33] F. Nau, *Rev. Or. Chrét.*, 2ième Série, T.8, vol. 18 (1913), 382.

details. The Nabataeans were ethnic Arabs who dominated Transjordan and the Negev for nearly five centuries. They were polytheists, whose cults were amalgamated to some degree to those of the Greeks after the transformation of their kingdom into a Roman province, first Arabia and later Third Palestine. Nabataean communities such as those at Petra and Avdat on opposite sides of the Arava have left ample evidence for the worship of their gods, of whom at least one was a deceased King Obodas.[34] Inscriptions identify him not only as a god but on occasion also as Zeus—Zeus Obodas.[35] The conflation of the supreme Greek deity with the king doubtless explains why the cult of Obodas served the Nabataeans for so long. As late as 267/8 a temple at Avdat still observed this cult, and an undated graffito not far away records the erection of a statue to the god-king by a writer whose text has four lines of Nabataean and, in the middle, two lines of Arabic.[36] This is a vigorous representation of a strictly ethnic cult in late Roman Palestine.

By the end of the third century polytheism had not much of a future in the Negev, but across the Arava in Third Palestine the Nabataeans maintained, according to Epiphanius, the cult of another of their gods at Petra. The birth of Dusares, the Nabataean divinity normally regarded as the chief god of the people, was celebrated annually in a mysterious rite with a text recited in the Arabic language. The god was represented as born by parthenogenesis, and since virgin birth is otherwise unexampled in Nabataean religion (and indeed until rather late in Greek religion) we would appear to have a stunning instance of the contamination of polytheism by Christianity in Palestine.[37] This is one of the last records of the Nabataeans as an ethnic group. It appears that the conversion to Christianity dispersed them into the larger society of the region, but even so the memory survived in names.

---

[34]   Uranius, *Frag. griech. Hist.* (Jacoby) III C 675, F 24.

[35]   A. Negev, "Obodas the God," *IEJ* 36 (1986), 56–60.

[36]   Negev, "Obodas," 56–60.

[37]   Epiphanius, *Panar.* 51.22.11. Cf. Bowersock, *Hellenism*, 24–25.

The newly discovered archive of papyri in a church at Petra has revealed members of the Christian community there with unmistakably Nabataean names in the middle of the sixth century: Obodianus, whose name was clearly formed from that of the deified king of the Nabataeans, was undoubtedly of Nabataean descent, and Dusarios, whose name recalls the god Dusares, must also have been another person of Nabataean origin.[38] Ethnicity proclaimed itself in this way over a millennium after the Nabataeans first settled in Petra. The end of the Nabataean *ethnos* forms a striking contrast with the proud survival of the Jews as a people, both in Palestine and abroad. It is worth asking whether that peculiar imperviousness of monotheism to assimilation may not account for the different destinies of Nabataeans and Jews. Jews took over Greek words into their language, and they enjoyed Greek myths and motifs in their synagogues, but the Jewish God could never have been worshipped as Zeus, as Obodas and Dusares both were. The Nabataeans were thus vulnerable to a loss of their narrower ethnic identity and disappeared into the more capacious ethnic category of Arabs, whose identity was soon to be defined by the monotheism of Islam.

Nonetheless, as we have seen in the case of Jewish and Christian communities, it can often happen that the partial appropriation of cultural motifs, images, and even ideas from another community or tradition deepens the understanding of one's own heritage. A mirror held up from the outside can help to clarify things. We may return to Numenius' appeal to Moses, because it was just such an appropriation. His own sense of the hierarchy of the gods in a polytheist universe made more sense to him when he could place the Jewish god as the father of all the others.

It was in a similar spirit that a Jewish physician and philosopher of the ninth century turned to Plato to enrich Jewish thought. Isaac ben Solomon Israeli introduced Neoplatonism into Judaism.[39] Writing as a

---

[38] L. Koenen, "Phoenix from the Ashes: The Burnt Archive from Petra," *Michigan Quarterly Review* 35 (1996), 513–31.

[39] See S. W. Baron, *A Social and Religious History of the Jews* (New York and Philadelphia: Columbia and JPS, 1952–83) 8, 57–61 and, above all, S. M. Stern and

Jew but in the Arabic language, drawing upon the pagan Greek Plato as mediated through the Muslim al-Kindi, he created a fruitful confusion of traditions to initiate the great legacy of Jewish Neoplatonism. Seven centuries after Numenius had proclaimed the Greek Moses, Isaac Israeli stepped forth to assume the role of the Jewish Plato. In doing so he reaffirmed, as Numenius had done, that the presence of other peoples and cultures, if not seen as a threat, can invigorate one's own people. This is what Palestinians of all stripes proved, in spite of occasional local turbulence, for the nearly five centuries before the Persians invaded Jerusalem.

A. Altmann, *Isaac Israeli*, Scripta Judaica 1 (Oxford: Oxford University Press, 1958).

II.

RELIGIOUS AND ETHNIC COMMUNITIES

THE SAMARITANS
IN ROMAN-BYZANTINE PALESTINE:
SOME MISAPPREHENSIONS

Leah Di Segni

The Hebrew University

WORKING AS I DO in close contact both with the ancient sources and with archaeological news, an uncomfortable feeling often creeps upon me, that we deal with the Samaritans as with a ghost people. On the one hand, sources—and first of all the Samaritan sources themselves—seem to me not to be doing justice to Samaritan history and realities. On the other hand, archaeological news, including new discoveries and reconsideration of long-known material data, tend to use the Samaritan entity as a solution for odd problems rather than setting it up as a historical-archaeological question to be explored, on a par with other ethnic groups in Palestine. Accordingly, archaeologists as well as historians occasionally evoke the Samaritan ghost in the most unexpected places and circumstances. The opposite also happens: that is, the option of a Samaritan presence is ignored in sites where it should be surmised, as it were, by geographical right. In what follows, I shall confine myself to a concise mention of a few examples, with the warning that, in my opinion, they should be considered as representative of a shallow approach to the whole question of Samaritan ethnicity rather than as interpretative faults of specific issues.

We have good reason to believe the unanimous evidence contributed by Procopius of Caesarea, Cyril of Scythopolis and John Malalas about the heavy damages caused to the Samarian countryside by the revolt of 529.[1] But this does not imply that all traces of destruction in any part of Palestine that can be approximately dated to the sixth century may be ascribed to the Samaritans. The misrepresentation is even worse when evidence of renovation of buildings is interpreted as proof of a prior damage, and the whole process is connected with the Samaritan revolt. This scenario has been suggested, for instance, for the Church of the Nativity at Bethlehem, which, according to Eutychius of Alexandria, was reconstructed by Justinian. If it was reconstructed, obviously it had been destroyed first, and by whom if not by the Samaritan rebels? This in spite of the fact that Eutychius, the only source for Justinian's intervention, states that the emperor himself had the church dismantled and rebuilt because it was too small.[2] Damage caused by the Samaritan revolt has been suggested also in the case of Emmaus.[3]

---

[1] Procop., *Historia Arcana* 11.29–30; Cyr. Scyth. *Vit. Sabae* 70, 73, ed. E. Schwartz (*Texte und Untersuchungen zur Geschichte der Altchristlichen Literatur* 49ii: Leipzig: J. Hinrichs Verlag, 1939), 173, 176–77; Joannes Malalas, *Chronographia* 50.18, ed. L. Dindorf (*CHSB* 13: Bonn: Weber, 1831), 447.

[2] Eutychius, *Annales* 17.3, trans. B. Pirone (Eutichio, *Gli Annali* [Cairo: Franciscan Printing Press, 1987] 293); M. Avi-Yonah, "Bethlehem," *EAEHL* I (Jerusalem: Israel Exploration Society and Massada Press; 1975), 201, 204. Procop. *Aed.* makes no mention of this work of Justinian, although he reports that the emperor restored the wall of Bethlehem and built the monastery of Abbot John: *Aed.* 5.9.12–13.

[3] L.-H. Vincent et F.-M. Abel, *Emmaüs, sa basilique et son histoire* (Paris: E. Leroux, 1932), 353–54: Abel speaks vaguely of damages to the buildings and the basilica of the *Fractio Panis* in the city at the hands of the Samaritans ("*Dans ces conditions, il sarait bien surprendant qu'Emmaüs n'ait pas eu à souffrir d'une telle effervescence...*"); he also states that the synagogue of Emmaus fell victim of the reaction of the authorities after the revolt; his statement is taken up by S. Winkler, "Die Samariter in den Jahren 529/30," *Klio* 43/45 (1965), 443. Admittedly, it seems that in the sixth century the earlier church was renovated and enlarged; however, *pace* the Dominican fathers, there is absolutely no trace of destruction or damage. Neither a synagogue nor any other building was excavated at all—so the statement remains pure fancy.

In another case, Samaritan rebels are conjured in the neighborhood of Gaza in order to explain an obscure passage of Choricius.[4] In his encomium of Bishop Marcianus the rhetor speaks of the passage of soldiers through the city on their way to fight some unspecified trouble-makers (*polemō sōphronisai tous hamartanontas*). Although the date of the encomium, between 535/6 and 548, fits more or less the period of Samaritan disturbances, especially if, as it seems, they were protracted for some years beyond the acute phase in 529–30, there is no real justi-fication for this surmise, and southern Palestine can hardly be seen as a favorable terrain for Samaritan guerrillas.

On the other hand, the option of a Samaritan presence is sometimes neglected when the epigraphical or archaeological finds would permit or even require that it should be explored. Admittedly, we have as yet no clear-cut criteria to define what constitutes Samaritan culture, if such a culture can be defined as a separate entity. The best known clue is the presence of the Samaritan script, that is, the ancient Hebrew writing used in Samaritan sacred inscriptions, even after Jews had adopted the variant of the Aramaic alphabet known as "Jewish script." However, on the one hand, there is no reason to believe that Samaritans consistently avoided the use of the Jewish script, at least in profane inscriptions and texts; and, on the other hand, the occasional use of the paleo-Hebrew script by Jews cannot be excluded: Epiphanius states that sacred texts in the ancient script were still in use among Jews in his time.[5] Another

---

[4]   Chor., *Laudatio Marciani* 2.23–24, eds. R. Foerster and E. Richsteig (Leipzig: Teubner, 1929), 34; A. Rabinowitz, "*Dibrê Koriqios ʿalʾereṣ yisrāʾēl*," in M. Schwabe and I. Gutman eds., *Commentationes Iudaico-Hellenisticae in memoriam Iohannis Lewy* (Jerusalem: Magnes Press, 1949), 181; F. K. Litsas, *Choricius of Gaza: An Approach to His Work* (diss.: University of Chicago, 1981), 69, 248–49, n. 28.

[5]   Epiph. *De gemmis*, *PG* 43, 357–58. The use of the old Hebrew script by the Samaritans is attested by Jerome (*Comm. in Ezech.* 3.9.4, *CCSL* 75, 106) and in the Babylonian Talmud (*b. San.* 21b). Z. Safrai, "Samaritan Synagogues in the Roman-Byzantine Period" [Hebrew], *Cathedra* 4 (1977), 86–87, suggested that the Samaritans may have used both scripts; R. Pummer, "Samaritan Material Remains and Archaeology," in A. D. Crown, ed., *The Samaritans* (Tübingen: J. C. B. Mohr, 1989),

well-known clue is the appearance of Samaritan amulets bearing quotations from the Samaritan Pentateuch in the Hebrew script; but these
amulets are often found in a mixed context. That indicates that, although
they may have been produced by Samaritans, they were certainly worn
by members of other ethnic-religious communities too.[6] Some valuable
work has been done on Samaritan lamps. Varda Sussman has shown
that the geographical distribution of these lamps, which make their
appearance in the third to fourth centuries, coincides with the region
that is known from historical sources and archaeological finds to have
been inhabited by Samaritans—although not exclusively by them—in
late antiquity.[7] But again, even if such lamps were indeed manufactured
in Samaritan workshops, there is no proof that they were not purchased
and used also by non-Samaritans. It follows that none of the above-
mentioned pointers can be accepted as an undisputed indication of

---

136–38, discusses the issue and finally rejects the suggestion, not quite convincingly
in my opinion.

[6]   R. Pummer, "Samaritan Amulets from the Roman-Byzantine period and their
Wearers," *RB* 94 (1987), 251–63. Pummer even goes so far as to maintain that the
Samaritan amulets were not used by Samaritans, but by Jews and Christians.

[7]   V. Sussman, "Samaritan Lamps of the 3rd–4th Centuries AD," *IEJ* 28 (1978),
238–50; *eadem*, "A Samaritan Oil Lamp from Apollonia-Arsuf" [Hebrew], *Tel Aviv*
10 (1983), 71–76. See also R. Pummer, "Samaritan Material Remains," 157–62.
Another element supposed to be typically Samaritan is the type or rather types of
2nd–3rd c. sarcophagi known as Samaritan. But the so-called Samaritan sarcophagi seem to be rather a feature of regional culture than of ethnic culture, and
there is no evidence that they were introduced by Samaritans or used exclusively by
them. For a survey of the question from opposed points of view, see R. Barkay,
"Four Samaritan Sarcophagi of the Roman Period" [Hebrew], *EI* 19 (1987), 6–18;
eadem, "A Roman-Period Samaritan Burial from Talluza," *Bulletin of the Anglo-
Israeli Archaeological Society* 7 (1987–88), 8–20; *eadem*, "Samaritan Sarcophagi of
the Roman Period in the Land of Israel," *Proceedings of the 1st International
Congress of the Societé d'Études Samaritaines, Tel Aviv 11–13.4.1988* (Tel Aviv:
Chaim Rosenberg School for Jewish Studies, Tel Aviv University, 1991) 83–95; Y.
Magen, "The 'Samaritan' Sarchophagi," in F. Manns and E. Alliata eds., *Early
Christianity in Context: Monuments and Documents* (*SBF Collectio Maior*, no. 38:
Jerusalem: The Franciscan Printing Press, 1993), 149–66.

Samaritan presence in a specific area. On the contrary, discoveries made in the last years indicate that elements formerly believed to be exclusively Jewish were no less characteristic of the Samaritan milieu. So, for instance, holy ark, menorah, shofar, bread-table, and other paraphernalia of the Temple cult have appeared in mosaic pavements of synagogues that are identified as Samaritan by their location and orientation.[8] *Miqwā°ôt* (ritual baths) have been discovered in the heart of the Samarian countryside.[9] Typical Jewish names, like Nahum, Bartholemy and Rebecca, appear in fourth-century dedications in the Samaritan holy place on Mount Gerizim.[10] A study I have conducted on the occurrence of the formula *heis theos* in Palestinian inscriptions has led me to the conclusion that this acclamation, usually considered a certain clue of the Christian or at least Jewish-Christian character of the monuments on which it appears, is neither Jewish nor Christian in the large majority of its occurrences in Palestine. On the contrary, it often appears in a pagan context, not only in the well-known instance of the acclamations of Emperor Julian, but also in earlier acclamations of Sarapis and Kore in Samaria. Moreover, it is most characteristic of Samaritan holy places, including the holiest of all, the temenos on Mount Gerizim.[11]

---

[8]   Y. Magen, "Samaritan Synagogues," *Early Christianity in Context,* 193–230.

[9]   Y. Magen, "Qedumim: a Samaritan Site of the Roman-Byzantine Period" [Hebrew], *Qadmoniot* 16 (1983), 76–83 (English version in *Early Christianity in Context,* 167–89); *idem,* "The Miqva°ot in Qedumim and the Purification Standards of the Samaritans" [Hebrew], *Cathedra* 34 (1985), 15–26 (English version "The Ritual Baths [Miqva°ot] at Qedumim and the Observance of Ritual Purity among the Samaritans," *Early Christianity in Context,* 181–92). See also R. Pummer, "Samaritan Material Remains," 162–65.

[10]   L. Di Segni, "The Church of Mary Theotokos on Mount Gerizim: the Inscriptions," in G. C. Bottini, L. Di Segni, and E. Alliata eds., *Christian Archaeology in the Holy Land: New Discoveries* (*SBF Collectio Maior,* no. 36: Jerusalem: Franciscan Printing Press, 1990), 343–50.

[11]   E. Peterson, ΕΙΣ ΘΕΟΣ (Göttingen: Vandenhoeck und Ruprecht, 1926); L. Di Segni, "Εἷς θεός" in Palestinian Inscriptions," *SCI* 13 (1994), 94–115.

Two conclusions follow. The first is that no one pointer can have decisive weight in the question of whether a specific monument or site is to be considered Samaritan. Only the combination of multiple clues, one being the geographical location, can incline the scale in one direction or the other. The second conclusion is that the appearance of traditionally Jewish elements in any area where a Samaritan presence is also attested must arouse at least the suspicion that the monument or site might after all be not Jewish but Samaritan. For instance, epitaphs in Greek found near Caesarea and characterized as Jewish because of the appearance of Jewish names, sometimes accompanied by a menorah or other Jewish symbols or formulas, cannot in my opinion be considered Jewish with absolute certainty, for the language, the names, and the symbols were common also among Samaritans.

The Sharon and the border area between Judaea and Samaria, around Lod, Emmaus, and Gophna were inhabited by Jews and by Samaritans, sometimes at the same time, sometimes in successive periods. When *miqwā'ôt* or tombs inscribed with Jewish names in Greek or in Aramaic are discovered, how are we to determine whether the site was a Jewish or a Samaritan settlement? A rule of thumb generally used is as follows. The *communis opinio* among historians is that after the First Revolt and especially after the Bar Kokhba war the Jewish population was in recession, while the Samaritans enjoyed a demographic growth that brought them to expand within the next two or three centuries outside the boundaries of Samaria and into the neighboring areas previously occupied by Jews. Therefore, any remains that can be dated to the Second Temple period or up to the mid-second century are ascribed to Jews, and later occupation to Samaritans, especially if evidence of an occupation gap can be shown. For instance, in burial caves at Jatt (map reference 1543/2005) Aramaic inscriptions were found with the names Joshua, Jacob, and Rebeccah, accompanied by Herodian lamps and potsherds of the Roman and Byzantine periods. According to the excavators, the place was first used by Jews, then taken over by Samaritans.[12]

---

[12]   Y. Porath, Y. Neeman and A. Boshnino, "Jatt," *ESI* 7–8 (1988–89), 83–84. The

The same sequence can be suggested for sites in the Modiin area where *miqwā'ôt* were discovered in close proximity to oil and wine presses—an arrangement required by the purity rules and typical of Samaritans as well as of Jews.[13] In this case, the issue is even more complicated because of the difficulty of dating the construction of *miqwā'ôt*. Now, the hypothesis of Samaritan expansion is certainly reasonable and probably sound. What is unreasonable and unsound is making use of it to interpret archaeological data whose significance is far from evident *per se*. Beside the obvious danger of misrepresenting the evidence, this kind of generalization may also lead into another pitfall, namely, exploiting the results of interpretation to strengthen the historical hypothesis, and then using the strengthened hypothesis to interpret the next excavation and so on in a circular fashion.

Another issue of Samaritan history that has repercussions in the interpretation of archaeological data is the revolt under Zeno, traditionally dated to AD 484. Evidence of damage to buildings and destruction or abandonment of settlements in Samaria has been explained as a result of either the first revolt of 484 or the second revolt of 529. Indeed a number of sites show signs of having come to a violent end in the late fifth or early sixth century. However, the dates of the two revolts being so close to one another, it is naturally generally impossible to ascertain which of the two events brought about the tragic results, except in the case of Kh. Buraq, where numismatic evidence proves that the destruc-

---

excavators cite parallels of this sequence in several other sites in the Sharon, e.g. H. Ra'ash, Umm Khaled, Maghar, esh-Sharaf (cf. Y. Porath, S. Dar and S. Applebaum, *The History and Archaeology of 'Emeq Ḥefer* [Hebrew] [Tel Aviv: Ha-Kibbutz ha-Me'uhad, 1985]). Later, another burial cave, with the same sequence and several 'Jewish' names (Berenike, Miriam, Agrippa, Zoilus, Paulus, Marcus etc.) inscribed in Greek, was discovered in the same site: Y. Porath, "Jatt, Burial Cave," *ESI* 9 (1989–90), 43.

[13] E.g., H. Hermeshit (map reference 1476/1509): Z. Greenhut, "Horvat Hermeshit (Ne'ot Qedumim)," *ESI* 7–8 (1988–89), 81–83; 9 (1989–90), 141–43. Later a chapel, possibly part of a monastery, was built on the site, indicating that it had been taken over by Christians: Z. Greenhut and M. Iron-Lubin, *ESI* 10 (1991), 123–24.

tion was not earlier than Justinian's time. Nevertheless, this does not prevent scholars from presenting these archaeological data as evidence of the cumulative damage caused by the two events on the settlement pattern of Samaria.[14] In my opinion, not only the archaeological finds but also the historical sources, if carefully read, do not support the hypothesis of a destructive uprising in the days of Zeno that may have affected the population of the countryside in a manner comparable with the results of the revolt of 529.

The sources on the events of 484 can be divided into three groups: A. Procopius of Caesarea in his work *De aedificiis*; B. different versions of the relevant chapter in Malalas' *Chronographia*, and an entry in the *Chronicon Paschale* that follows Malalas or his source; and C. Samaritan sources, whose historical value is uncertain for they preserve a rather foggy and confused popular tradition and were put into writing not earlier than the Middle Ages. The description of the events is so different in Procopius and Malalas that, were it not for the identity of the conclusion—the erection of the Church of Mary Theotokos on Mount Gerizim—it would be impossible to refer the reports to the same crisis. The divergence originates partly from the use of different sources, and partly from a different approach to the available information due to the difference in literary genre between the two works. Malalas as a chronographer was interested in the juiciest news items, while Procopius was intent on relating the history of the church of the Theotokos and touched on the surrounding circumstances only inasmuch as they were relevant to his restricted perspective. Moreover, since his work was in fact a panegyric, the Caesarean historian may have been reluctant to

---

[14]   For a survey of the evidence and its interpretation, see S. Dar, "Additional Archaeological Evidence of the Samaritan Rebellions in the Byzantine Period," in A. D. Crown and L. Davey eds., *Essays in Honour of G.D. Sixdenier: New Samaritan Studies of the Société d' Études Samaritaines* III and IV (*University of Sydney Studies in Judaica*, no. 5: Armidale: Mandelbaum, 1995), 157–68, and, for Kh. Buraq, p. 163. A first version of this article appeared in Hebrew in D. Jacoby and Y. Tsafrir eds., *Jews, Christians and Samaritans in Byzantine Palestine* (Jeruslem: Yad Izhak Ben-Zvi, 1988), 228–37.

give too much space to events whose recollection was potentially disagreeable to the imperial authority.

Procopius (*Aed.* 5.7) opens his report on Mount Gerizim with a remark on the sanctity of the mountaintop in the eyes of the Samaritans, who regularly came there to pray, not because of having ever built a sacred edifice there, but out of veneration for the site itself. But when Jesus passed through the place and talked with the Samaritan woman, he prophesied that in future not the Samaritans but the Christians would worship on Mount Gerizim. This is a hint to the episode narrated in John 4:5–28, but it must be noted that the evangelical message is definitely twisted in Procopius' version, for what Jesus really said was that "the hour is coming when neither on this mountain nor in Jerusalem will you worship the Father... but the true worshippers will worship the Father in spirit and truth" (John 4:21–23). Procopius goes on to say that the prediction came true in the following way. During the reign of Zeno the Samaritans attacked the Christians in Neapolis, while they were in church celebrating the Pentecost. They disturbed the religious ceremony, killed many, and slashed at Bishop Terebinthus who was standing at the altar and cut off the fingers of his hand. The bishop went to Byzantium, begged the emperor to avenge the injury and reminded him of Jesus' prophecy. Zeno then decided to punish the perpetrators of the outrage: he drove out the Samaritans from Mount Gerizim and handed it over to the Christians. He built a church dedicated to the Mother of God and surrounded it with a wall, and he placed a large garrison in Neapolis, with a guard post of ten soldiers at the fortifications of the church. The Samaritans bitterly resented the action but did not resist, out of fear of the emperor. Then Procopius relates an attack made on the church by a group of Samaritans led by a woman during Anastasius' reign, and the suppression of this aborted uprising by the governor, Procopius of Edessa. Finally the historian reports Justinian's decision to convert the Samaritans and to fortify the church so that it would effectively resist any further assault.

Summing up, Procopius' account contains a number of precise details that reveal a first-hand knowledge of local circumstances and topography and of the personages involved in the several episodes. Moreover, the twisted version of the evangelical story given by the historian seems to be an innovation of the local church, for, to my knowledge, it does not appear in any text or commentary of the Gospel of John, and on the other hand, according to Procopius' testimony it was used by Bishop Terebinthus to induce the emperor to take away the holy mountain from the Samaritans. Procopius, born in Caesarea about 15 years after the erection of the church on Mount Gerizim, and a youth at the time of the aborted uprising under Anastasius, can reasonably be expected to have had inside information on the events. Procopius' version seems therefore reliable as far as it goes, in spite of his silence about the facts reported by Malalas, which have no direct bearing on the specific angle dealt with by him.

As for Malalas, he ignores the episode of Neapolis and gives a completely different version of the events. I shall quote his words, combining the slightly different versions that have come down to us.[15]

> During the reign of Zeno members of the Samaritan nation rebelled against the legitimate authority (*etyrannēsan*) with some pretext, and crowned a brigand chieftain named Justasas the Samaritan. He came to Caesarea, attended the chariot races, and killed many [Christians][16]

---

[15]   *Chron.*, ed. Bonn 382–83; *Excerpta historica iussu Constantini Porphyrogeneti, Excerpta de insidiis*, 32, ed. C. de Boor (Berlin, 1905), 162; *Chronicle of John Malalas, Books VIII–XVIII, Translated from the Church Slavonic*, ed. M. Spinka and G. Downey (Chicago: University of Chicago Press, 1940), 100–1. The text of the *Chronographia* that has come down to us is an abridged version of the original, which is lost.

[16]   The translation is my own: I chose not to use E. Jeffrey, M. Jeffreys, R. Scott, *The Chronicle of John Malalas* (Melbourne and Sydney: Australian Association for Byzantine Studies and the Department of Modern Greek, University of Sydney, 1986), because, in my opinion, the relevant passage in it (Book 15.8, p. 212) is vitiated by interpretation. According to the translators Justasas "presided over the chariot-races and killed many Christians," but I believe that this translation of *etheōrēsen hippikon*, though permissible in a context that may justify it, is forced in this case. As to the addition *Christianous*, only the text of the *Chronographia* has it, while the *Excerpta* and the Slavonic version both say only that "he killed many people (*pollous*)."

during the administration of *Palaestina Prima* by Porphyry. The same
Justasas also set fire to the Church of St. Procopius, at the time of Timothy,
bishop of Caesarea. And the *dux Palaestinae* Asclepiades immediately
came with his forces, and the sheriff (*lēstodiōktēs*) Reges, the officer in
charge of Caesarea, [came] with the Arcadiani, and they went in pursuit
with their soldiers, caught up with Justasas, and captured and beheaded
him, and his head with the diadem was sent to Emperor Zeno. And immediately Zeno converted their synagogue that was on Mount Gerizim into
a church of the holy Mother of God. He also restored St. Procopius and
issued an edict that no Samaritans be admitted into the army, after having
confiscated the property of the wealthy among them. And so there was
fear and peace.

To complete the survey of the sources, the *Chronicon Paschale* follows
Malalas closely, while, curiously enough, pseudo-Zacharias and Theophanes say nothing of the rebellion under Zeno, though both write full
accounts of this emperor's reign.[17] The Samaritan sources describe the
chain of events that led to the expulsion of the Samaritans from Mount
Gerizim in terms of a violent struggle for the control of the holy places,
but they say nothing of a rebellion.[18] Their account of the struggle begins
with the reign of Marcian. In order to avoid a war, the two sides each
put forth a champion to duel. The Samaritan champion, the hero Justas,
fought against the representative of the Christians; the latter made use
of black magic but was defeated notwithstanding. Later Zeno came to

---

[17]   *Chron. Pasch.*, *PG* 92, 840–44; *The Syriac Chronicle known as that of Zacharias
of Mitylene, Books V–VI*, trans. F. J. Hamilton and E. W. Brooks (London: Methuen,
1899), 101–46; Theophanes, *Chronographia* I, ed. C. de Boor, (Leipzig: Teubner,
1883), 120–26. Since both pseudo-Zacharias and Theophanes were duly aware of
the facts and political implication of the 529 revolt, their silence about the events of
484 may indicate that in their eyes those events had not the magnitude supposed by
modern historians.

[18]   E. N. Adler, "Une nouvelle chronique samaritaine," *REJ* 45 (1902), 235–36;
Abu'l Fath, *Annales Samaritani*, ed. E. Vilmar (Gotha: Perthes, 1865), 169–72.
Admittedly the Samaritan chronicles are rather sketchy from the late fifth century
on, to the point that they say nothing of the revolt of 529: cf. J. A. Montgomery, *The
Samaritans* (Philadelphia: Winston, 1907; rpt. New York: Ktav Publishing House,
1968), 114.

Shechem, persecuted the Samaritans, took the synagogue of Helqat Sade in the city away from them, and converted it into a monastery. Then he took over the whole of the holy mountain, with the synagogue of Baba Rabba and the water reservoir that were at the foot of Gerizim, and built a tomb and many buildings on the summit.

Returning to the versions of Malalas and Procopius, the former seems to be much fuller than the latter, and it is the one generally used by modern historians for their reconstruction of the facts. Some scholars, for example, Montgomery and Abel,[19]also attach considerable weight to the Samaritan sources and stress the issue of the holy places as the main cause of the revolt. Yet even for these scholars, Procopius' report of the incident in Shechem is left in the shadow. Most scholars not only use but abuse Malalas' account by enriching it with elements borrowed from the revolt of 529. For instance, Yaron Dan, following Stein, maintained that the Samaritans planned the rebellion in view of political events on the imperial and even international scale, riding the wave of Illus' revolt, in the hope of availing themselves of the help of those enemies of the empire, Armenians and Persians, who had promised their support to the usurper.[20] According to this interpretation, the Samaritan uprising was not a spontaneous outbreak, but a well-planned campaign, at the beginning of which the rebels enjoyed some successes and even chose a king, gained control of Neapolis, conquered the capital of the province, Caesarea, and celebrated games there as a mark of the triumph of Justasas.[21] Justasas also persecuted the Christians and their

---

[19]   Montgomery, *The Samaritans,* 110–12; F.-M. Abel, *Histoire de la Palestine depuis la conquête d'Alexandre jusqu'a l'invasion arabe* (Paris: Gabalda, 1952) 2, 350.

[20]   E. Stein and J. R. Palanque, *Histoire du Bas-Empire* (Paris: Desclée de Brouwer, 1949), 31–32; Y. Dan, "The Circus and Its Factions in Eretz Israel during the Byzantine Period" [Hebrew], *Cathedra* 4 (1977), 134–35; *idem,* "Eretz Israel in the Fifth and Sixth Centuries" [Hebrew], in Z. Baras, S. Safrai, Y. Tsafrir and M. Stern eds., *Eretz Israel from the Destruction of the Second Temple to the Muslem Conquest* (Jerusaelm: Yad Izhak Ben-Zvi, 1982) 2, 282–83.

[21]   K. G. Holum, "Caesarea and the Samaritans," in R. H. Hohlfelder, ed., *City, Town and Countryside in the Early Byzantine Period* (Boulder: East European

cult. Only later did the *dux* succeed in rallying his forces and quenching the revolt.

This interpretation is clearly influenced by the events of 529, which included national aspirations and the crowning of a king, the conquest of Neapolis, the intervention of the rebel chief in the direction of the chariot races, and an attempt of the Samaritan leaders to enlist the help of the Persians. Curiously enough, Avi-Yonah even compressed the narration of the two revolts in one, claiming that both took the same course.[22] But in fact Malalas' account, if it is not read through the lens of the later events, does not support the above-mentioned interpretation, even if his version is accepted as reliable. Moreover, the reliability of Malalas' narration cannot be taken for granted, inasmuch as it is contradicted in several points by Procopius' testimony. Procopius states or implies the following facts that stand in contrast with Malalas' account: A. there was no general revolt of the Samaritans under Zeno, but only a local clash on religious grounds; B. the incident in Neapolis was not dealt with on the provincial level for the Christian party sought redress in Byzantium; C. the church on Mount Gerizim did not supplant a Samaritan sacred building, neither was it a converted synagogue; on the contrary, the Samaritans had no sacred building on the summit within memory of their neighbors, of whom Procopius was one. In view of these contradictions it is necessary to re-read Malalas' account criti-

---

Monographs no. 120, 1982), 69–70 maintains that the coronation of Justasas, his conquest of the capital and the celebration of chariot races indicate the degree of Romanization of the Samaritan people, who viewed the seizing of power in Byzantine-imperial terms. However, even if we take Malalas' words in this sense, the description of the Samaritan leader in terms of a Byzantine usurper does not necessarily reflect reality. This conception of power may have been in the eyes of the chronicler: he was the one that could not conceive the seizing of power in other terms than the coronation of a *basileus*, the conquest of the capital, and the celebration of triumphal games.

[22]   M. Avi-Yonah, *The Jews under Roman and Byzantine Rule* (Jerusalem: Magnes, 1984), 242–43.

cally and ascertain what he really says and how much of it can be accepted.

First of all, the involved wording of the opening sentence of the story in the *Excerpta* version (*hoi ek tou ethnous tōn Samareitōn*) seems to attest that the original text was nearer the restrained phrase of the Slavonic translation ("some [members] of the nation of Samaritans in Palestine") than the blunt (*hoi Samareitai en Palasteinē*) of the pre-served version of the *Chronographia*. Malalas indeed states that the Samaritans crowned a king, but not that he conquered Caesarea or organized chariot races. Justasas was a spectator at the races, stirred disorders in which many were killed and a church burnt. These facts do not differ from ordinary riots caused by the circus factions.[23] The sequel is more specific: the pursuit by the *dux*, the capture of the rebel leader, his decapitation, and the sending of his crowned head to the emperor. Unfortunately, all these details are so similar to the events of 529—the latter much better documented through the testimony of Procopius of Caesarea, Cyril of Scythopolis, and Pseudo-Zacharias[24]—that one is led to suspect a doublet: indeed, part of the phrasing in the accounts of 484 and 529 is identical. But even if we accept Malalas' narration at face value, in conjunction with Procopius' report of the events in Neapolis, the resulting picture is not that of a popular revolt that swept the coun-tryside and caused the destruction of settlements. All is reduced to two riots arising from ethnic enmity in the two main cities with a mixed Christian and Samaritan population.

As to the question of the punitive measures taken by the emperor against the Samaritans—expulsion from Mount Gerizim, confiscation

---

[23] Cf. the description of the riots in Antioch under Zeno and Anastasius in Malalas, *Chron.* 389–90 and 396. It will be remembered that two of the three versions of the episode of Justasas in Caesarea speak of casualties in general and do not specify that the dead were Christians.

[24] Procop., *Historia Arcana* 11.14–33; 27.6–10; Cyr. Scyth., *Vit. Sabae* 70, ed. Schwartz, 171–73; *The Syriac Chronicle of Zacharias* 9.8 (trans. Hamilton and Brooks), 231–32.

of property, and introduction of legal disabilities—only the first can be taken as an established fact. Malalas' statement about the other steps may be influenced by the sanctions that followed the revolt of 529.[25] The exclusion of Samaritans from the civil service and the army was first sanctioned in a law issued by Honorius in 404 (*Cod. Theod.* 16.8.12) and repeated by Theodosius II in Novella 3 (438 or 439); Justinian re-enacted it in *Cod. Just.* 1.5.18, issued between 527 and 531, but there is no trace in the Novellae or in the Justinian Code of a re-enactment by Zeno. As a matter of fact, Samaritan tradition says that Zeno did issue a discriminatory law, depriving the Samaritan people of jurisdictional autonomy and making them subject to the Christian courts. However, this information is not confirmed by any source, nor is there any trace of Samaritan jurisdiction ever having been recognized by the Roman law.[26]

If any legal disabilities followed the disturbances under Zeno, they obviously did not last long, for the socio-economic status of the Samaritan upper class under Anastasius had not degenerated. This is illustrated by the condition of the family of Arsenius in Beth Shean. Arsenius

---

[25]   Cyr. Scyth., *Vit. Sabae* 71 (ed. Schwartz, 173). According to Cyril, the legal disabilities imposed by Justinian on the Samaritans were a punitive measure and followed the revolt. This view seems to be confirmed by the introductory remarks of Novella 129. On the other hand, Procopius states that the revolt broke out because Justinian extended to the Samaritans a law that deprived heretics of the right of willing their property to non-orthodox heirs (*Hist. Arcana* 9.14–15, 24). Procopius in the *Hist. Arcana* was determined to paint Justinian in the blackest colours, so he may have bent the truth; on the other hand, Cyril was eager to ascribe the merit of the anti-Samaritan measures to St. Sabas' visit to the emperor after the revolt. The law in question, *Cod. Just.* 1.5.17, bears no date. Possibly both authors are partly right: the deprivation of the *ius testandi* may have preceded the revolt, while the other disabilities (*Cod. Just.* 1.5.18–21) followed it.

[26]   Roman law recognized Jewish jurisdiction (*Cod. Theod.* 2.1.10; *Cod. Just.* 1.9.8, 15) but there is no mention of Samaritan jurisdiction. However, since arbitration was encouraged by Roman law, a measure of jurisdictional autonomy may perhaps have been achieved by the Samaritans through recourse to arbitrators within their own community.

himself had perhaps formally converted to Christianity in order to achieve the illustrate and a seat in the senate at Constantinople under Justin.[27] However, the rest of the family had kept their ancestral faith and this did not prevent Arsenius' father, Silvanus, from holding a high magistrature in the city in 518.[28] Recently inscriptions have come to light that show that Silvanus himself and his brother Sallustius, both *skholastikoi*, acted as patrons of the city under Anastasius and obtained grants from the emperor for the erection of public buildings in Scythopolis. Their father, Arsenius, is styled *skholastikos* too, and probably held office during the reign of Zeno himself.[29]

---

[27] So, at least, states Procopius (*Hist. Arcana* 27.6–10), although according to Cyril he only received baptism at the hands of St. Sabas in 531 (*Vit. Sabae* 71, ed. Schwartz, 174).

[28] Cyr. Scyth., *Vit. Sabae* 61 (ed. Schwartz, 163).

[29] The inscriptions are as yet unpublished. I am grateful to Y. Tsafrir and G. Foerster for permission to mention them here.

"Chancel" Screens in Late Antique Palestinian Synagogues: A Source from the Cairo Genizah*

Steven Fine

Baltimore Hebrew University

OBJECTS IDENTIFIED as synagogue "chancel screens" and "chancel screen posts" have been discovered throughout the Land of Israel, from Dalton in the Upper Galilee to the vicinity of Gaza in the south. Such screens have been uncovered in both apsidal basilicas and in a broadhouse-type synagogue.[1] The remains of a wooden screen were identified in the Ein Gedi synagogue,[2] and E. L. Sukenik posited a wooden fence surrounding the *bêmâ* of the Beth Alpha synagogue.[3] In basilical synagogues that date

---

* This essay is dedicated in honor of Professor Elieser Slomovic of the University of Judaism.

[1] G. Foerster, "Decorated Marble Chancel Screens in Sixth-Century Synagogues in Palestine and Their Relation to Christian Art and Architecture," *Actes du XIe Congrès International d'Archéologie Chrétienne* (Rome: Potoficio Istituto di Archeologia Cristiana, 1989), 1809–20; L. I. Levine, "From Community Center to Small Temple: The Furnishings and Interior Design of Ancient Synagogues" [Hebrew], *Cathedra* 60 (1990), 74–75; J. R. Branham, "Sacred Space under Erasure in Ancient Synagogues and Churches," *Art Bulletin,* 74 (1992), 380, n. 24, suggests that "about twenty" synagogues in Israel show evidence of chancel arrangements, "all south of the Kinneret." Add to these the screen post from Dothan. See J. Naveh, *On Stone and Mosaic: The Aramaic and Hebrew Inscriptions from Ancient Synagogues* [Hebrew] (Jerusalem: Maariv, 1978), 144–46; S. Fine in S. Fine, ed., *Sacred Realm: The Emergence of the Synagogue in the Ancient World* (New York: Oxford University Press and Yeshiva University Museum, 1996), cat. no. 50, fig. 6.6b.

[2] D. Barag, Y. Porat, E. Netzer, "The Synagogue at En-Gedi," in L. I. Levine, ed., *Ancient Synagogues Revealed* (Jerusalem: Israel Exploration Society, 1981), 117.

[3] E. L. Sukenik hypothesizes a "wooden grating." *The Ancient Synagogue of Beth Alpha* (Jerusalem and London: Oxford, 1931), 19.

to the late fifth and sixth centuries, the chancel screen served to enclose an often broad *bêmâ*, which stood before an apse on the Jerusalem-aligned wall. Within the apse stood the Torah shrine, and, in some, one or more large stone or metal menorahs. Chancel screens have been uncovered in apsidal basilicas at Beth Shean A, Rehov, Maʿoz Hayyim, Ein Gedi, Gaza, Ashkelon, Hammath Tiberias, and elsewhere.[4] The broadhouse-type synagogue at Khirbet Susiya in Judea contains a unique arrangement. There an ornate screen surrounded the main podium before the Torah shrine of a broadhouse-type synagogue.[5]

In both the apsidal basilicas and the Susiya broadhouse, the screen served to emphasize and distance the area of the Torah shrine from the assembled community.[6] The chancel screen, together with the entire arrangement of the Torah shrine compound within apsidal basilicas, was borrowed from contemporary churches.[7] In fact, M. Avi-Yonah has shown that the chancel screen uncovered in the Hammath Gader synagogue was made in the same workshop as the screen discovered in the Monastery of the Lady Mary in Beth Shean. At Beth Shean a cross appears within a wreath at the center of the screen, while at Hammath Gader a menorah appears in that space.[8]

---

[4]   Above, n. 1.

[5]   The most recent survey of archaeological evidence of synagogues in late antique Palestine is R. Hachlili, "The Art and Architecture of Late Antique Synagogues in the Land of Israel," in Fine, ed., *Sacred Realm*, 96–129.

[6]   See Z. Yeivin, "Khirbet Susiya, the Bima and Synagogue Ornamentation," in R. Hachlili, ed., *Ancient Synagogues in Israel* (BAR International Series: Oxford, 1989), 93–100.

[7]   Y. Tsafrir, "The Byzantine Setting and Its Influence on Ancient Synagogues," in L. I. Levine, ed., *The Synagogue in Late Antiquity* (New York: ASOR and Jewish Theological Seminary, 1987), 151. See also A. Ovadiah, "Reciprocal Influences between Churches and Synagogues in the Land of Israel During Late Antiquity" [Hebrew], in M. Broshi, ed., *Between Hermon and Sinai: Memorial to Amnon* [Hebrew] (Jerusalem: Yedidim, 1977), 163–64.

[8]   So Hachlili, "Art and Architecture." See Branham, "Sacred Space under Erasure," 379.

Synagogue screens have received considerable attention from modern scholars, who have generally discussed the style and iconography of these objects.[9] J. Branham has made a major step forward, addressing the religious significance of the "chancel screen" in terms of the sanctity of the Jerusalem Temple.[10] In 1978, S. Hopkins published a text (T-S A45.6) from the Taylor-Schechter Genizah collection of Cambridge University titled *Pereq māšîaḥ*.[11] This text provides a literary context in which to interpret screens that were uncovered in Palestinian synagogues. This essay will begin by interpreting this tradition within the context of rabbinic literature and institutions. We will then turn to the religious meaning of synagogue screens and conclude with some thoughts on a medieval variant of this text and its implications for the history of the synagogue.

The Genizah text reads as follows:

> R. Eliezer son of Jacob says: The great study house of the Holy One, Blessed be He, in the future will be eighteen thousand myriad parsangs [in size], for it is written: "Its circumference [will be] 18,000" (Ezek. 48:35). The Holy One, Blessed be He, sits on the chair among them, and David sits before him, for it is said: "His chair is like the sun before me" (Ps. 89:37). All the teaching women who teach[12] and pay so that their sons may be taught Torah, Scripture, and Mishnah, manners, pious sincerity and honesty *stand by [or, within] reed mats made as a partition for the bêmâ* and listen to the voice of Zerubbabel son of Shealtiel when he stands as interpreter (*metûrgĕmān*)....[13]

---

[9]   Above, n. 1.

[10] Branham, "Sacred Space under Erasure," 393.

[11] S. Hopkins, *A Miscellany of Literary Pieces from the Cambridge Genizah Collection* (Cambridge: Cambridge University Library, 1978), 12–13.

[12] "Teach," *mĕlamdôt*, clearly bears the nuance of facilitating study in *t. Ket.* 4:7 and parallels. See S. Lieberman, *Tosefta Ki-Fshuṭah* (New York: Jewish Theological Seminary, 1955–88) 6, 243–44 (Hebrew). The medieval version of this text, discussed below, was seemingly altered so as to accentuate this interpretation.

[13] The Genizah text actually reads *metûrgĕmān mišpāḥâ*. The notion of a "family translator" is unknown elsewhere in rabbinic literature. The text continues in a

The Heavenly Study House and Rabbinic Literature

According to *Pereq māšîaḥ,* pious women who facilitate the education of their sons and husbands are promised a reward in kind in the
messianic (or heavenly) *bēt ha-midrāš.* While implicit in our tradition,
this notion is stated explicitly in *b. Berakot* 17a:

> Our Rabbis taught:[14] Greater is the promise which the Holy One, Blessed
> be He, made to the women than that which He made to the men. For it
> is written: "Rise up you *ša°ănannôt* women, hear my voice, promised
> (*bôṭḥôt*) daughters hear my voice" (Isa. 32:9).

> Said Rav to R. Hiyya: How do women gain merit for the world to come?
> By bringing their sons to study Scripture in the synagogue,[15] by sending
> their husbands to study in the study house, and by waiting for their
> husbands until they return from the study house (*bê rabbānān*).

The behavior for which the *ša°ănannôt* women receive the divine promise of merit before God is their willingness to educate their sons and
husbands. *Ša°ănannôt* is read as *šānôt,* "teaching."[16] The first half of the

---

manner that is quite unrelated to the study house context and may suggest that a
corruption has occurred. To the best of my knowledge, this document is not
preserved in its entirety, and this precludes further evaluation. Cf. The medieval
versions cited below, read: "Zerubbabel son of Shealtiel who translates (*mĕtargēm*)
before the Holy One, Blessed be He." On the *mĕturgĕmān* in rabbinic sources, see
A. D. York, "The Targum in the Synagogue and in the School," *JSJ* 10 (1979), 75–
86; D. Urman, "The House of Assembly and the House of Study: Are They One and
the Same?" in D. Urman, V. M. Flesher, eds., *Ancient Synagogues: Historical
Analysis and Archaeological Discovery* (Leiden: Brill, 1995) 1, 232–55.

[14] According to the Munich manuscript and other medieval manuscript traditions. See R. Rabbinowicz, *Variae Lectiones in Mischnam et in Talmud Babylonicum*
[*Diqdûqē sôprîm*] (Munich, 1867–86; rpt. New York: M.P. Press, 1976) 1, 16, n.
dalet. For other variants, see note *hēh.* See also *Exodus Rabba,* Vilna, 28:2; *b. Soṭa*
21a.

[15] See Rabbinowicz, *Diqdûqē sôprîm* 1, 16, n. *hēh.*

[16] The middle *°alep* of *ša°ănannôt* was apparently not vocalized by the author of
this tradition. Manuscripts and inscriptions that reflect late antique Hebrew and
Aramaic orthography suggest that the use of the letter *°alep* as medial letter was
quite fluid. It was discarded in some cases, and inserted into other words. See J. N.

verse is thus interpreted: "Rise up you teaching women," or more correctly, you "facilitators of teaching." This is clearly the intended meaning of *ša⁽ănannôt* in our *Pereq māšîaḥ* text as well.

Projections of synagogues and study houses into the world to come are known beginning in the third or fourth century, although no text is so explicit as *Pereq māšîaḥ* in its description of the divine realm.[17] The promise of eternal synagogue and study house attendance for the pious is stated explicitly in a tradition preserved in a post-Amoraic collection, *Deuteronomy Rabba* 7:1:[18]

> Anyone who enters synagogues and study houses in this world merits to enter synagogues and study houses in the world to come.
>
> Whence this?
>
> For it is said: "Happy are those who dwell in your house, they will again praise you, selah" (Ps. 84:6).

The promise of heavenly synagogue and study house attendance is here based on the exegesis of Psalm 84:6: "those who dwell in your house ... will again praise you." When will this "again" happen? In the world to come. The possibility of synagogues and study houses in the world to come was completely believable to the authors of these traditions and their audience(s).[19]

"Synagogues and study houses," paired in a formula that appears in all strata of rabbinic literature, were closely related institutions during late

---

Epstein, *Mābô⁽ lĕ-nûsaḥ ha-mišnâ* (Jerusalem, 1948) 1234–37; E. Y. Kutscher, *Studies in Galilean Aramaic*, trans. M. Sokoloff (Ramat Gan: Bar Ilan, 1976) 82, 83; Naveh, 1978, 31; M. Sokoloff, "The Hebrew of Genesis Rabba, Manuscript Vatican 30" [Hebrew], *Leš.* 33 (1969), 25–42, 135–49, 270–79.

[17] See S. Fine, *This Holy Place: On the Sanctity of the Synagogue During the Greco-Roman Period* (Notre Dame: Notre Dame University Press, 1998), 65–66, 110–11.

[18] The passage has a parallel at *Midrash Psalms* 84:3. Cf. *Targum Psalms* to Ps. 84:8 and Rashi, *ad. loc.*

[19] Compare S. J. D. Cohen, "The Temple and the Synagogue," in T. G. Madsen, ed., *The Temple in Antiquity* (Provo: Brigham Young University, 1984), 170 and n. 50.

antiquity.[20] In general, synagogues were the institutions of people who were not sages, while study houses served the rabbinic community. Within the walls of the same institution, study, prayer, and legal judgment were carried out. The importance of this institution is expressed sparingly in Tannaitic sources. One of the rare examples of this phenomenon appears in *Sipra* to Leviticus 26:31, "I will destroy your temples":[21]

> Temple, my temple, your temples—
> to include synagogues and study houses.

The word *miqdĕšêkem*, "your temples," provides the stimulus for this midrash. In Leviticus 26:31 *miqdĕšêkem* refers to "your (local, illicit) temples." Tannaitic exegetes attempted to reconcile the fact that *miqdāš*, "temple," elsewhere appears in the Pentateuch only with regard to the ordained temple of God yet appears in a plural form in this verse.[22] They found referents for the plural form among the institutions of their own time.[23] The *Sipra* text projects synagogues and study houses back into the mythic reality ordained by the Torah itself, setting these institutions on the same level as the Temple. Such projection backward in time was often used in Tannaitic sources to legitimize contemporary institutions.[24] The study house became more important during the course of the third century, drawing much of its conceptual underpinnings from the synagogue. In *y. Megilla* 3:1 (73d), study houses are called "holy" for

---

[20] See Fine, *This Holy Place*, chs. 3, 4; F. G. Hüttenmeister, "The Synagogue and the Beth Ha-Midrash and their Relationship" [Hebrew], *Cathedra* 18 (1981), 38–44; L. I. Levine, "The Sages and the Synagogue in Late Antiquity: The Evidence of the Galilee," in L. I. Levine, ed., *The Galilee in Late Antiquity* (New York: Jewish Theological Seminary, 1992) 201–22; see especially Urman, "House of Assembly and House of Study."

[21] *Sipra, Bĕḥuqôtaî* 6 (ed., I. H. Weiss).

[22] E. Kautzsch, *Gesenius' Hebrew Grammar*, trans. A. E. Cowley (Oxford: Clarendon Press, 1910), 264, 399–400.

[23] See B. Epstein, *Tôrâ tĕmîmâ* (Vilna: Romm, 1902) 3, 566–67, n. 42.

[24] Fine, *This Holy Place*, ch. 2.

the first time. This sanctity is derived by placing it on a hierarchy of holiness that derives from contact with the Torah scroll. Some rabbis considered the study house to be more sacred even than the synagogue.[25]

In our *Pereq māšîaḥ* text, God is portrayed as having his own study house, just as numerous Talmudic sages (and certain biblical characters) had their own study houses.[26] It is likely that from the third century onward synagogues and some study houses bore an architectural resemblance to one another. An architectural relationship, minimally as two varieties of Jewish public buildings, is assumed in paired traditions in *y. Šeqalim* 5:5 (49b):

> Rabbi Hamma son of Haninah and Rabbi Hoshayah were walking in a synagogue in Lod.
> Said Rabbi Hamma son of Haninah to Rabbi Hoshayah: My ancestors donated much money here!
> He responded: How many souls have your ancestors dimmed here! Were there no people studying Torah [for them to support]?
>
> Rabbi Abun donated the arches of the *sidrā' rabbā'* [that is, the great study house of Tiberias].
> Rabbi Mani came to him.
> He [Rabbi Abun] said to him: Look at what I have done!
> He [Rabbi Mani] responded: "Israel has abandoned its creator and built shrines!" (Hos. 8:14) Were there no people studying Torah [for you to support]?

Unfortunately, the only secure archaeological evidence for a study house from late antiquity is an inscription from Dabbura in the Golan Heights that reads, "This is the study house of Rabbi Eliezer ha-Qappar."[27] The numerous "study houses" that have been identified by scholars adjacent to synagogues, as for example at Gamla, Meroth, and Khirbet Shema, are projections backward from the European communal synagogue com-

---

[25] See *m. Meg.* 3:1; Fine, *This Holy Place*, 38–39, 68–69.

[26] See L. D. Gordon, "Becoming a Rabbi in First-Century Palestine," *Proceedings of the Eastern Great Lakes Biblical Society* 7 (1987), 105–15.

[27] D. Urman, "Jewish Inscriptions from the Village of Dabbura in the Golan," in L. I. Levine, ed., *Ancient Synagogues Revealed*, 155–66.

plex onto the ancient synagogue.[28] Elsewhere I have suggested in a very tentative way that the "Beth Shean B" synagogue may have been a study house, basing my suggestion on terminology that appears in one of its dedicatory inscriptions and the unusual square plan of the hall.[29] The strong relationship between synagogues and study halls that is asserted in literary sources renders it almost impossible to distinguish the presumably few study houses[30] from the presumably many synagogues in late antique Palestine. Only where explicit epigraphic sources are available can one be certain that a study house has been uncovered.

"Reed Mats Made as a Partition for the Bêmâ"

The use of the term *bêmâ* in our text is significant. *Bêmâ* is a term that often appears in rabbinic literature for the podium where Scripture is read. *t. Sukka* 4:6 portrays the "double colonnade of Alexandria," the great synagogue of that city, as having "a wooden platform (*bêmâ*) in the center."[31] This text is a projection by the Tannaitic sages of the second or early third century onto the Alexandrian synagogue and teaches more about synagogues and story-telling techniques in the Land of Israel during the late Roman period than it does about Roman Alex-

---

[28] Z. Ilan and E. Damati, *Meroth: The Ancient Jewish Village* [Hebrew] (Tel Aviv: Society for the Preservation of Nature, 1987), 72–82; E. M. Meyers, A. T. Kraabel, J. F. Strange, *Ancient Synagogue Excavations at Khirbet Shemaʿ—Upper Galilee, Israel, 1970–1972* (AASOR: Durham: Duke University Press, 1976), 87. See Fine, "Gamla," in E. M. Meyers, ed., *Oxford Encyclopedia of Near Eastern Archaeology* (New York: Oxford University Press, 1997), 2, 382.

[29] Fine, *This Holy Place*, 100–1.

[30] Note the small numbers of rabbinic sages mentioned in rabbinic literature (L. I. Levine, *The Rabbinic Class of Roman Palestine* [Jerusalem and New York: Jewish Theological Seminary, 1989], 66–69).

[31] See Fine, *This Holy Place*, 43–45. Z. Safrai discusses whether there was a central platform in "the middle of the prayer hall," coming to conclusions similar to our own. See Z. Safrai, "Dukhan, Aron and Teva: How was the Ancient Synagogue Furnished?" in Hachlili, ed., *Ancient Synagogues in Israel*, 74–77.

andria.[32] This wooden *bêmâ* seems to be modeled upon the wooden platform (*migdāl ʿēṣ*) from which Ezra reads Scripture in Nehemiah 8:4, and it parallels the *bêmâ* upon which *m. Soṭa* 7:8 says the king stood in the Temple to read publicly from the Torah on the first day of Sukkot after a Sabbatical year (*haqhēl*).[33] Unfortunately, neither of the Palestinian Talmud texts that refer to *bêmôt* in synagogues are useful in locating the *bêmâ* spatially. All we can tell from *y. Megilla* 3:1 (73d) is that there was a question as to whether the synagogue *bêmâ* had the greater "holiness of the ark" or the lesser "holiness of the synagogue." *y. Yebamot* 13 (13a) refers to a large podium, a *bêmâ gĕdôlâ*, that a community constructed for its newly appointed religious leader, presumably in the synagogue. It is not clear, from this text, however, where in the synagogue the *bêmâ* stood.

Central platforms are unknown from synagogue ruins in the Land of Israel, although one is known from the Diaspora. Evidence that has been interpreted as the foundation of a central podium was discovered in the fourth-century synagogue at Sardis.[34] While wooden podia might have fit comfortably in the naves of Galilean-type synagogues like Capernaum or Baram, no evidence for such structures is extant. It is unlikely that central *bêmôt* existed in Palestinian synagogues that were paved with intricate mosaic floors, whether of the type known from Hamat Tiberias B and Beth Alpha, or of the inhabited scroll that is extant at Beth Shean B and in Maon (Nirim). Large platforms on the Jerusalem aligned wall are, however, particularly common. In fact, these platforms continually increased in size during antiquity. A good example is the synagogue *bêmâ* of Maʿoz Hayyim in the Beth Shean valley. The development of the shrine area at Maʿoz Hayyim is representative of the general expansion of shrine compounds in basilica-type synagogues:

---

[32] Fine, *This Holy Place*, ch. 2.

[33] *t. Soṭ.* 7:13–14.

[34] A. R. Seager, "The Synagogue at Sardis," in L. I. Levine, ed., *Ancient Synagogues Revealed*, 182.

Torah shrine on the Jerusalem wall in the first phase (third century) was replaced by a shrine set within an apse in the second phase (fourth century), with a raised platform enclosed by a chancel screen appearing in the third phase (fifth to sixth century).[35] Within the church context this platform was called a *bēma*.[36] This term appears in no Jewish epigraphic source, but the Christian parallel, as well as the use of this term in two Palestinian Talmud passages in reference to synagogues and the common use of this term in regard to podia in other rabbinic sources,[37] makes it likely that this was the name used by synagogue communities as well.

The Babylonian Talmud does not refer to a *bêmâ* within Babylonian synagogues, and no Gaonic source of which I am aware uses this term either.[38] Sources from Fatimid Egypt do not use the term *bêmâ*[39] nor do they seem to refer to a platform before the Torah shrine.[40] This is the case in documents from the Cairo Genizah as well, where we hear instead of an *ʾanbōl*, a construction in the hall from which "special sections of the service and the reading of [scriptural] lections" took place. The *ʾanbōl* was architecturally distinct from the Torah shrine, and, like the Christian *ambo*, it may have been constructed toward the

---

[35]   V. Tzaferis, "The Ancient Synagogue at Maʿoz Hayyim," *IEJ* 32 (1982), 215–44; Branham, "Sacred Space under Erasure," 384–85. R. Hachlili, *Ancient Jewish Art and Archaeology in the Land of Israel* (Leiden: Brill, 1988), 160, 221–24.

[36]   G. W. H. Lampe, *A Patristic Greek Dictionary* (Oxford: Oxford University Press, 1961), 295–96; C. Delovye, "*Bema*," *Reallexikon zur byzantinischen Kunst,* ed. K. Wessel (Stuttgart: A. Hiersemann, 1966), 583–99.

[37]   E. Ben Yehuda, *Complete Dictionary of Ancient and Modern Hebrew* [Hebrew] (Jerusalem and Berlin, 1902–59) 1, 522.

[38]   Z. Safrai, "Dukhan, Aron and Teva," 75–77, discusses Gaonic sources.

[39]   Maimonides (*Mišneh tôrâ, Laws of Prayer,* 11:3), influenced by the tradition in *t. Sukk.* 4:6, speaks of a central *bêmâ*. This use of *bêmâ* reflects his well known preference for Hebrew terminology over loan words in this work.

[40]   Compare S. D. Goitein, "Ambol—The Raised Platform in the Synagogue" [Hebrew], *EI* 6 (1960), 162.

center of the room.[41] The fact that the term *bêmâ* does not appear in Babylonian, Gaonic, or Genizah sources may support the interpretation that our text is, as Z. Safrai has suggested, of Palestinian origin.[42]

The term *gādēr* is used for many types of partitions in rabbinic sources.[43] The use of this term to describe the structure by (or within) which the women would stand is consistent with rabbinic usage. It is used, for example, in *y. Berakot* 4:1 (7d) to describe the addition of benches to the rabbinic assembly (*bēt ha-waᶜad*) at Yavneh after the deposition of Rabban Gamaliel:[44]

> How many benches (*sapsālin*) were there?
> R. Jacob son of Sisi said: There were three hundred there, excluding those who stood behind the partition (*ʾaḥôrê ha-gādēr*).
> R. Jose son of R. Abun said: There were three hundred there, excluding those who stood behind the partition (*ʾaḥôrê ha-gādēr*).

The partition mentioned in this text is not so high that those who stand behind it cannot hear and, perhaps, see as well.[45] This is also the case for

---

[41] Greek: *ambōn*, Latin: *ambo*, Syriac: *ʾambōnāʾ*. For a full linguistic discussion, see Goitein, "Ambol," 162–67, esp. 163; *idem*, *A Mediterranean Society* (Berkeley: University of California, 1971) 2, 146, nn. 9–11. See also J. Mann, *The Jews in Egypt and in Palestine under the Fatimid Caliphs* (London: Oxford, 1920, 1922; rpt. New York: Ktav, 1970) 1, 222, n. 2; B. Narkiss, "The Hekhal, Bimah and Teivah in Sephardi Synagogues," *Jewish Art* 18, 31–47; Z. Safrai, "Dukhan, Aron and Teva," 76–77; L. Bouras and R. F. Taft, *ODB*, 75–76, *s.v.* "Ambo."

[42] See Z. Safrai, "Dukhan, Aron and Teva," 78–79; *idem*, "When Was Gender Segregation Introduced in the Synagogue," *Moment*, 15.2 (1990), 8.

[43] For examples, see Ben Yehuda, *Dictionary* 2, 705–7.

[44] The passage has a parallel at *y. Taan.* 4:1, 67d. See also *Deut. Rabb.* 1:8 (ed. Lieberman, 5). On the sources for this event, see R. Goldenberg, "The Deposition of Rabban Gamaliel II: An Examination of the Sources," *JJS* 23 (1972), 167–90.

[45] *Gĕdārîm* ranged in height from low walls of ten handbreadths to tall structures. Examples are cited by Ben Yehuda, *Dictionary* 2, 705–7. See especially *b. Sanh.* 75a, where the partition is clearly of a height as to block vision and allow the person on the other side to hear. See also *b. Sanh.* 67a.

the women in the *Pereq māšîaḥ* source.[46] Reed mats that might have served as partitions for *bêmôt* like those mentioned in our tradition are not extant from Palestine.[47] However, genizah documents do speak of "reed mats" within Fatimid-period synagogues, some of which were "large" and used for seating on the floor.[48]

"Chancel" screens in Palestinian synagogues provide a reasonable context for interpreting the *geder la-bêmâ* of *Pereq māšîaḥ*. In our text we find that mothers who support their sons' studies in this world are promised reward in kind, *middâ kě-neged middâ*, in the world to come. In this world these exemplary "teaching women" may have little status in the rabbinic study house,[49] but in the world to come they are promised a place front row center before the *bêmâ*.

The Meaning of Synagogue Chancel Screens in Late Antique Palestine

Scholars agree that the chancel screen, together with the broad frontal podium and apse, were borrowed directly from Christian church architecture. Y. Tsafrir reflects the consensus when he states that for Jews "the *bêmâ*, apse and chancel screen were not imbued with special status, as they were in the church, where they were reserved for the priesthood and for the mystical and 'awesome' rites that were hidden from lay worshippers."[50] The meaning for Jews is less clear. It is obscured

---

[46] A "partition" is not discussed in the Babylonian recension of our story (*b. Ber.* 27b–28a). This detail seems to reflect the ambiance of the late antique Palestinian storyteller.

[47] A tradition preserved in *b. ʿErub.* 62a, which is unrelated to the synagogue contexts, which mentions *maḥăṣālôt gôdrôt*.

[48] Goitein, "Ambol," 166; *idem*, "The Synagogue Building and Its Furnishings According to the Records of the Cairo Geniza," *EI* 7 (1964), 82, 90–92; *idem*, *A Mediterranean Society* 1, 149–50.

[49] Sources are collected by S. Safrai, "Female Torah Sages in Rabbinic Literature" [Hebrew], *Maḥanayim* 98 (1964), 58–59.

[50] Y. Tsafrir, "Byzantine Setting," 152. On chancel screens in churches, see Branham, "Sacred Space under Erasure," 380–83.

by the use of the term "chancel," a term with a specific ecclesiastical connotation, in reference to the synagogue and its furnishings.[51]

What Jewish purpose did the screen serve when it was taken over into the synagogue? Clearly it was intended to separate the *bêmâ* from the hall, though it is unclear why this might be necessary in late antique Palestinian Judaism.[52] One avenue for interpretation is suggested by a text preserved in *y. Megilla* 3:1 (73d). This text, redacted circa 400 C.E., gives concrete expression to a notion first mentioned two centuries earlier in *m. Megilla* 3:1.[53] According to the Mishnah, the Torah scroll is the source of holiness in a synagogue. Objects that are closer to the scroll are considered to be holier. Thus, the cloths wrapped around a Torah scroll are holier than the chest (*tēbâ*) in which the scrolls are stored, and the scrolls chest is holier than the synagogue building. The Jerusalem Talmud divides the synagogue interior into two distinct realms, those parts of the synagogue that are in close and constant contact with the Torah scrolls and those which are more distant:

> All the furnishings of the synagogue are like [in holiness to] the synagogue. Its bench and its couch (*qalṭîra*)[54] are like [in holiness to] the synagogue.

---

[51] Sukenik and Goodenough seem to refer to "synagogue screens" and not to "chancel screens." See E. L. Sukenik, *The Ancient Synagogue of el-Hammeh (Hammath-by-Gadara)* (Jerusalem: Rubin Mass, 1935), 58–69; E. R. Goodenough, *Jewish Symbols in the Greco-Roman Period* (New York: Pantheon, 1953–68) 1, 240–41.

[52] There is no conclusive evidence that "chancel" screens were used in Diaspora synagogues. See Fine and L.V. Rutgers, "New Light on Judaism in Asia Minor during Late Antiquity: Two Recently Identified Inscribed Menorahs," *Jewish Studies Journal* 3 (1996), 20; L. V. Rutgers, "Diaspora Synagogues: Synagogue Archaeology in the Greco-Roman World," in S. Fine, ed., *Sacred Realm*, 67–95. Cf. J. Branham, *Sacred Space in Ancient Jewish and Early Medieval Christian Architecture* (diss., Emory University, 1993), 106, n. 26.

[53] See Fine, *This Holy Place*, ch. 3.

[54] M. Sokoloff, "The Hebrew of Genesis Rabba, Manuscript Vatican 30," in *Anthology of Articles in Rabbinic Hebrew*, ed. M. Bar-Asher [Hebrew] (Jerusalem, 1971), 1, 493, 435; S. Krauss, *Griechische und lateinische Lehnwörter* (Berlin: S. Calvary, 1898–99), 545. M. Jastrow, *Dictionary of the Targumim, the Talmud Babli,*

The curtain ($k\hat{\imath}l\hat{a}$)[55] on the ark ($\hat{\jmath}ar\hat{o}n\bar{a}\hat{\jmath}$) is like [in holiness] to the ark.

R. Abbahu put a cloak ($g\hat{o}lt\bar{a}\hat{\jmath}$)[56] under the curtain ($b\hat{\imath}lan$).[57]

Rab Judah in the name of Samuel: The $b\hat{e}m\hat{a}$[58] and planks ($l\breve{e}w\bar{a}\d{h}\hat{\imath}n$)[59] do not have the sanctity of the ark, and do have the sanctity of the synagogue.

The reading table ($\hat{\jmath}ing\bar{a}l\hat{\imath}n$)[60] does not have the sanctity of the ark, and does have the sanctity of the synagogue.

Objects within the synagogue are divided into the superior "sanctity of the ark" or the lower "sanctity of the synagogue." Our third-century text therefore discusses ambiguous objects. It is possible that when the frontal $b\hat{e}m\hat{a}$ surrounded by a chancel screen developed some centuries later there were some Jews who broadened the categories set out in our text (or others like them that are unknown to us) so as to include the $b\hat{e}m\hat{a}$. The enlarged $b\hat{e}m\hat{a}$ of the fifth to sixth centuries would thus have paral-

---

and Yerushalmi, and the Midrashic Literature (London and New York: Luzac & Co. and Putnam, 1982), 1375, translates "teacher's litter." L. Y. Rahmani, "Stone Synagogue Chairs: Their Identification, Use, and Significance," *IEJ* 40 (1990), 197–99, suggests that this is the equivalent of the Greek/Aramaic *qatedra*. Levine, "Community Center to Small Temple," 54–56 collects the various interpretations of the synagogue appurtenances mentioned in this pericope.

55   Sokoloff, *Dictionary*, 256. On the usage of this curtain, see *y. Šabb.* 20:1 (17c); *Esth. Rab.* 2:7. See Z. Safrai, "Dukhan, Aron and Tevah," 74, 89, n. 29.

56   Sokoloff, *Dictionary*, 123. Krauss, *Lehnwörter*, 235.

57   Krauss, *Lehnwörter*, 235–36, and Sokoloff, *Dictionary*, 96, read *bîlan* from Greek *bēlon*.

58   Krauss, *Lehnwörter*, 150.

59   Levine suggests that "planks" probably refers to a reading table. Cf. Elbogen, *Jewish Liturgy*, 359. Compare *b. Meg.* 32a. Rashi's comment (*ad loc.*) that "I do not know what they are ..." is still quite true.

60   From the Greek, *analogion*. Opinions regarding this object are collected by L. I. Levine, "From Community Center to Small Temple," 56–57. See Lampe, *Patristic Greek Dictionary*, 111, and D. Sperber, *Greek and Latin Legal Terms in Rabbinic Literature* (Ramat Gan: Bar Ilan University, 1984), 37, n. 1. Archdeacon Seraphim, formerly of the Monastery of the Cross in Jerusalem, informs me that the pedestal upon which the Scriptures are read in contemporary Greek Orthodox churches is called an *analogeion*.

leled an expanding notion of the Torah shrine's sanctity. All of this, of course, is only conjecture on a subject for which we would like to know much more than we do.

J. Branham has suggested that the synagogue chancel screen was related to the fence that surrounded the Temple of Jerusalem, beyond which gentiles were forbidden to enter.[61] In *m. Middot* 2:3 this fence, which is said to have been "ten handbreadths high," is called a *sôrēg*.[62] This term is today used to describe synagogue chancel screens. As far as I can ascertain, the first scholar to use this term to denote a synagogue screen was E. L. Sukenik in his 1934/5 description of a screen from the Hammath Gader synagogue. Sukenik referred to this construction somewhat tentatively. First he mentioned "this area in which the holy ark was separated (*gādûr*) with a *maʿăqeh* [partition]." Later in the same paragraph he refers to the partition as "a *maʿaqeh* or *sôrēg*," grasping for a term that in his English publication he usually called a "screen."[63] In the conclusion of his Hebrew discussion Sukenik settled upon the term *sôrēg*, describing the "marble panels of the *soreg* which was beside the holy ark."[64] This choice of *sôrēg*, the term commonly used in discussions of chancel screens in Hebrew since Sukenik, has had unfortunate consequences. Branham forges an ahistorical philological relationship between the ancient *sôrēg* of the Jerusalem Temple and the modern term *sôrēg* for the screen of the ancient synagogue. This connection is

---

[61]   See E. J. Bickerman, "The Warning Inscriptions of Herod's Temple," in *idem, Studies in Jewish and Christian History* (AGJU 9: Leiden: Brill, 1980) 2, 210–24.

[62]   See A. S. Kaufman, ed., *Tractate Middot* [Hebrew] (Jerusalem: Har Yeraeh, 1991), 45. On the size of a handbreadth, see J. Z. Lauterbach, "Weights and Measures in Rabbinical Literature," *JE* 12, 486, 489. E. Z. Melamed, *Eshnav ha-Talmud* [Hebrew] (Jerusalem: Kiryat Sefer, 1976), 86, suggests that a handbreadth in rabbinic literature measures 9.3 cm. See also *Měgillat taʿanît* 17 (B. Z. Lurie, ed., *Megilath Taʿanith* [Jerusalem, 1964], 150–53).

[63]   E. L. Sukenik, "The Ancient Synagogue of Hamath Gader" [Hebrew], *Journal of the Jewish Palestine Exploration Society* 3 (1934/35), 48; *idem, Synagogue of el-Hammeh*, 37–38, 58–69.

[64]   Sukenik, "The Ancient Synagogue of Hamath Gader," 59.

strengthened by the fact that many of the extant synagogue screens are approximately "ten handbreadths high," roughly the same size as the Temple *sôrēg*.[65] Branham is correct to note that the expanding use of Temple motifs to define the interior space of late antique synagogues might have come to include synagogue screens, but like many scholars she overstresses the importance of the Temple-synagogue relationship during late antiquity.[66] It was during this period that the Torah shrine came to be called an "ark" after the biblical "Ark of the Covenant,"[67] its curtain a *paroktā* after the Temple veil,[68] and seven-branched menorahs[69] often stood on the *bêmâ*. Although it is possible that some Jews conceptualized the synagogue partition in terms of the Temple partition, there is no positive archaeological or literary evidence to support this interpretation. In fact, the phrase *geder la-bêmâ*, does not in any way suggest a relationship with the Temple.

A Medieval Version of the Pereq māšîaḥ

A medieval version of *Pereq māšîaḥ*, first attested in a manuscript that was copied in Ashkenaz during the fifteenth century,[70] contains a reading of our text that demonstrates that we are not the first to have

---

[65]   For example, Z. Yeivin, "Khirbet Susiya, the Bima and Synagogue Ornamentation," 94, figs. 6, 8, reports that two chancel screens from Susiya, are 90 cm in height. According to Melammed's measure of one handbreath=9.3 cm, these pieces are equal to 9.56 handbreadths. On the inherent flexibility of rabbinic measures, however, see H. H. Cohn, "The Fictions of Measurements," in A. I. Katsch, L. Nemoy, eds., *Essays on the Occasion of the Seventieth Anniversary of Dropsie University* (Philadelphia: Dropsie University, 1979), 39–47.

[66]   This is discussed in detail in Fine, *This Holy Place*, 7–8, n. 35..

[67]   *y. Taʿan.* 2:1 (65a), discussed by Fine, *This Holy Place*, 79–80, 199, n. 127.

[68]   *y. Yoma* 7:1 (44b); *Meg.* 4:5 (75b); *Soṭ.* 8:6 (22a). Discussed by Fine, *This Holy Place*, 80.

[69]   Fine, *This Holy Place*, 47–49, 76, 80, 117–21.

[70]   Bayerische Staatsbibliothek, Munich, ms. 222. See also the version of our text that appears in a manuscript which, according to its colophon, was copied in

difficulty determining the correct denotation for "reed mats made as a partition for the *bêmâ*." According to this text the women "stand by [or, within] reed partitions and listen to the voice of Zerubbabel son of Shealtiel when he stands as translator before the Holy One, Blessed be He ...."[71] The differences between the Genizah and the later version are clear. Where the Genizah version reads *maḥṣĕlôt qanîm*,[72] the medieval version reads *mĕḥîṣôt qanîm*. Both of these constructs appear in rabbinic idiom. More important, however, is what is left out by the medieval version. Here the women stand by "reed *mĕḥîṣôt*," and the word that follows in the Genizah version, *la-bêmâ*, "for the podium" is deleted. It is likely that the copyist of this tradition omitted the phrase *la-bêmâ* because he could not imagine a context in which a *bêmâ* could have a fence around it. In addition, it is likely that he transformed the word *maḥṣĕlôt* into *mĕḥîṣôt*, a simple orthographic procedure, because synagogues during his own period had partitions called by this name that were used to separate women from men within synagogue contexts. *Mĕḥîṣôt* of various materials that separated men from women within synagogues are attested from the thirteenth century onward. The earliest source to which scholars point for the use of the term *mĕḥîṣâ* within the synagogue context is Mordecai son of Hillel (d. 1298), who mentions the "*mĕḥîṣâ* that is made at the time of the homily between the men and the women."[73] The revisions to our text during the Middle

---

Mantua in 1643 (Russian State Library, Moscow, Ginzberg Collection no. 688: 87). This text was published by A. Jellinek, *Bet ha-Midrasch* (Leipzig: Wahrmann, 1853–58; rpt. Jerusalem 1967) 3, 75; followed by Y. Ibn-Shmuel, *Midrashei Geula* (Jerusalem: Bialik, 1954), 341. Ibn-Shmuel, 301, discusses the printed editions of this text.

[71]   Z. Safrai, "Dukhan, Aron and Teva," 78–79.

[72]   E.g., *m. Kil.* 4:4; *m. B. Bat.* 4:8, 9.

[73]   *Pisqê mordĕkaî* (printed in the Vilna edition of the *Babylonian Talmud*, Vilna, 1880–86), *Šabbat*, no. 311. Sources on the separation of men and women in synagogue contexts are collected by D. Golinkin, "The *Mehiza* in the Synagogue," *The Rabbinical Assembly of Israel Law Committee Responsa* (Jerusalem: Rabbinical Assembly of Israel, 1987), esp. 14 and n. 7. See J. M. Rosenthal, "The History of the

Ages reflect the separation of men and women with a *měḥîṣâ* in late medieval synagogues. This separation, however, does not reflect the state of synagogues in late antique Palestine, as Ze'ev Safrai has suggested.[74] Not understanding the denotation of our text, the medieval scribe simply changed it, a well-known procedure that was bemoaned by medieval and modern scholars alike. While an important source for the history of the medieval synagogue, this variant has no significance for the history of the ancient synagogue.

To conclude, it is my contention that the Genizah version of *Pereq māšîaḥ* preserves an important source for our understanding of screens that have been uncovered in late antique synagogues. On the basis of this text and parallel terminology in rabbinic sources, it is reasonable to suggest that such a screen constructed in a late fifth- or sixth-century Palestinian synagogue might have been called a *geder la-bêmâ*. There is no evidence, however, that such a screen might have been called a *sôrēg* on the model of the Temple partition or otherwise treated as a Temple appurtenance. The synagogue partition served to differentiate the realm of the Torah from the rest of the hall, to create a sacred precinct. This is the place where the interpreter might have stood, and where women in this world did not regularly tread. In the world to come, however, their merit in support of their sons' education would be repaid, and they would be brought to the very focal point of the hall, next to the interpreter. The pious women, we are told, will stand right next to the partition of the *bêmâ*. In the course of making this pious promise, the author of our text has done us the enormous favor of mentioning this synagogue appurtenance, and thus provided a literary context through which to interpret the numerous synagogue screens that have been discovered during this century. The screen, modeled upon the church chancel screen, was considered to be so basic to the architecture of the study house that *Pereq māšîaḥ* projects the screen into the divine domain,

---

Partition in the Synagogue (*Mehiza*)" [Hebrew], *Studies and Texts* (Jerusalem: Mossad Harav Kook, 1966) 2, 162–67.

[74]   Z. Safrai, "Dukhan, Aron and Teva," 78–79.

into the future "great study house of the Holy One, Blessed be He." This in itself is worthy of note, as one more example of the complex inter-relationships between religious and ethnic communities in late antique Palestine.

JEWS AND CHRISTIANS IN
A LATE ROMAN CEMETERY AT BETH GUVRIN

Jodi Magness / Gideon Avni

Tufts University / Israel Antiquities Authority

IN 1985, a late Roman cemetery was discovered by archaeologists near the Ahinoam Cave, approximately half a kilometer south of the site of Beth Guvrin in Israel. The following year, the cemetery was intensively surveyed and mapped. Seventy-four burial caves were located, cut into the soft chalk of the rolling hills. Most of the caves have a single room containing several burials, though some large complexes were also discovered. In a number of the simpler caves crosses were carved or painted on the walls, and in others, usually the more complex ones, Jewish symbols were found on the walls or on oil lamps inside. Rescue excavations were conducted in several caves under the direction of Gideon Avni, Uzi Dahari, and Amos Kloner on behalf of the Israel Department of Antiquities (now the Israel Antiquities Authority).[1] This paper describes the results of a study of the oil lamps from four of the excavated burial caves.

The numismatic and ceramic evidence indicates that the Ahinoam Cave Cemetery was in use from the late second or third century through the first half of the eighth century.[2] In historical terms, this corresponds with the late Roman, the Byzantine, and the beginning of the early Islamic periods in Palestine. Beth Guvrin is located in the ancient district

---

[1] G. Avni, U. Dahari, and A. Kloner, "Notes and News: Beth Guvrin: The Ahinoam Cave Cemetery," *IEJ* 36 (1986), 72–74.

[2] Unless otherwise indicated, all dates refer to the Common Era.

of Idumaea. Prior to 586 B.C.E., this area was part of the kingdom of Judah, and its main city was Lachish. After the fall of Judah, an Edomite population settled in the area, whence it became known as Idumaea. During the Hellenistic period, the capital city of the district was Marissa (or Mareshah), next to Beth Guvrin. Idumaea was annexed by the Hasmonean kings, and its inhabitants were forcibly converted to Judaism.[3] When Marissa was destroyed by the Parthians in 40 B.C.E., Beth Guvrin replaced it as the capital of the district. In the year 200, Septimius Severus refounded Beth Guvrin as the *polis* of Eleutheropolis. It served as the capital of Idumaea and controlled the largest city territory in late Roman Palestine. Eleutheropolis flourished through the Roman and Byzantine periods. After the Muslim conquest in the seventh century it again became known as Beth Guvrin (or in Arabic, Beit Jibrin).[4]

Different types of burial caves in the Ahinoam Cave Cemetery can be distinguished on the basis of size, arrangement, and decoration. Most are simple arcosolium caves, which consist of a rectangular burial chamber with an arcosolium (arched niche) cut into three of the walls: in each arcosolium are one to three burial troughs cut in the shape of coffins. Usually the troughs are arranged in the shape of the letter "U," with a passage to facilitate access to each one. The troughs were covered with rectangular stone slabs and sealed with plaster. The most elaborate caves are hall caves, which consist of a rectangular hall with arcosolia and gable-shaped depressions containing burial troughs cut into the walls (see, for example, Figures 1–3). In some cases, coffins were hewn out of the rock and left attached not to the walls but to the floor. Hall caves have richly carved architectural elements such as columns, pillars, capitals, and wall reliefs. They contain a large number of burial troughs: thirty-eight were counted in one cave of this type. The location and shape

---

[3]   M. Avi-Yonah, *The Holy Land from the Persian to the Arab Conquest (536 B.C.–A.D. 640), A Historical Geography* (Grand Rapids: Baker Book House, 1977), 25–26, 61; M. Avi-Yonah, "Mareshah (Marisa)," *NEAEHL*, 3, 948.

[4]   Avi-Yonah, *The Holy Land*, 159–62; A. Kloner, "Beth Guvrin," *NEAEHL*, 1, 195.

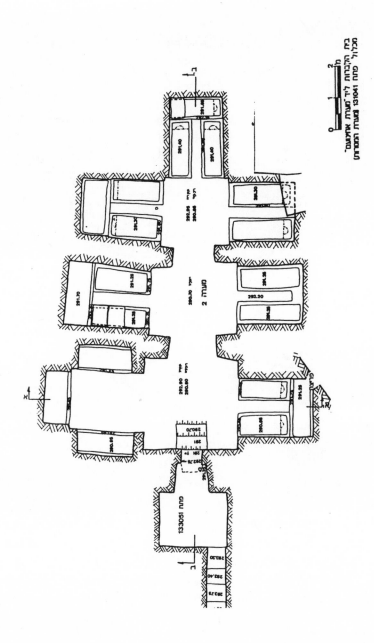

FIGURE 1

Plan of the Menorah Cave

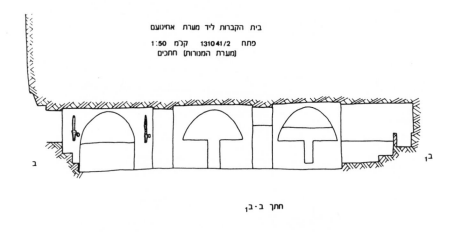

בית הקברות ליד מערת אחינועם
פתח 131041/2   קנם 1:50
(מערת המנורות) חתכים

חתך ב - ב₁

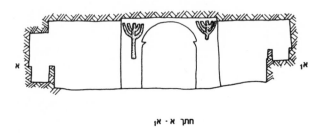

חתך א - א₁

FIGURE 2
Sections through the Menorah Cave

of the troughs indicate a certain hierarchy, with the largest and most
elaborate usually cut into the wall opposite the main entrance.[5]

Some of the burial caves in the Ahinoam Cave Cemetery are paralleled in the famous necropolis at Beth Shearim, in Israel's Lower Galilee.
Rabbi Judah Ha-Nasi, who carried out the redaction of the Mishnah or
Oral Law, resided at Beth Shearim and was buried there when he died at
the beginning of the third century. A necropolis sprang up around his

---

[5]   Avni, Dahari, and Kloner, "Notes and News: Beth Guvrin"; Kloner, "Beth Guvrin,"
198–99.

FIGURE 3

Reconstruction of the interior of a hall cave

tomb, as Jews from around Palestine and the Middle East were brought to the site for burial.[6] Excavations from the 1930s to 1950s uncovered twenty-seven elaborate catacombs in the necropolis at Beth Shearim. The catacombs have courtyards with built entrances providing access into underground burial halls. Some of the catacombs have several stories of burial halls placed on either side of a long corridor; Catacomb 1, for example, has sixteen halls containing four hundred burial places. The burial halls are of various sizes, and some consist of several rooms. The graves are usually either arcosolia, loculi cut into the walls, or pit graves cut into the floors. Sometimes the bodies were placed in large

---

[6] N. Avigad, *Beth She'arim. Report on the Excavations During 1953–1958, Volume III: Catacombs 12–23* (New Brunswick: Rutgers University, 1976), 2–3.

stone sarcophagi along the walls of the burial halls and corridors. Reliefs carved on some of the walls of the catacombs and on the stone sarcophagi depict Jewish ritual objects such as the menorah, *lûlāb*, *'etrôg*, and shofar, as well as other motifs such as people, animals, and architectural and geometric designs. There are also inscriptions in Hebrew, Aramaic, Greek, and other languages on the walls of the catacombs and on the sarcophagi.[7] Many of the features of the Ahinoam Cave Cemetery, such as the plans of some of the burial caves, the use of arcosolia, and carved reliefs depicting Jewish ritual objects, are paralleled at Beth Shearim. However, the Ahinoam Cave Cemetery differs in other respects, probably because it served a local, mixed population and remained in use for a longer period.[8]

Hundreds of oil lamps and lamp fragments were recovered in the excavation of the Ahinoam Cave Cemetery at Beth Guvrin. Together with the coins, they provide a chronological framework for the cemetery's use. In addition, Jewish and Christian motifs or inscriptions found on several lamps probably reflect the religious orientation of some of the tombs' occupants. They might also reflect changes in the composition of the local population over time, an issue that will be examined later. The fact that these lamps come from a controlled archaeological excavation is of great importance for typological reasons. Many represent types paralleled at Beit Nattif, a site to the north of Beth Guvrin excavated by D. C. Baramki in 1934 that yielded unused lamps and molds for their production.[9] While the same types have been found in other excavations, the primary studies are based on private collections of lamps of unknown or uncertain provenience. Our lamps provide excavated parallels for many of the latter, and greatly enrich the known corpus.

---

[7]   N. Avigad and B. Mazar, "Beth She'arim," *NEAEHL*, 2, 241–48.

[8]   For a recent reevaluation of the chronology of Beth Shearim, see F. Vitto, "Byzantine Mosaics at Bet She'arim: New Evidence for the History of the Site," *'Atiqot* 28 (1996), 115–46.

[9]   D. C. Baramki, "Two Roman Cisterns at Beit Nattif," *QDAP* 5 (1936), 3–10.

Oil Lamp Types

A number of different lamp types are represented in the Ahinoam Cave Cemetery. The earliest are round lamps with decorated discus of Roman type.[10] These Palestinian versions of Broneer Type 25 have a round, handleless body, a small nozzle, a flat base, and a closed, sunken discus. The discus is decorated with a design in relief, and the base may have potter's marks (see, for example, Figure 6, upper right). There are often volutes flanking the nozzle, and double axes or other motifs on the shoulder. A slightly later variant of this type has a larger filling hole in the center of an undecorated discus, and a knob handle (see, for example, Figure 6, upper left).[11]

Round lamps with decorated discus of Roman type have a range from the second half of the first century through the third century.[12] However, the absence of clearly first- to second-century types such as "Herodian" and mold-made Southern lamps points to a late second- to third-century date for our round lamps with decorated discus of Roman type, and thus for the beginning of the use of the Ahinoam Cave Cemetery.[13] This is further indicated by the relative rarity of round lamps with decorated discus of Roman type in our assemblage, which must have been uncommon by the time the first burials were made.

The majority of lamps from the Ahinoam Cave Cemetery represent types that date from the third to the fifth centuries. Most belong to one of three types associated with the workshop at Beit Nattif: round lamps with decorated discus of Beit Nattif type; lamps with bow-shaped nozzle;

---

[10] R. Rosenthal and R. Sivan, *Ancient Lamps in the Schloessinger Collection* (*Qedem* 8: Jerusalem: Hebrew University, 1978), 85, 95. We use the term "round lamps with decorated discus of Roman type" to distinguish these from the "round lamps with decorated discus of Beit Nattif type," discussed below.

[11] Rosenthal and Sivan, *Ancient Lamps*, 96, nos. 389–90.

[12] Rosenthal and Sivan, *Ancient Lamps*, 85.

[13] Rosenthal and Sivan, *Ancient Lamps*, 79–84.

and ovoid lamps with large filling hole.[14] Round lamps with decorated
discus of Beit Nattif type are made of unslipped, light brown or cream
colored ware. They have a round body with a flat top, a slightly sunken,
closed discus with small central filling hole, a pyramidal handle, and a
broad, flat (or sometimes sloping) shoulder. Geometric and/or figured
designs in a delicate linear style cover the discus and shoulder (see, for
example, Figure 4, lower right). At Beit Nattif, almost all of the round
lamps with decorated discus came from Cistern I. The associated coins
suggest a range of ca. 250–350 for this type.[15] Our lamps represent the
only published specimens found outside Beit Nattif.[16] One bears the
first published example of Jewish motifs (a seven-branched menorah
flanked by incense shovel and shofar) on such a lamp (Figure 4, upper
left). By contrast, Baramki noted the "entirely pagan" motifs on those
he found at Beit Nattif.[17]

Cistern II at Beit Nattif contained mostly lamps with bow-shaped
nozzle.[18] This type has a round body, a large central filling-hole surrounded by a ridge, and a curved shoulder. In a few examples, there is a
closed, sunken discus with or without decoration. The manner in which
the sides of the nozzle are pinched creates the appearance of volutes.
There is a ring base and a pyramidal handle (or, rarely, a loop handle).
The shoulder and nozzle are decorated with geometric and floral designs.
The ware is light brown in color and is very soft and friable in texture. A
drippy dark red or dark orange-red slip covers the upper part of the
exterior. Rosenthal and Sivan noted a typological development in these
lamps, corresponding to a degeneration in quality over time. The earlier

---

[14]   Baramki, "Two Roman Cisterns"; Rosenthal and Sivan, *Ancient Lamps*, 99–
110.

[15]   Baramki, "Two Roman Cisterns"; Rosenthal and Sivan, *Ancient Lamps*, 104–5.

[16]   Baramki, "Two Roman Cisterns"; Rosenthal and Sivan, *Ancient Lamps*.

[17]   Baramki, "Two Roman Cisterns," 8.

[18]   Baramki, "Two Roman Cisterns," 8; Rosenthal and Sivan, *Ancient Lamps*,
104–5.

examples are better proportioned and have clear reliefs; the later ones are crude and were often made in poor molds.[19] The evidence from Beit Nattif and elsewhere suggests a range from the second half of the third century to the fifth century for this type. The fact that one of our lamps has an exact parallel from Beit Nattif attests to contacts between the sites.[20] Baramki noted that many of the motifs decorating the lamps with bow-shaped nozzle from Cistern II at Beit Nattif are Jewish.[21] At the Ahinoam Cave Cemetery, both Jewish and Christian motifs appear on lamps of this type (Figure 4, upper right; Figure 5, upper right).

Ovoid lamps with large filling-hole were found with the round lamps with decorated discus in Cistern I at Beit Nattif.[22] They are closely related in ware and decoration to the lamps with bow-shaped nozzle. Their main characteristics are an ovoid body, a relatively large filling hole, a knob or pyramidal handle, and a short nozzle. The clay is often light brown or yellow-brown, although in some cases it is red-brown. The ware tends to be thinner and harder-fired than that of the lamps with bow-shaped nozzle. The upper part of the exterior is usually covered with a red slip that may be fired brown or black. Many of the motifs decorating the shoulder and nozzle are the same as those found on the lamps with bow-shaped nozzle (such as wreaths across the nozzle and a rinceau on the shoulder; see, for example, Figure 6, lower right). In addition, the manner in which the nozzle is sometimes pinched can blur the distinction between the two types. For these reasons, it is often difficult to make a definite typological assignment, especially in the case of small fragments. Ovoid lamps with large filling-hole were dated by Rosenthal and Sivan to the third to fourth centuries, but the evidence from the City of David indicates that production

---

[19] Rosenthal and Sivan, *Ancient Lamps*, 105.

[20] See Baramki, "Two Roman Cisterns," pl. 11:13.

[21] Baramki, "Two Roman Cisterns," 8.

[22] Baramki, "Two Roman Cisterns," 8; Rosenthal and Sivan, *Ancient Lamps*, 99.

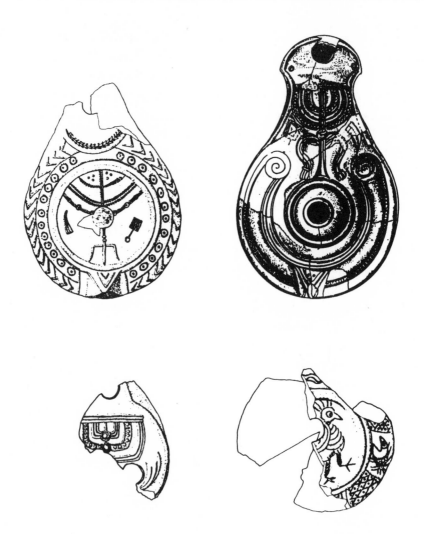

FIGURE 4
Round lamp with decorated discus of the Roman type (lower left);
Round lamps with decorated discus of Beit Nattif type (upper left and lower right);
Lamp with bow-shaped nozzle (upper right).

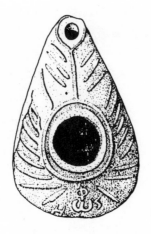
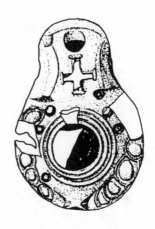

FIGURE 5
Large candlestick lamp (upper left);
Lamp with bow-shaped nozzle (upper right);
Early channel-nozzle lamps (lower right and left).

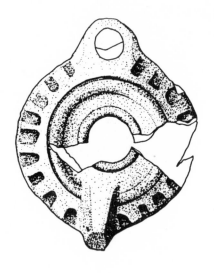

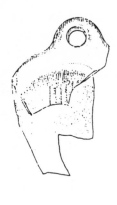

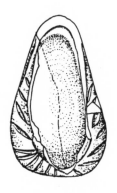

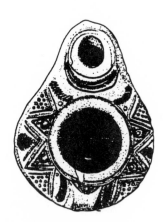

FIGURE 6

Round lamp with decorated discus of Roman type (upper right);
Variant of round lamp with decorated discus of Roman type (upper left);
Ovoid lamp with large filling-hole (lower right);
Small candlestick lamp (lower left).

continued into the fifth century.[23] Thus, all three lamp types associated with Beit Nattif fall within a range from the third to fifth centuries.

Small and large candlestick (or slipper) lamps, which are the standard types of the Byzantine period in Judea, are well represented in the Ahinoam Cave Cemetery. Small candlestick lamps have an oval body, a low circular ring base, and a medium-sized filling-hole. These features and the relief pattern of radiating lines around the filling-hole are shared with the large candlestick lamps (see, for example, Figure 6, lower left). There is often a cross on the nozzle, though other designs occur. The filling-hole and sometimes the wick-hole are encircled by a single raised ring. There is either a loop handle, a "pellet" in place of the handle, or no handle at all. The ware is hard-fired and light brown in color. Small candlestick lamps are dated from the second half of the fourth to the mid-sixth century.[24]

Large candlestick lamps resemble the small candlestick lamps in shape and decoration, but are larger in size and have a more elongated nozzle. The medium-sized filling-hole is surrounded by two ridges, with the inner one forming a closed circle. The outer ridge extends onto the nozzle in a straight line down to the wick-hole. There is a low circular ring base, and the hard-fired ware is light brown, orange-brown, or pink-brown in color. Large candlestick lamps are dated from the mid-sixth century to the late seventh or early eighth century. All of those from the Ahinoam Cave Cemetery represent the variant with a pattern of radiating lines around the filling-hole.[25] One bears an inscription reading "the light" (hē phōs), which is an abbreviated version of the common formula "the light of Christ shines for all" (Figure 5, upper left).[26]

---

[23] Rosenthal and Sivan, *Ancient Lamps*, 99; J. Magness, *Jerusalem Ceramic Chronology circa 200–800 C.E.* (Sheffield: Sheffield Academic Press, 1993), 161–65.

[24] Rosenthal and Sivan, *Ancient Lamps*, 112–13; Magness, *Jerusalem Ceramic Chronology*, 250; Oil Lamps Form 2.

[25] See Magness, *Jerusalem Ceramic Chronology*, 252; Oil Lamps Form 3A.

[26] See S. Loffreda, *Lucerne bizantine in Terra Santa con iscrizioni in greco* (Jerusalem:

The latest oil lamps found in the Ahinoam Cave Cemetery are of the early channel-nozzle type.[27] The distinguishing features of this type are the channel connecting the filling-hole and wick-hole (which often contains a decorative pattern), and the low knob handle. The ware varies in color, but is usually coarse and very hard-fired. Several variants can be distinguished on the basis of morphology and decoration. One lamp is decorated with the pattern of radiating lines characteristic of the candlestick lamps, but has a channel formed by two parallel lines running from the filling-hole to the wick-hole.[28] Another example of this variant carries a Greek inscription around the filling-hole that reads "your law is a lamp to my feet" (*lykhnos t<o>is posin mou ho [no]mos <so>u(?)*) (from Psalms 119:105) (Figure 5, lower left).[29] Examples of the most common Judean variant of the early channel-nozzle lamp are represented, which have a pattern of raised dots and lines surrounding the filling-hole (Figure 5, lower right).[30] There are also slightly later variants of this type.[31] One is decorated with a fish on the nozzle.

Early channel-nozzle lamps date from the seventh to early eighth centuries. The rarity or absence of clearly later types, such as channel-nozzle lamps, suggests that burials in the Ahinoam Cave Cemetery ceased by the middle of the eighth century.[32] This accords well with the early Islamic date proposed for the quarrying of the bell-shaped caves, which cut into and thus must postdate the tombs in the cemetery.[33] It is now time to examine the four excavated burial caves and their contents.

Studium Biblicum Franciscanum, 1989); J. Magness, "Blessings from Jerusalem: Evidence for Early Christian Pilgrimage," *EI* 25 (1996), 37*–45*.

[27] Magness, *Jerusalem Ceramic Chronology*, 255–58; Oil Lamps Form 4.

[28] Magness, *Jerusalem Ceramic Chronology*, 255; Oil Lamps Form 4A.

[29] For a close parallel, see Loffreda, *Lucerne bizantine*, 121–22; Type C1.1.

[30] Magness, *Jerusalem Ceramic Chronology*, 255; Oil Lamps Form 4B.

[31] Magness, *Jerusalem Ceramic Chronology*, 255; Oil Lamps Form 4C.

[32] Magness, *Jerusalem Ceramic Chronology*, 258; Oil Lamps Form 5.

[33] Kloner, "Beth Guvrin," 200–1.

The Four Excavated Burial Caves

THE INSCRIPTION CAVE (L092052)

This relatively simple cave consists of a single room containing three arcosolia with two burial troughs each. Fragments of a stone lintel found in the room were decorated with a carved seven-branched menorah, flanked by inscriptions in Greek listing the names of the interred: "Ioses Tanhuma and Zenon Zacharias" (Figure 7).[34] The cave contained a large number of lamps and lamp fragments, the earliest of which are round lamps with decorated discus of Roman type. The discus of one

FIGURE 7
Greek inscription mentioning "Ioses Tanhuma and Zenon Zacharias,"
from the Inscription Cave.

---

[34] Avni, Dahari, and Kloner, "Notes and News: Beth Guvrin," 73–74; Kloner, "Beth Guvrin," 199. The names as they appear in Greek are:

ΙΩΣΗΣ		ΖΗΝΟΝ
	(Menorah)	
ΘΑΝΟΥΜΑ		ΖΑΧΑΡ[ ]

(see Fig. 7). It is not clear whether the second name in each pair is a patronymic (especially since the ending of the last is not preserved), and whether the names should be read horizontally (e.g., "Ioses Tanhuma") or vertically (e.g., "Ioses Zenon").

was apparently decorated with a human figure. Two feet facing left are still visible at the bottom of the discus, with the base of another object, perhaps a staff, to the left (Figure 6, upper right). One lamp base bears an incised potter's mark that has an exact parallel from Aphek-Antipatris.[35] As noted above, the round lamps with decorated discus of Beit Nattif type found here represent the first published examples of this type from an excavated context outside Beit Nattif. The shoulders are decorated with a variety of geometric and floral designs in a delicate linear style. On one, a bird occupies the center of the discus, and there is a fish in a panel on the shoulder (Figure 4, lower right). Birds are found on lamps of this type from Beit Nattif, although there are no exact parallels.[36] We have also noted that one lamp is decorated with the first Jewish motifs attested on this type (Figure 4, upper left). A seven-branched menorah with tripod base is prominently displayed in the discus, flanked on the right by an incense shovel and on the left by a shofar, or ram's horn. Two groups of three dots each occupy the spaces between the uppermost branches of the menorah.

One of the lamps with bow-shaped nozzle has an exact parallel from Beit Nattif.[37] Though this is the only case of an exact parallel, typological similarities suggest that Beit Nattif was the source for other third- to fifth-century lamps in the Ahinoam Cave Cemetery. The motifs found on our specimens are common on lamps with bow-shaped nozzle: a leaf on the nozzle, a curved wreath across the nozzle, an egg-and-dart or tongue pattern on the shoulder, and a row of circles enclosing raised dots on the shoulder.

The decorative motifs on the shoulders of our ovoid lamps with large filling-hole are characteristic of this type: a leaf and vine pattern; a leaf pattern interrupted by a double ax or "maltese cross" motif; a row of

---

[35]   See W. Neidinger, "A Typology of Oil Lamps from the Mercantile Quarter of Antipatris," *Tel Aviv* 9 (1982), pl. 23:12; number 38 in the catalogue.

[36]   Baramki, "Two Roman Cisterns," pls. 7:6–9; 11:19, 24.

[37]   See n. 20 above.

concentric circles enclosing dots; an ovolo pattern; a row of hooks; swastikas, concentric circles, and other geometric motifs; and radiating lines. V. Sussman and M. Gihon have each suggested that some of the geometric motifs found on Palestinian lamps of the Roman and Byzantine periods might be schematic representations of objects.[38] For examples, circles with dots inside could represent shields.[39] Hooks like those decorating the shoulder of one of our lamps, called "gammas" by Sussman, are interpreted by Gihon as a military structure.[40] In addition, examples of small and large candlestick lamps were found in this cave.

THE COLUMNS CAVE (L113045)

The Columns Cave consists of a rectangular chamber with deep arcosolia along the walls. The chamber contains nine burial troughs, some in the arcosolia and others carved out of the floor as standing sarcophagi. A single sarcophagus connected to the floor flanked by round carved columns stands in the center of the arcosolium opposite the entrance. Small arcosolia in the tomb were probably used for bone collection (*ossilegium*). Two troughs carved into the floor on either side of the entrance may have been used for this purpose.[41] The cave contained a large number of lamps and lamp fragments. One is a round lamp with decorated discus of Beit Nattif type, showing a bird standing beneath a tree. Most of the lamps are of the type with bow-shaped nozzle; one has a cross on the nozzle (Figure 5, upper right). The nozzle of another bears a representation of an arcade consisting of two columns with

---

[38]   V. Sussman, *Ornamented Jewish Oil-Lamps* (Warminster: Aris and Phillips, 1982); M. Gihon, "The Ground Plan of a Military Camp on a Jewish Lamp," in M. Heltzer, A. Segal, and D. Kaufman, eds., *Studies in the Archaeology and History of Ancient Israel in Honour of Moshe Dothan* (Haifa: Haifa University Press, 1993), 181–94.

[39]   Sussman, *Ornamented Jewish Oil-Lamps*, 84, no. 136; 109, no. 204; Gihon, "The Ground Plan," 191–93.

[40]   Gihon, "The Ground Plan," 190–91.

[41]   Avni, Dahari, and Kloner, "Notes and News: Beth Guvrin," 73.

diagonal flutes that frame a three-branched object.[42] The Columns Cave also has examples of ovoid lamps with large filling-hole and the most common Judaean variant of early channel-nozzle lamp.

THE MENORAH CAVE (L131041/2) (Figures 1–2)

This tomb consists of a large rectangular hall, subdivided into three square areas along its long axis. The areas are separated by wide passage-ways lined with decorated pilasters. On three sides of each area are carved arcosolia, with two or three burial troughs apiece, for a total of nineteen troughs. The troughs had been sealed with large square stone slabs that were plastered together. On the pilasters opposite the cave entrance are two five-branched menorahs carved in relief, and on each side of the arcosolium to the left of the entrance, are *lulābîm* and *ʾetrôgîm*, also carved in relief. Next to the entrance another relief on the wall, which was removed by looters, seems to have depicted a shofar. The finds from the tomb include a great number of lamps and lamp fragments, and a cylindrical bronze amulet with a long, still undeci-phered inscription in Hebrew.[43]

Perhaps the most spectacular lamp found in the excavation comes from this cave (Figure 4, upper right). It is an unusually large example of the type with bow-shaped nozzle and closed discus of the highest quality (now restored). Its orange-brown ware is smooth and well-levigated, and the upper part of the exterior is covered with an orange-red slip. A seven-branched menorah with tripod base rendered in fine relief occu-pies the space from the nozzle to the edge of the closed discus. Its branches are beaded or jewelled, and it is flanked by a shofar on the right

---

[42]   For other examples of this motif, see Rosenthal and Sivan, *Ancient Lamps*, 107, no. 435; Y. Israeli and U. Avida, *Oil Lamps from Eretz Israel, The Louis and Carmen Warschaw Collection at the Israel Museum, Jerusalem* (Jerusalem: Israel Museum, 1988), 132, nos. 384–86.

[43]   Avni, Dahari, and Kloner, "Notes and News: Beth Guvrin," 72–73.

and an incense shovel on the left. A scroll whose rolled-up ends frame the base of the menorah curves around the top of the shoulder. The edges of the scroll are delineated by a row of raised dots.[44]

The designs on the nozzles of other lamps with bow-shaped nozzle from this cave include peacock tails and an oil flask.[45] One ovoid lamp with large filling-hole has concentric circles enclosing dots and whirled spokes or rosettes on the shoulder. There are also examples of wheel-made (or "Persian") lamps, which represent a type common in southern Palestine during the sixth to seventh centuries.[46] The other Byzantine lamps are of the small and large candlestick type; as noted above, one bears an inscription in Greek reading "the light" in place of the handle (Figure 5, upper left). The early channel-nozzle lamps have also been discussed, including one that bears a Greek inscription on the shoulder reading "your law is a lamp unto my feet" (Figure 5, lower left). Loffreda has suggested that the design in the nozzle of another lamp of this type is a *phi*, representing the Greek word "light" (*phōs*) (Figure 5, lower right).[47] We may also note again the fish decorating the nozzle of another lamp of this type.

THE BONE COLLECTION CAVE (L893144)

This complex has a large central hall with deep arcosolia along the walls. The hall gives access to seven more rooms, which contain many burial troughs and niches for the collection of bones (*ossilegium*). The large number of bones, lamps and lamp fragments attests to the intensive use of the cave. The earliest pieces are round lamps with decorated discus of Roman type. No parallels were found for a lamp with a closed discus

---

[44] For lamps of the same type decorated with menorahs, see V. Sussman, "Astragal Menorah on Clay Lamps" [Hebrew], *Qadmoniot* 51–52 (1980), 119–21.

[45] For an oil flask on a Southern lamp, see Sussman, *Ornamented Jewish Oil-Lamps*, 66, no. 85.

[46] Magness, *Jerusalem Ceramic Chronology*, 129.

[47] Loffreda, *Lucerne bizantine*, 161–62 no. 712; Type D6.3.

decorated with a seven-branched menorah, flanked by a shofar on the right (Figure 4, lower left). The short nozzle and circular discus with small, off-center filling-hole, suggest that it is a round lamp with decorated discus of Roman type. Thus, while the menorah and shofar resemble those depicted on lamps with bow-shaped nozzle, this is a different type. Other types represented are lamps with bow-shaped nozzle and early channel-nozzle lamps.

Conclusion

A total of 483 lamps or lamp fragments was recovered in the excavation of the Ahinoam Cave Cemetery. The number and percentage of types found in each cave is provided in Tables 1 and 2. The distribution of types reflects the occupational history of each cave. The presence of round lamps with decorated discus of Roman type indicates that the Inscription Cave and Bone Collection Cave came into use first. These lamps are completely absent from the Columns Cave and the Menorah Cave, where the earliest types are the round lamp with decorated discus of Beit Nattif type, the lamp with bow-shaped nozzle, and the ovoid lamp with large filling-hole. In all four caves, it is these three types that predominate. Large radiated candlestick lamps and early channel-nozzle lamps were also found in all the caves, though they are represented in substantial numbers only in the Menorah Cave. This fact, together with the presence of clearly Christian symbols and inscriptions on the large radiated lamps and early channel-nozzle lamps found in it, indicate that the Menorah Cave was used much more intensively than the other caves during the seventh and early eighth centuries.

The presence of both Jewish and Christian symbols and inscriptions on the lamps and in the caves raises the intriguing question of the occupants' religious orientation. Specifically Jewish or Christian motifs or inscriptions appear on the following lamps:

The Inscription Cave:

- A menorah on a round lamp with decorated discus of Beit Nattif type (Figure 4, upper left).

The Columns Cave:

- A cross on a lamp with bow-shaped nozzle (Figure 5, upper right).

The Menorah Cave:

- A menorah on a lamp with bow-shaped nozzle (Figure 4, upper right).
- A Christian inscription on a large candlestick lamp (Figure 5, upper left).
- A Christian inscription on an early channel-nozzle lamp (Figure 5, lower left).
- A possible Christian inscription (the letter *phi*) on an early channel-nozzle lamp (Figure 5, lower right).
- A possible Christian motif (a fish) on an early channel-nozzle lamp.

The Bone Collection Cave:

- A menorah on a lamp with decorated discus, apparently of Roman type (Figure 4, lower left).

In addition, clearly Jewish symbols and inscriptions decorated the walls and lintels of the Inscription Cave and the Menorah Cave.

In the case of the Inscription Cave and the Bone Collection Cave, only Jewish symbols are attested. In the case of the Columns Cave, there is just one Christian symbol. It is reasonable to assume that the presence of clearly Jewish or Christian symbols reflects the religious orientation of the caves' occupants. As Avigad stated in his discussion of the catacombs at Beth Shearim, "a menorah on a grave ... primarily represented

TABLE 1: NUMBERS OF LAMPS ACCORDING TO TYPE					
Burial Cave	L092052	L113045	L131041/2	L893144	Total
Round lamps with decorated discus of Roman type	28	0	0	8	36
Probably/perhaps round lamps with decorated discus of Roman type	4	0	0	3	7
Round lamps with decorated discus of Beit Nattif type	7	5	1	0	13
Probably/perhaps round lamps with decorated discus of Beit Nattif type	5	1	1	1	8
Lamps with bow-shaped nozzle	38	82	44	13	177
Probably/perhaps lamps with bow-shaped nozzle	33	35	13	9	90
Ovoid lamps with large filling-hole	24	2	4	3	33
Probably/perhaps ovoid lamps with large filling-hole	11	3	3	4	21
Lamps with bow-shaped nozzle OR ovoid lamps with large filling-hole	10	4	6	7	27
Small radiated candlestick lamps	2	1	2	1	6
Large radiated candlestick lamps	3	1	8	1	13
Wheelmade (Persian) lamps	1	0	3	0	4
Early channel-nozzle lamps (including possible channel-nozzle lamps)	1	2	29	4	36
Type: NOT CLEAR	6	2	1*	3	12
TOTAL NUMBER	173	138	115	57	483

* Mamluke?

TABLE 2: PERCENTAGES OF LAMPS ACCORDING TO TYPE					
Burial Cave	L092052	L113045	L131041/2	L893144	Total %
Round lamps with decorated discus of Roman type	16%	0%	0%	14%	7%
Probably/perhaps round lamps with decorated discus of Roman type	2%	0%	0%	5%	1%
Round lamps with decorated discus of Beit Nattif type	4%	3%	.8%	0%	3%
Probably/perhaps round lamps with decorated discus of Beit Nattif type	3%	.7%	.8%	1%	2%
Lamps with bow-shaped nozzle	22%	60%	38%	22%	37%
Probably/perhaps lamps with bow-shaped nozzle	19%	25%	11%	16%	19%
Ovoid lamps with large filling-hole	14%	1%	3%	5%	7%
Probably/perhaps ovoid lamps with large filling-hole	6%	2%	2%	7%	4%
Lamps with bow-shaped nozzle OR ovoid lamps with large filling-hole	5%	3%	5%	12%	5%
Small radiated candlestick lamps	1%	.7%	2%	1%	1%
Large radiated candlestick lamps	2%	.7%	7%	1%	3%
Wheelmade (Persian) lamps	.5%	0%	2%	0%	.8%
Early channel-nozzle lamps (including possible channel-nozzle lamps)	.5%	1%	25%	7%	7%
Type: NOT CLEAR	3%	1%	.8%	5%	2%

affiliation and identification with the Jewish people."[48] Avigad also pointed out that the menorah is much more common during the late Roman period in Jewish cemeteries in the Diaspora (such as the catacombs at Rome) than in Jewish cemeteries in Palestine. Evidently, Diaspora Jews felt a stronger need to display their Jewish identity than did Palestinian Jews who lived among their own people in their own country.[49] On the other hand, the absence of Jewish or Christian symbols in the Ahinoam Cave Cemetery does not necessarily mean that these caves were used during their entire occupational history only by people of one faith or another. In fact, the evidence provided by the lamps suggests that the religious orientation of the caves' occupants changed over time. This is clearest in the case of the Menorah Cave, which is the only one where a mixture of Jewish and Christian symbols is represented.

Jewish symbols decorate the walls of the Menorah Cave and are found on a lamp with bow-shaped nozzle. Christian symbols and inscriptions are found on large radiated candlestick lamps and on early channel-nozzle lamps. Thus, the Jewish symbols seem to be associated with the Menorah Cave's initial use during the third and fourth centuries. The Christian symbols from this cave are found on lamps dating to the late sixth to early eighth centuries. This picture is complemented by the evidence from the other caves.

Jewish symbols are attested only on lamps dating from the late second to fourth centuries. They do not appear on lamps that postdate the fourth century (the latest examples are the round lamp with decorated discus of Beit Nattif type [Figure 4, upper left] and the fine lamp with bow-shaped nozzle [Figure 4, upper right]). The earliest Christian symbol is on the lamp with bow-shaped nozzle (Figure 5, upper right), whose poor quality suggests a slightly later date (fourth to fifth century) than the lamp of the same type with the menorah. Again, the absence of

---

[48]   Avigad, *Beth She'arim*, 268.

[49]   Avigad, *Beth She'arim*, 268.

clearly Jewish or Christian symbols does not necessarily reflect the absence of that religious group. However, the evidence from the Menorah Cave and the distribution of clearly Jewish and Christian symbols on lamps from the other caves is suggestive of a change over time in the religious orientation of the cemetery's occupants. It seems that the initial (late second to fourth century) burials in these caves were Jewish. The first evidence for Christian presence dates to the fourth or fifth century, and is most common during the late sixth to early eighth centuries.

Not all of the burial caves in the cemetery underwent this process of transformation; some appear to have been Christian from the start. The excavators have noted that the large hall tombs were usually originally Jewish, whereas the caves in which only Christian symbols were found have a simple plan. Thus, at least some of the simpler burial caves were probably constructed by Christians during the Byzantine period. Jewish or Christian presence can be identified definitely only when religious symbols or inscriptions are present, rather than on the basis of tomb layout or architecture. Still, tombs decorated with Christian symbols do not appear to be attested in the Ahinoam Cave Cemetery before the fifth century. In addition, tombs with Jewish symbols provide evidence for the custom of bone collection (*ossilegium*) in niches or pits, which continued from the Second Temple period. In tombs with Christian symbols, and in those without a clear religious identification, the bones were collected in a corner of the cave or on a bench, to provide space for newly interred. The apparent distinction between the larger, more elaborate Jewish burial caves and the simpler Christian ones may reflect different religious beliefs. Christianity attaches less significance to the body after death, since only the soul is immortal and is assigned a place in the world to come. Jewish tradition, however, takes care to preserve the deceased's bodily remains, which will be physically resurrected with the coming of the Messiah.[50] This distinction in burial cave types may

---

[50]   Kloner, "Beth Guvrin," 199.

also reflect a greater degree of prosperity among the local Jewish community.

Another distinction between the caves concerns the lamps. The caves with Jewish symbols contained many more lamps than the simple ones with Christian symbols. This may again reflect differences in religious beliefs and practices. One possible explanation for this phenomenon is that according to Jewish law, pottery vessels cannot be purified. Since an oil lamp becomes impure when it is brought into contact with a corpse, it cannot be used again and must be left in the cave or smashed near the door. Thus, the large hall caves contained hundreds of lamp fragments.[51]

The lamps provide one piece of evidence for the transformation of the Ahinoam Cave Cemetery from a Jewish one to a Christian one. However, this raises more problems than it solves. For example, does this transformation reflect the conversion of Jewish families to Christianity, or the replacement of a Jewish population by an unrelated Christian one? Or, did a Jewish element continue to co-exist alongside the Christian population? If the last is true, why are no Jewish symbols attested after the fourth century? Why were the Christians buried in the Menorah Cave not disturbed by the Jewish symbols decorating the walls, and why is it the one with the most intensive and clearest Christian use?

The phenomenon of Christian reuse of formerly Jewish tombs has been noted elsewhere in Palestine. Gideon Avni has demonstrated that a number of Jewish tombs of the late Second Temple period in Jerusalem were reused during the late Roman and Byzantine periods.[52] They

---

[51] Kloner, "Beth Guvrin," 199. This explanation is hypothetical since we do not know how widespread purity practices were among the Jewish population in Byzantine Palestine, and how such practices may have related to the oil lamps used in burial caves. We are grateful to Hayim Lapin for his helpful comments on this matter.

[52] G. Avni, "Christian Secondary Use of Jewish Burial Caves in Jerusalem in the Light of New Excavations at the Aceldama Tombs," in F. Manns, E. Alliata, eds.,

contained the remains of cremated pagans interred during the second to fourth centuries, and/or clearly Christian burials of the fifth to seventh centuries. One interesting aspect of this phenomenon is the respect shown by subsequent burials for the previous remains, which were usually not disturbed to make way for the newly interred. Avni proposes that this deference represents a more complex concept than merely the functional utilization of existing space.[53]

The process of transformation suggested here for the Ahinoam Cave Cemetery receives indirect support from historical sources. We know that during the second and third centuries, Beth Guvrin (Eleutheropolis) was a Roman urban center with a predominantly pagan population mixed with some Jews. Its Jewish community was one of a number that were established in the southern Shephelah after the Bar Kokhba Revolt and flourished during the late Roman period. In fact, Eleutheropolis was among the cities with a predominantly non-Jewish population where Jews were permitted and encouraged to settle. Our evidence complements that obtained by E. Oren in his survey of the necropolis at Beth Guvrin, which demonstrated that Jews reused Hellenistic tombs during the second to fourth centuries.[54] The population adopted Christianity early on: in the year 325 a bishop from Beth Guvrin participated in the Council of Nicaea. By the sixth century, the city was clearly Christian in character. It is not known whether a Jewish population continued to exist during this period, as the historical and archaeological sources are silent.[55]

The lamps from the Ahinoam Cave Cemetery greatly enrich the known corpus of types, especially those associated with the site of Beit

---

Early Christianity in Context: Monuments and Documents (Jerusalem: Studium Biblicum Franciscanum, 1993), 265–76.

[53] Avni, "Christian Secondary Use of Jewish Burial Caves," 275.

[54] E. D. Oren and U. Rappaport, "The Necropolis of Maresha-Beth Guvrin," *IEJ* 34 (1984), 114–53.

[55] See J. Schwartz, *The Jewish Settlement in Judaea after the Bar-Kochba War until the Arab Conquest* [Hebrew] (Jerusalem: Magnes, 1986), 87–91.

Nattif. The fact that these lamps derive from a controlled archaeological context constitutes an important fixed point for comparative purposes. Finally, the lamps provide valuable information on the nature of the population that used the cemetery, and shed light on the historical, religious, and demographic changes at work in late Roman and Byzantine Beth Guvrin.

THE SOCIAL WORLD OF
CHRISTIAN JEWS AND JEWISH CHRISTIANS*

Anthony J. Saldarini
Boston College

THE FRAGMENTARY and tendentious ancient sources that speak of followers of Jesus who retained their Jewish identity make a description and evaluation of these movements very difficult. This study will approach Jewish Christian groups from their social context in the eastern Roman empire. Recent studies of the Roman Near East and of ethnic groups will contribute to the description of the social and cultural relationships that bound the peoples and groups of the Near East. Within this context one rich and detailed case study of Jews in the Roman empire will be developed, using the so-called Babatha Archive, a collection of legal documents from just before the Bar Kosiba (Bar Kokhba) war against Rome (132–35). Some early Jewish and Jewish Christian groups will then be related to the picture of second century society derived from these documents. The results of this exploration will both complement and critique the usual views of the second century derived from rabbinic and Christian literature.

Ideally, we could begin with a brisk review of Jews who followed the teachings of Jesus, accepted him as Messiah and continued to observe the law. Regrettably the evidence for most early Jewish and Christian groups, especially for Jewish Christians, is notoriously fragmentary and

*Part of the research for this paper was carried out during a semester leave of absence supported by grants from the Endowment for Biblical Research, Boston, Mass., the Memorial Foundation for Jewish Culture, New York, N.Y., and Boston College.

tendentious. The Pseudo-Clementine *Homilies* and *Recognitions* have
been mined for earlier, Jewish-Christian sources since the last century,
with limited success.[1] Early Christian writers described Ebionites, Naza-
renes, Elkasaites, and other less known groups in order to attack them as
heretics because of their low Christology or adherence to Jewish law.[2]
Irenaeus, Hippolytus, Eusebius, and Epiphanius tendentiously characterized Jewish Christian groups to serve their apologetic purposes. They
often cited reports they did not understand and used the same term,
such as Ebionite or Nazarene, for manifestly different groups.[3] Because
of these confusions, the definitions and descriptions of Jewish Christians are alarmingly hypothetical and controversial.

---

[1]   For a review of a century and a half of research, see F. Stanley Jones, "The
Pseudo-Clementines: A History of Research [2 Parts]," *Second Century* 2 (1982), 1–
33; 63–96. References to the original texts and translations can be found there. The
most influential study in recent decades is Georg Strecker, *Das Judenchristentum in
den Pseudoklementinen* (2 ed.; Berlin: Akademie, 1981; orig. ed. 1958). Post-World
War II study was prompted by Hans Joachim Schoeps, *Theologie und Geschichte des
Judenchristentums* (Tübingen: Mohr, 1949), and popularized in the English speaking world by the translation of his abbreviated treatment in *Jewish Christianity:
Factional Disputes in the Early Church* (Philadelphia: Fortress, 1969; German
original 1964).

[2]   For a brief but cogent overview, see S. G. Wilson, *Related Strangers: Jews and
Christians 70–170* C.E. (Minneapolis: Fortress, 1995), 143–68. The standard collec-
tion of sources is A. F. J. Klijn and G. J. Reinink, *Patristic Evidence of Jewish-Christian
Sects* (Leiden: Brill, 1973) and the recent collection by Klijn, *Jewish-Christian Gospel
Tradition* (Leiden: Brill, 1992). Klijn's interpretations of the sources have been
frequently disputed. See also the older study of Joseph Thomas, *Le mouvement
baptiste en Palestine et Syrie* (Gembloux, 1935) and the more recent one by Kurt
Rudolph, *Antike Baptisten zu den Überlieferung uber fruhjudische und -christliche
Taufsekten* (Berlin: Akadamie, 1981). Daniel Vigne, *Christ au Jourdain. Le Baptême
de Jésus dans la tradition judéo-chrétienne* (EB NS 16; Paris: Gabalda, 1992) is
seriously flawed, but still useful.

[3]   See Ray Pritz, *Nazarene Jewish Christianity* (Jerusalem and Leiden: Magnes
and Brill, 1988), 11–47 for the confusion in the use of Ebionite and Nazarene.
Irenaeus, *Adv. Haer.* 1.26.2 used the term "Ebionite" for all Jewish Christians and
was followed by many later writers.

Jean Danielou treated all early Christianity as Jewish Christianity in his well-known study, *The Theology of Jewish Christianity.*[4] While his approach stressed the Jewish roots of Christianity, it did not adequately differentiate among the diverse ways Christianity appropriated or rejected Jewish laws, interpretations, customs, and understandings. Subsequently some scholars have limited the term "Jewish Christian" to ethnic Jews who followed Jesus, or to ethnic Jews who followed Jesus and kept the Jewish law; others enlarged it to include law observant gentile followers of Jesus and still others have reserved the term for those who had theological views at variance with the increasingly strong Christological claims of the early church.[5] The title of this study assumes that some of these groups identified themselves as Jews who follow Jesus, and thus can be anachronistically labeled "Christian Jews," and that others identified themselves as Christians who were ethnically Jewish or Jewish in practice and thus can be anachronistically labeled "Jewish Christians." Useful and tight definition(s) of these groups can only emerge from an accurate understanding of the historical phenomena in context, not from logical and conceptual distinctions. In the meantime, in this study the conventional term "Jewish Christian" will be used.

---

[4]   Jean Danielou, *The Theology of Jewish Christianity* (London: Darton, Longman, 1964).

[5]   The term "Jewish Christian" has been variously defined and distinguished from "Christian Jew." Literature on the definition of Jewish Christianity includes Bruce Malina, "Jewish Christianity or Christian Judaism: Toward a Hypothetical Definition," *JSJ* 7 (1970), 46–57; A. F. J. Klijn, "The Study of Jewish Christianity," *NTS* 20 (1974), 419–31; S. K. Riegel, "Jewish Christianity: Definitions and Terminology," *NTS* 24 (1978), 410–15; Joan E. Taylor, "The Phenomenon of Early Jewish-Christianity: Reality or Scholarly Invention?" *VigChr* 44 (1990), 313–34; S. C. Mimouni, "Pour une définition nouvelle du judéo christianisme ancien," *NTS* 38 (1992), 161–86; F. Stanley Jones, *An Ancient Jewish Christian Source on the History of Christianity. Pseudo-Clementine Recognitions 1.27–71* (Texts and Translations 37; Atlanta: Scholars, 1995), 164, n. 21.

Since all Christians, including Jewish Christians, emerged from late Second Temple and early rabbinic Judaism, and since Christianity as a distinct religion can be distinguished from Judaism only gradually and at different times in different places, definitions, and descriptions of Judaism and Christianity are also necessary. However, the last three decades of scholarship on Second Temple and early rabbinic Judaism have established the diachronic and synchronic diversity of Jewish communities and overturned many definitions and categories of Judaism and our assumptions about the social settings, behaviors, and mental worlds of ancient Jews. The same is true for Christians. Nineteenth and twentieth century scholars often retrojected clear, comfortable definitions of "Jew" and "Christian" into the first two or three centuries. But the sharp boundaries and robust identities of these historical reconstructions cannot contain the varied and messy evidence found in ancient history, literature, inscriptions, and even the "orthodox" sources when read with a discerning eye.

First, then, some remarks on the diversity of early Judaism and Christianity and their relationships to one another. Scholars have long recognized that Christianity began as a Jewish movement or sect, but many, both Jewish and Christian, have hastened to separate them from one another as quickly as possible. Some suggest that the Jewish followers of Jesus in Jerusalem were killed or fled to Pella (according to a story of doubtful historicity in Eusebius[6]) during the war with Rome in 66–

---

[6]   Eusebius, *Hist. Eccl.* 3.5.3 contains the basic story. Epiphanius refers to the story three times in *Panar.* 29.7 and 30.2 and *de Pond. et Mens.* 15. Strecker, *Judenchristentum,* 229–31, argues against its historicity. Gerd Luedemann, *Opposition to Paul in Jewish Christianity* (Minneapolis: Fortress, 1989; original German 1983), 200–13, has the most detailed recent discussion of the Pella tradition. Like many recent scholars, he does not take the tradition as historically accurate. Luedemann understands the story as stemming from a gentile Christian community in Pella claiming legitimacy through a connection to Jerusalem. Pritz, *Nazarene Jewish Christianity,* App. 3, pp. 122–27, takes the basic tradition as accurate because he can find no other motive for its creation. Craig Koester, "The Origin and the Significance of the Flight to Pella Tradition," *CBQ* 51 (1989), 90–

70. The loss of prestige caused by dislocation from Jerusalem and Jerusalem's very destruction, according to this theory, led eventually to the community's end or at least loss of influence. Others have looked to the devastation of Judaea during the Bar Kosiba (or Bar Kokhba) war against Rome in 132–35, which resulted in the devastation of Judaea, the exclusion of Jews from Jerusalem, and various other liabilities, as the point where Jews and Christians went their separate ways and Jewish Christianity died out. Still others link the end of the Jewish Christianity with the ascendancy of the rabbinic movement in the late first and early second century or more vaguely with the passage of time and the shift of power to non-Jewish followers of Jesus during the late second century.

The separation of Jews and Christians probably did not happen as quickly or neatly as most theories envision. Something there is that loves a high, sharp boundary, but seldom do the boundaries hold, except in the minds of their creators. Both Jews and Christians struggled to define a normative orthodoxy that marginalized various groups as heretics. As time went on Jewish Christians attracted censure from both Jews and Christians. Yet, despite the intentions of the writers, many diverse groups of Christians are recorded in polemics against heretics.[7] Among Jews, the rabbinic way of life eventually triumphed

---

106, responds to Luedemann with detailed arguments suggesting the historicity of the basic claim. According to the summary in J. Wehnert, "Die Auswanderung der Jerusalemer Christen nach Pella—historisches Faktum oder theologische Konstruktion?" *ZKG* 102 (1991–92), 231–55, Jozef Verheyden, *De vlucht van de Christenen naar Pella* (Brussels: Paleis der Academiën, 1988) argues that Eusebius created the Pella tradition to support his theological history. Wehnert himself argues for its historicity, as does Wilson, *Related Strangers*, 145–48. For further views on both sides, see the references in Wilson, *Related Strangers*, pp. 353–54, nn. 13–14. The evidence is probably too sparse to allow a convincing interpretation of the passages concerning the flight to Pella. Even if the historical event could be established, it would not tell us much about early Jewish Christians.

[7]   The importance of dissident voices for the history of Christianity was established decisively by Walter Bauer, *Orthodoxy and Heresy in Earliest Christianity*, ed. R. Kraft, G. Krodel from 2nd German ed.; tr. Philadelphia Seminar in Christian Origins,

over other interpretations of law and custom by absorbing or ignoring its opponents and their views. Even so, a sophisticated analysis of rabbinic literature, balanced by equal attention to inscriptions and archaeology, has led to a recognition of the diversity of Jewish communities and groups and the severe limits of rabbinic influence in the Roman period.[8]

The Eastern Roman Empire

Studies of early Jewish and Christian groups often minimize the most important reality in the ancient Mediterranean, the Roman Empire. Many discussions of Jewish and Christian history, beliefs, practices, and communities have treated these groups as cultural isolates, substantially free of entangling Graeco-Roman influences and relationships, clearly defined by normative *halākâ* or doctrine. In such accounts Jews and Christians, their ideas, behaviors, and conflicts are described and traced through a history oblivious to the majority of the imperial populace and deaf to the voices of the ruling classes and indigenous peoples. But the story of ancient Jews, Christians, and Jewish Christians must be understood as part of the history of the Roman empire.

Fergus Millar has described the cultural complexity of the eastern empire and of its gradual Romanization over several centuries in *The*

(Philadelphia: Fortress, 1971; original German 1934). Large segments of the ancient Christian churches held views that were later labelled as unorthodox or heretical. Though many church writers celebrate the triumph of orthodox truth, dissident views endured for centuries and cannot be ignored by historians.

[8]   The limited influence and power of the rabbis on Palestinian Judaism (as well as diaspora Judaism) runs counter to many Talmudic stories and traditional assumptions but it has been increasingly accepted by historians who have recognized the diversity of Jewish groups and communities and have taken a critical approach to the sources. See excellent accounts in Martin Goodman, *State and Society in Roman Galilee, A.D. 132–212* (Totowa, N.J.: Rowman and Allanheld, 1983), esp. chs. 7 and 10 and Lee I. Levine, *The Rabbinic Class of Roman Palestine in Late Antiquity* (Jerusalem and New York: Yad Izhak Ben-Zvi and Jewish Theological Seminary, 1989; earlier Hebrew edition 1985).

Roman Near East 31 BC–AD 337.[9] It is in this arena, in Syria and Palestine, that Jews, Christians, and Jewish Christians lived and worked out their early relationships. In the East diverse and changing populations, linked to one another by commercial relationships and well-traveled trade routes, emerge from the sparse literary and inscriptional evidence and the scattered archaeological ruins. Cities and networks of villages, geographical regions and linguistic zones both linked and separated peoples at the same time. The eastern Mediterranean inland as far as the Euphrates and the desert was heavily populated but lacked stable, clear regional boundaries. The Roman army conquered part of the East and repeatedly fought to expand and to retain control. However, Rome took until the third century to police inland Syria consistently and Romanize it in any thorough sense.[10]

In the Roman empire local customs merged with Greek and Roman expressions and practices. Surprisingly, neither inscriptions nor surviving literature and architecture testify to a vital indigenous Semitic cultural tradition,[11] other than that of the Jews, which is amply communicated in the Bible, literature from the Second Temple period and rabbinic literature from the third century and beyond. Even in the interior of Syria, temples were built in the Greek style with Greek inscriptions.[12] The language and symbolism of political, social, and religious expression in the eastern empire was Greek.

G. W. Bowersock, too, has stressed the omnipresence of Greek modes of expression and their integral coexistence with local traditions.[13] He correctly argues that the usual question concerning the degree of

---

[9] Fergus Millar, *The Roman Near East 31 BC–AD 337* (Cambridge: Harvard University, 1993).

[10] Millar, *Roman Near East,* 525–27.

[11] Millar, *Roman Near East,* 319, 510, 525.

[12] Millar, *Roman Near East,* 523.

[13] G. W. Bowersock, *Hellenism in Late Antiquity* (Ann Arbor: University of Michigan, 1990), ch. 1. See also his essay "The Greek Moses: Confusion of Ethnic

Hellenization, in the East is misconceived. Most studies see Hellenization and local cultures in conflict, a tendency that is especially true in modern histories of Israel. But the Greek language does not have a word for Hellenization, and Greeks did not see themselves in opposition to anything else. The Greek and Near Eastern worlds were accommodating and adaptable. Local cultures, temples, and governments accepted outside cultural influences, including the Greek and Roman, with little tension. The benign influence of Hellenism need not have led to and most often did not lead to loss of identity.[14]

Jews and Christians fit within this stream of eastern culture. Jews in Palestine spoke Greek along with Hebrew and Aramaic. Inscriptions in Greek appear in Jerusalem and dominate in the third and fourth century Jewish tombs in Beth Shearim. No place can be said to be entirely Jewish, as opposed to Graeco-Roman.[15] The culture flowed from Jews to Greeks also. Herod the Great, through his patronage and benefactions, fostered the construction of Greek cities in the east, including Caesarea and Sebaste in his homeland. Tiberias and the rebuilt Sepphoris as well as the network of Galilean villages, some of them large and fortified, helped shape the Roman East. All through the Roman period the relationships between Jews and gentiles were substantial and complex.[16]

Significantly, both rabbinic Judaism and Christianity in the east developed in the villages and cities of Palestine and contiguous areas

---

and Cultural Components in Later Roman and Early Byzantine Palestine," in this volume.

[14]   Bowersock, "The Greek Moses."

[15]   Millar, *Roman Near East*, 343–46.

[16]   See the mass of evidence collected by Louis H. Feldman, *Jew and Gentile in the Ancient World: Attitudes and Interactions from Alexander to Justinian* (Princeton: Princeton University, 1993). Feldman's interpretations of texts are often forced in the direction of separating Judaism and Hellenism and finding a tradition of law observance among all Jews, but the evidence he adduces leads in many other directions.

such as Transjordan, the Negev, and southern Syria. Archaeological studies of Galilee and other areas in Syria-Palestine have stressed integral studies of regions.[17] Galilee and it contiguous neighbors in the early through late Roman period formed a well-articulated and complex socio-economic society in which multiple geographic and ethnic groups interacted in multiple ways. Rabbinic Judaism is firmly associated with the villages and then cities of Galilee. Jewish Christianity, with much less historical certitude, is linked to the Decapolis, including Pella, in Transjordan, and Kokhaba, probably in Batanaea west of the Sea of Galilee (as well as Beroea [Aleppo] in northern Syria) by Epiphanius in his *Panarion* 29–30. Eric Meyers argues for the likelihood of continuity in early Jewish Christian settlement on the basis of the admittedly controversial literary and archaeological evidence and against a total migration of the Jerusalem community to Pella.[18] Though this conclusion is far from certain due to lack of evidence, the presence of Jewish Christians along with Jews and many other ethnic groups in southern Syria and Palestine in the second century and beyond would be coherent with what we understand of the region. The villages of greater Syria were the backbone of settlement. Galilee and the Golan were notable for their strong village cultures.[19] Even the desolate area between Damascus and Palmyra had villages whose boundaries were clearly marked out, and the Hauran south of Damascus had villages integrated into the

---

[17]   See the regional studies by Eric M. Meyers, some of which are "Galilean Regionalism as a Factor in Historical Reconstruction," *BASOR* 221 (1976), 93–101; "Galilean Regionalism: A Reappraisal," in W. S. Green, ed., *Approaches to Ancient Judaism*, 5 (Atlanta: Scholars Press, 1985), 115–31; "An Archaeological Response to a New Testament Scholar," *BASOR* 297 (1995), 17–26, esp. 22–23.

[18]   Eric M. Meyers, "Early Judaism and Christianity in the Light of Archaeology," *BA* 51 (1988), 69–79, esp. 69, 71, 73, 75, 79. The so-called Franciscan school of archaeology has tried to find evidence of Jewish Christians in Galilee and Judaea. Their dubious claims have been definitively refuted in Joan E. Taylor, *Christians and their Holy Places: The Myth of Jewish-Christian Origins* (Oxford: Clarendon Press, 1993).

[19]   Millar, *Roman Near East*, 350–51.

imperial system.[20] Similarly, the Negev south of the Dead Sea was populated by a network of villages and families living in them.[21] Though the
roles of Greek cities in the life of the east have often been stressed, village
culture formed the backbone of the region.

Though all peoples in the eastern Roman Empire lived in a common,
loosely defined, constantly changing cultural milieu,[22] real tensions
often arose between the Romans and their subject peoples, as the history
of many regions and ethnic groups testifies.[23] Among Jews and Christians, sharp tensions arose with the prevailing eastern culture because of
the exclusive claims of monotheism in contrast to the open, flexible
world of polytheism.[24] Jewish literature universally marked itself off
against polytheism, and the followers of Jesus participated in that tradition. The rabbis resisted many aspects of the prevailing culture by their
involvement in the laws and intellectual world of the Mishnah. The
Jewish author of the Gospel of Matthew, though he sought to attract
gentiles to his Jewish group of followers of Jesus, nevertheless characterized non-Jews as ethnics (*ethnikoi*).[25] But the boundaries among groups
and between them and the culture of the eastern empire shifted often.
The terms used for the "other" were not stable or all-encompassing. In
Christian texts from gentile followers of Jesus, the term *ethnikoi* does
not refer to gentiles, but to non-Christians with whom one should not

---

[20]   Millar, *Roman Near East*, 317, 426–27.

[21]   Millar, *Roman Near East*, 404–5.

[22]   Bowersock, "The Greek Moses."

[23]   Richard D. Sullivan, *Near Eastern Royalty and Rome, 100–30 B.C.* (Toronto:
Toronto University Press, 1990) traces numerous monarchies, along with districts
and peoples in Asia Minor and greater Syria.

[24]   Bowersock, *Hellenism*, 6, 9–11.

[25]   Matthew 5:47; 6:7. For the place of the Gospel of Matthew in first-century
Judaism, see Anthony J. Saldarini, *Matthew's Christian-Jewish Community* (Chicago:
University of Chicago Press, 1994).

associate.[26] Among later Christians the word "Greek" became the term for a polytheist. Rabbinic texts often use the designation *mîn* (heretic) to refer to a variety of groups, including Jewish Christians.[27] Non-Jews are characterized as gentiles ("the nations") or idolators.

As we sort through the population of Syria, Palestine, and Arabia in the Roman period, how shall we designate various groups in a less polemical way? How shall we understand the social location, relations, and self-definition of Romans, Greeks, peoples in south Syria, Nabataeans, Jews, Christians, and Jewish Christians? By village of origin? Geographical region? Language or dialect? Gods and customs? Historical associations? Imperial governmental districts and provinces? Can we ferret out how people identified or thought of themselves? Is "Jew" a recognized, univocal and primordial label everywhere in the eastern Roman empire? Would a Jewish resident of Philadelphia or Caesarea identify himself as a resident of his city or as a *Ioudaios*? What would he mean by *Ioudaios*: an adherent of religious and social customs originating in Judaea or a person associated by kinship with people in Judaea, or a person ultimately originating in Judaea? Would he be an adherent of a particular way of life promoted by a community of Jews in his city? It is difficult to discern the importance of the label "Jews" both to Jews and to their neighbors.[28] Similarly, and more problematically, how would followers of Jesus think of themselves, identify themselves and relate to other individuals and groups? The designation *Khristianos* is not on a par with *Ioudaios*. Christian does not designate a people with a common geographic origin, nor an established way of life, nor a common language or paternity. In the modern world we often think of Christians and Jews

---

[26]   3 John 7; *Herm. Mand.* 10.1.4.

[27]   See Christine E. Hayes, "Displaced Self-Perceptions: The Deployment of *Minîm* and Romans in *b. Sanhedrin* 90b–91a," in this volume.

[28]   Ross S. Kraemer, "On the Meaning of the Term 'Jew' in Graeco-Roman Inscriptions," *HTR* 82 (1989), 35–53, shows that most of the people whom scholars have reasonably identified as Jews in inscriptions are not designated by the term "Jew" (*Ioudaios*) in the inscriptions themselves.

as members of religious communities, but no such encompassing category existed in antiquity. Were Christians identified by their place of
origin or language? Were Jewish Christians considered to be an ethnic
group, or to be part of the Judaean ethnic group?

The social and historical context of Jewish Christianity within the
Roman empire depends upon an understanding of Jewish groups in the
Roman empire. But the very nature of groups within the empire is problematic. The innocent looking and attractive title of this volume, "Religious and Ethnic Communities," complicates the discussion even more
because it brings with it historical and sociological disputes over the
nature of a community, the relationships of communities to empires,
the very nature of an ethnic group, and the dubious hypothesis of a religious community in ancient Roman society, a society in which what we
call religion and economics are embedded in the family and political
society.[29]

---

[29]   For a standard overview of Roman and ancient society, see Peter Garnsey and
Richard Saller, *The Roman Empire: Economy, Society and Culture* (Berkeley:
University of California, 1987). The standard book on the ancient economy is
Moses I. Finley, *The Ancient Economy* (Berkeley: University of California, 1973).

Greeks and Romans had voluntary associations, some of which had religious
purposes. Christian assemblies may have been understood as such associations. See
Marcus N. Tod, *Sidelights on Greek History* (Oxford: Blackwell, 1932), 76–77;
Ramsey MacMullen, *Roman Social Relations 50 B.C. to A.D. 284* (New Haven: Yale,
1974), 18–20; 73–80; Finley, *The Ancient Economy*, 138; Franz Poland, *Geschichte
der griechischen Vereinswesens* (Leipzig: Teubner, 1909), esp. 152–68 for terminology. Robert L. Wilken, *The Christians as the Romans Saw Them* (New Haven:
Yale, 1984), ch. 2, gathers evidence for outsiders' views that Christianity was a
private association. For an application of these associations to the Pauline evidence,
see Wayne Meeks, *The First Urban Christians* (New Haven: Yale, 1983), 77–80;
Abraham J. Malherbe, *Social Aspects of Early Christianity* (Baton Rouge: Louisiana
State University, 1977; 2 ed.; Philadelphia: Fortress, 1983). For the Pharisees, see
Anthony J. Saldarini, *Pharisees, Scribes and Sadducees in Palestinian Society*
(Wilmington: Glazier, 1988), 67–70.

The Sociology of Ethnic Groups

To understand Jews and Christians as groups within the Roman empire we must first ask what a group is. "Group" is perhaps the most general, and least loaded, term for a social aggregation. A group is a number of individuals gathered in some way or perceived as having common characteristics. Sociology usually understands groups to be aggregates of people who interact with one another. "Group" has been used especially for small gatherings whose members know one another personally and interact closely (primary groups).[30] Social psychology defines a group as "a social unit that consists of a number of individuals who, at a given time, have role and status relations with one another, stabilized in some degree, and who possess a set of values or norms regulating the attitude and behavior of individual members, at least in matters of consequence to them."[31]

Groups are not static. Many scholars stress synchronic diversity and diachronic change in groups and religious traditions and some write of Judaisms and Christianities. Others, however, still treat Romanness or Hellenism or Judaism as essentially unchanging realities. The modern romantic concept of community as a face-to-face assemblage of people with multiple, close ties to one another exercises a subtle but powerful influence on how we conceive of religious groups and traditions, village and small town life, ethnic groups, nations and peoples. For example, a primordial ethnic group is conceived of as a natural grouping of people or as an independent cultural unit with its own territory, language, customs, and social, political, and religious attitudes, convictions, and practices. Such a group is pictured as coming into existence, reproduc-

---

[30]   George Homans, "Groups," in David L. Sills, ed., *International Encyclopedia of the Social Sciences* (New York: Macmillan, 1968) 6, 259–65; G. Duncan Mitchell, "Group; social group," *A New Dictionary of the Social Sciences* (New York: Aldine, 1979), 91.

[31]   Muzafer Sherif, *Group Conflict and Cooperation: Their Social Psychology* (London: Routledge, 1966), 12. For the terminology of groups applied to the Gospel of Matthew, see Saldarini, *Matthew's Christian-Jewish Community*, ch. 5.

ing itself and enduring for a long time based on the natural affinity of the group members themselves. According to this view an ethnic group is a relatively stable aggregate that fulfills natural human needs for self-definition, social interaction, procreation, production of food, and mutual assistance.[32]

This traditional, primordial definition of an ethnic group, which is commonly presumed in scholarly discussion, has been effectively challenged and modified in the last twenty-five years. Most anthropologists and sociologists do not treat social, political, or ethnic groups as if they were pre-existing, natural, unchanging, clearly defined social entities. Groups have histories and undergo change. Attitudes, boundaries, practices, characteristics, and membership vary in relationship to both internal and external social, political, and economic circumstances. Even ethnic groups are not static and permanent social entities. They begin, evolve, and change; they must be maintained and interact with outsiders; they deteriorate and sometimes go out of existence.[33]

---

[32] The seminal article for understanding ethnic groups as primordial is by Edward Shils, "Primordial, Personal, Sacred and Civil Ties," *British Journal of Sociology* 8 (1957), 130–45. For a review of this approach to ethnicity, see Richard H. Thompson, *Theories of Ethnicity: A Critical Appraisal* (New York: Greenwood, 1989), ch. 3. Charles F. Keyes, in "Towards a New Formulation of the Concept of Ethnic Group," *Ethnicity* 3 (1976), 202–13 and in "The Dialectics of Ethnic Change," in Charles F. Keyes, ed., *Ethnic Change* (Seattle: University of Washington, 1982), 3–30 joins the primordial approach with the newer social organization approach.

[33] Donald L. Horowitz, "Ethnic Identity," in Nahum Glazer and Daniel P. Moynihan, eds., *Ethnicity, Theory and Experience* (Cambridge: Harvard University Press, 1975), 111–40, esp. 113, argues on the basis of seven Indian groups that boundaries between groups are more fluid than has often been admitted. In general, a group may change. It may become more or less ascriptive, more or less acculturated to norms of another group, more or less internally cohesive, ethnocentric, hostile. These factors affect boundaries. For example, if a group loses internal cohesion, it may split into components. If it becomes less ascriptive, it is likely to widen its boundaries and expand its numbers.

The traditional view of a static, relatively unchanging ethnic group ignored the reality that virtually all social groups, including ethnic groups, constantly interact with and are influenced by other groups, change substantially over time, and both lose and gain members regularly. Consideration of the usage of the Greek word *ethnos*, which is certainly not determinative for sociological meaning in English, will illustrate the social complexity of group categorization. In Homeric times an *ethnos* was a band of soldiers. Subsequently, for example in the historian Herodotus, an *ethnos* was a people or nation, especially one of the non-Greek nations he described. As a result of this usage *ethnos* came to refer to other, non-Greek nations (i.e., barbarians); analogously among Greek-speaking Jews it meant the non-Jewish nations. For the Romans, the *ethnē* were provinces of the empire peopled by non-Romans. Used thus *ethnos* became a social category marking off "others" from the speaker and as such, was thoroughly relational. These tendencies have been replicated in modern usage of the term "ethnic group."

Ethnic studies in the last thirty years have stressed a picture of ethnic groups as social organizations that are defined and characterized by both internal processes and ascription of characteristics by outsiders.[34] Consequently, any group, even an ethnic group, must constantly be redefined in light of changing social circumstances.[35] To set the

---

[34] The shift in focus to ethnic groups as social organizations and to the importance of group boundaries began in sociology, but reaches anthropology in a collection of essays edited by Fredrik Barth, *Ethnic Groups and Boundaries: The Social Organization of Cultural Difference* (Boston: Little, Brown, 1969), esp. 13.

[35] The most recent studies of ethnicity in pluralistic societies argue that an ethnic identity is adopted by an immigrant or less powerful group for political and social purposes in its struggle against the more powerful groups. See for example, "Ethnicity" in Ellis Cashmore *et al.*, eds., *Dictionary of Race and Ethnic Relations*, 3 ed. (London and New York: Routledge, 1994), 102–7 and Benjamin B. Ringer and Elinor R. Lawless, *Race-Ethnicity and Society* (New York and London: Routledge, 1989).

problem in sharp focus, though we think of ethnic groups as linked by descent, in fact people constantly join and leave ethnic groups by initiating or ceasing contact, by intermarriage, and by identifying or refusing to identify with the group. Association with an ethnic group requires effort. Cultural traditions, language, practices, expectations, norms, understandings of social relationships must all be taught to children and newcomers and maintained by adults. Since an ethnic group depends upon the passing on of traditions, descent through an ethnic group is not the same as biological procreation. Descent involves social relationships and recognition. An outsider can be made part of a descent group.[36] An ethnic group is also formed by outside forces when others highlight or attribute characteristics in such a way as to mark out a group as different.[37]

Ancient society was hardly pluralistic in the modern sense, so groups functioned differently than they do in contemporary society. However, ancient society was complex and diverse in the eastern Mediterranean during Roman times, so modern analyses of ethnic groups

---

[36]   See Keyes "Dialectics of Ethnic Change," 5–10. Many Americans identify the seventeenth-century Pilgrims and eighteenth-century Founding Fathers as their ancestors even if their own biological ancestors emigrated to the United States in the nineteenth or twentieth century. Talcott Parsons, "Some Theoretical Considerations on the Nature and Trends of Change of Ethnicity," in Keyes, *Ethnic Change*, 53–83, contextualizes the ethnic group in the United States as a "fiduciary group" that is expected to exercise responsibility for the maintenance or development of a transgenerational tradition. It is a collectivity with a diffuse, enduring solidarity (which is characteristic of American kinship) (pp. 59–62). An ethnic group is a fusion of kinship and community types (62). George De Vos and Lola Romanucci-Ross, *Ethnic Identity: Cultural Continuities and Change* (Palo Alto: Mayfield, 1975) take a social psychological approach to ethnic groups: "An ethnic group is a self-perceived group of people who hold in common a set of traditions not shared by others with whom they are in contact. Such traditions typically include 'folk' religious beliefs and practices, language, a sense of historical continuity, and common ancestry or place of origin" (p. 9). The group sees itself as independent and is endogamous, though newcomers can be initiated.

[37]   Barth, *Ethnic Groups*, 13–15.

can be adapted for the analysis of ancient groups. Then as now people were simultaneously members of several groups based on kinship, ethnicity, region, village, class, and status in relation to the government or empire.[38] A broad spectrum of various types of ethnic boundaries, boundary maintaining mechanisms, and inter-ethnic strategies are used by ethnic groups within their social contexts. Various traits may be significant or not, depending on internal and external circumstances. Ethnic distinctions, stratification, and dichotomization are part of the groups' strategies for preserving or increasing control of resources and social status. Cultural content does not define an ethnic group in interactional contexts such as these.[39]

The meaning of the category *Ioudaios*, "Jew," varied in its social connotations and importance.[40] Even if someone were a Jew or Judaean,

---

[38] Barth, *Ethnic Groups*, 10, notes that "stable, persisting, and often vitally important social relations are maintained across [ethnic] boundaries." In the same volume Karl E. Knutsson, "Dichotomization and Integration," 86–100 argues that inter-ethnic relations and ethnic distinctions are multiple and complex. Hence ethnicity is "not a single universally applicable term but rather the representation of a wide range of inter-relations in which the dominant reference is to an ethnic status ascribed on the basis of birth, language, and socialization" (p. 99).

[39] Karl E. Knutsson, "Dichotomization and Integration," 86–100.

[40] Kraemer, "The Term 'Jew'." Traditionally a Jew has been defined halakhically, but this is to impose the rabbinic view of what a Jews should think and do on all Jews, sometimes anachronistically. For a defense of the halakhic view applied to the Jewish-Christian question, see Lawrence H. Schiffman, *Who was a Jew? Rabbinic and Halakhic Perspectives on the Jewish-Christian Schism* (Hoboken: Ktav, 1985). Jewish historians still sometimes insert parochial views into historical accounts. Doron Mendels, *The Rise and Fall of Jewish Nationalism* (Anchor Bible Reference Library; New York: Doubleday, 1992), accepts unquestioningly Josephus' Hasmonean prejudice and treats Herod as not really a Jew (pp. 214–23) and refers to the deterioration of "genuine" Jewish kingship from Herod to Agrippa II (p. 223). Although he allows that groups of Jews had different reactions to Herod (p. 223) he also judges that because Herod encouraged a multinational, multiethnic Palestine, he could not have been acknowledged as legitimate by "believing" or "religious" Jews (pp. 248–49). One has the feeling that these believing and religious Jews are not first century realities, but an orthodox ideal created by Mendels.

that might not have made much significant difference in the course of life, in daily activities, or in social and political relationships. In other circumstances it might have been determinative of one's social status and even physical safety. Scholars often ponder whether the Mishnah was a practical law code or an ideal and whether Jews observed these laws or not. But these dyads are inadequate. Jews had many choices in the Roman empire, and we cannot assume but must determine, often indirectly, how people reconciled their many social relationships, public roles, and group memberships. The firmness and importance of group boundaries and the weight given to communal practices varied greatly with time and place. We often tend to treat being a Jew as a primary or exclusive or primordial commitment, but it often was not, much to the chagrin of the community leaders.[41] Christian is an even more ephemeral category. In fact, in most of the New Testament documents the followers of Jesus have no group name. The terms "Jewish Christian" and "Christian Jew" were not used in antiquity. In general, neither ancient nor modern categories should be assumed to be obvi-

---

[41] Joseph Mélèze Modrzejewski, "How to be a Jew in Hellenistic Egypt?" in Shaye J. D. Cohen, ed., *Diasporas in Antiquity* (*BJS* 288; Atlanta: Scholars, 1993), 65–91, esp. 77–80 argues that the primary group identity was not necessarily "Jew" for someone who was Jewish. "We see that to be a *Ioudaios* in Ptolemaic Egypt is not very different from being a *Makedōn*. Facing the native Egyptians, both are 'Hellenes.' ... Neither 'citizens' nor 'autonomous aliens,' the Jews are one of the various elements composing the society of Greek speaking conquerors. Nothing but his religion distinguishes a Jew from his Graeco-Macedonian neighbors. He is a full-fledged member of the dominant group of 'Hellenes,' the equal of any other Greek speaking immigrant" (p. 80). See also *idem, The Jews of Egypt from Ramses II to Emperor Hadrian* (Philadelphia: Jewish Publication Society, 1995), ch. 3.

For the general lack of distinctive social marks of Jews in the diaspora, see in the same volume Shaye J. D. Cohen, "'Those Who Say They are Jews and Are Not': How Do You Know a Jew in Antiquity When You See One?" pp. 1–45. On the other hand, in Rome the Jewish community seems to have functioned more as an immigrant group, among many other immigrant groups. For a convenient and recent summary of the evidence, see James C. Walters, *Ethnic Issues in Paul's Letter to the Romans* (Valley Forge: Trinity, 1993).

ously or inevitably clear, appropriate, or reflective of how all the ancients viewed themselves or how they acted.[42]

The Babatha Archive

Some of the letters and contracts found in the Judaean desert, the Babatha Archive, will illustrate the complexity of ancient society and provide a way out of overly general or rigid ethnic and religious categories. These documents also provide a provocative test case for Jews in a Graeco-Roman context in and near the land of Israel. The documents give us a narrow but fascinating window into the culture and ethos of the villages and cities in the land of Israel and its environs. This limited but very concrete information provides a control for the more tendentious historical notices and stories that speak of early Jews and Jewish Christians in the villages and cities of Syria-Palestine.

A packet of Greek and Aramaic documents found in the so-called Cave of Letters in Nahal Hever (on the western shore of the Dead Sea about three miles south of Ein Gedi) belonged to a woman named Babatha daughter of Simon from the village of Maoza (*Maḥoza*²— Aramaic for "harbor"; a village in the district of Zoara on the southern shore of the Dead Sea in the Roman province of Arabia [established 106 C.E.]). From the documents we can deduce the following dates, facts, and relationships pertinent to her. Though we do not know her year of birth, by 124 she was a young widow with a son, Jesus son of Jesus, for whom two

---

[42]   See Harjot Oberoi, *The Construction of Religious Boundaries: Culture, Identity and Diversity in the Sikh Tradition* (Oxford, New York and Delhi: Oxford University Press, 1994), 1–19 for instructive examples from northern India where colonial divisions of the populace in to Hindus, Moslems and Sikhs were woefully inadequate to peoples' understandings, practices and attitudes. See also E. K. Francis, *Interethnic Relations: An Essay in Sociological Theory* (New York: Elsevier, 1976), 147–48, 296, for the importance of the larger cultural context for studying ethnic groups. "Ethnicity is fundamentally a relational concept. The emergence of groups on account of ethnic differentiation implies changes in the relations of a population to the societal environment" (p. 168).

guardians were appointed (*P. Yadin* 12).[43] In 128 she married a second time to Judah son of Eleazar Khthousion of Ein Gedi who was then resident in her village of Maoza (*P. Yadin* 18). Judah already had a wife, Miriam bat Beianos of Ein Gedi and a daughter, Shelamzion, when he married Babatha. He died several years later, about 130. The last document in the packet is dated 132, at the beginning of the Bar Kosiba war against Rome. Babatha was probably one of the victims of the Roman army found in the caves where her documents were discovered.[44]

The families of both Babatha and Judah were moderately wealthy and are probably typical of the more prosperous residents of the Dead Sea area. They provide a good corrective to the instinctive tendency to think of the Dead Sea as barren or inhabited only by the sectarians at Qumran. The Greek documents mention four date palm orchards, houses and courtyards, a trust fund of 400 denarii, a loan of 500 denarii, and other loans and deposits received and made. The caves where the documents were found also contained expensive clothes and artifacts. When Babatha fled to the cave hideout during the Bar Kosiba war, she brought both some of her possessions and also her carefully packaged documents (the contents of her safety deposit box, as it were) in order to protect her rights to properties, money, and contracts. Her papers record

---

[43] The Greek documents along with Aramaic and Nabataean signatures and subscriptions have been published in Naphtali Lewis, ed., *The Documents from the Bar Kokhba Period in the Cave of Letters: Greek Papyri* (Jerusalem: Israel Exploration Society, 1989). The Aramaic documents have not yet been published as a whole, though some of them are discussed in periodical literature. The Greek documents are referred to by the siglum *P. Yadin* plus the number of the document in honor of their deceased discoverer and first editor, Yigael Yadin.

[44] For a popular account of the discoveries in the caves, see Yigael Yadin, *Bar-Kokhba* (London and Jerusalem: Weidenfeld and Nicolson, 1971). The complete report on the finds from the Cave of Letters (excluding the documents) is Yigael Yadin, *The Finds from the Bar-Kokhba Period in the Cave of Letters* (Jerusalem: Israel Exploration Society, 1963). Preliminary reports on other caves are in *IEJ* 11 (1961) and 12 (1962).

marriages, the guardianship of her minor son, legal suits over payments and property, petitions to the court, summons, etc. She preserved copies of transactions and trusteeships that had been recorded in the imperial registry. In these documents property lines were precisely described in relation to abutters and the changes in names of abutters testify to property transfers. Legal disputes recorded in the documents show that Babatha and the network of families with which she did business and interacted were in full contact with the Roman provincial courts in Rabbatmoab and Petra. She and her colleagues appeared before the Roman governor and other officials to settle their affairs. The legal system in the Dead Sea area was fully operational and covered a wide variety of relationships. The names, places, and types of transactions are consistent with and in some cases related to a similar assortment of documents found in other caves in Wadi Murabba'at along the shore of the Dead Sea.[45]

What do we learn about these residents of the Dead Sea area? The names found in the Greek documents are a combination of traditional Jewish names, along with Nabataean and Roman names. Judah, Simon, Jesus, Shelamzion, and Miriam are all Jewish names. In accordance with longstanding custom, some people had both Jewish and Greek names, such as Eleazar Khthousion and Judah Cimber.[46] Among the witnesses to the documents we find presumed friends, neighbors, associates, and Roman officials. Signing a loan document in Greek (*P. Yadin* 11) are Gaius Julius Proclus, Kallaios son of John, Simon son of Simon, Onesimos, John, Joseph, and Theodore. Witnessing an extract from acts of the council of the metropolis of Petra that appoints two guardians for Babatha's son are, among others, Nubi son of Walat, 'Abd'obdath son of Shuheiru, and Abdereus son of Soumaios, whose names are Naba-

---

[45]   P. Benoit, J. T. Milik and Roland de Vaux, *Les Grottes de Murabba'ât: Textes* (*DJD* II: Oxford: Clarendon Press, 1961). Documents from this find are identified by the abbreviation "*Mur*" plus the number of the document in the official list.

[46]   John Hyrcanus and Alexander Jannaeus are perhaps the most famous Jewish leaders with double names.

taean and Greek. The two guardians of young Jesus are 'Abdobdas son of Illouthas, a Nabataean, and John son of Eglas, a Jew (*P. Yadin* 12). When Babatha sold a date crop in Maoza to Simon son of Jesus, she had as her required legal guardian for the transaction Yohana son of Makhoutha, a Nabataean (*P. Yadin* 22). A judicial summons written back home in Maoza was witnessed in Aramaic by Elazar son of Shim'on, and Yehosef and Elazar sons of Mattat and in Greek by Thaddeus son of Thaddeus (*P. Yadin* 23). In general Jews and non-Jews seem to have transacted business together as necessary.

Interestingly, in the Greek documents only one person, the very young minor child Jesus (who still needs a guardian in 132, eight years after his first guardianship), is identified as a Jew (*Ioudaios*): "Jesus a Jew son of Jesus of the village of Maoza" (*P. Yadin* 12). *Ioudaios* is often used in Greek to describe an adherent of the Judaean way of life or for people commonly construed as Jews, no matter where they are.[47] *Ioudaios* is also used to designate a Judaean in the sense of an inhabitant of Judaea. But here the child is not from Judaea, but from Maoza.[48] Interestingly, Ross Kraemer has noted that the identifying epithet "Jew" appears relatively seldom in Jewish inscriptions, including funerary and dedicatory synagogue inscriptions.[49] So the question is why Babatha's minor child is identified in an official city council document as a Jew when none of

---

[47] Similarly and much earlier in an Aramaic divorce document (*Mur* 19; also in Joseph Fitzmyer, *A Manual of Palestinian Aramaic Texts* [Rome: Pontifical Biblical Institute, 1978], 40, pp. 138–41) the man leaves the woman free to marry a *gĕbar yĕhûdî*. The date of this document is the sixth year either of the war against Rome (i.e., 71–72) or of the Province of Arabia (i.e., 111).

[48] In Egypt in the Ptolemaic period terms like "Jew" and "Macedonian" were used to identify the ultimate geographical and ethnic origin of a person's ancestors and to mark a person as, therefore, superior in status to native Egyptians who were identified by their villages, according to Joseph Mélèze Modrzejewski, *Jews of Egypt*, 80–81. However, this usage of *Ioudaios* is not pertinent here because the Romans abolished such distinctions (pp. 161–65) and thus the Jews, Nabataeans and others inhabiting the Dead Sea area are identified by villages.

[49] Kraemer, "The Term 'Jew'," 37–38.

the other Jews involved in this transaction (and others) are so identified. Kraemer has the same problem with several inscriptions in which either a three year old deceased foster daughter or her mother is identified as a Jew (*Eioudea*)[50] and a deceased eighteen-year-old woman is designated *Iudeae* in Latin by her mother.[51] In these and other inscriptions Kraemer suggests that a person is called a Jew if their Jewishness is not obvious, for example, in the case of a proselyte or a gentile observer of Jewish customs or the member of a non-Jewish family. Alternatively, Jew in its various Greek and Latin forms may also have been given as a proper name.[52] All these suggestions are very hypothetical, but they witness to the lack of clarity in the usage of a term as simple as Jew.

In the case of Babatha's son Jesus, he is the son of two Jews, so he is not a proselyte, he is not a Judaean in his origin, and *Ioudaios* is almost certainly not a name since all the people in these documents are identified by their own name and that of a parent. Since the guardianship document is an extract from the minutes (*acta*) of the town council (*boulē*) of Petra, a Nabataean city and the capital of the Roman province of Arabia, perhaps the identification of the ethnic origin of the minor child was made on his behalf because he was not old enough to have established his group membership by his own customs, language, and actions. Even if this is so, it does not testify to Jewish community boundaries since one of the two guardians appointed is a Nabataean, 'Abdobdas son of Illouthas.

In their public dealings, at least, adult Jews were not overdetermined as Jews. The had recognizably Jewish names and presumably acted and worshipped in customary ways. But at the same time they also acted as citizens of the Roman province and as residents of their villages, along with all other residents and citizens. The documents do

---

50   Kraemer, "The Term 'Jew'," 38–41. The inscription also uses the epithets "proselyte" and "Israelite" and it is not at all clear which epithets refer to which people.

51   Kraemer, "The Term 'Jew'," 41–42.

52   Kraemer, "The Term 'Jew'," 48–50.

not reveal specific communal or religious customs or affiliations that differentiate these people from other residents of the Dead Sea area. People are identified primarily by their place of birth and retain connections to those places even when they are residing elsewhere. Babatha's second husband resided in Maoza, but is still identified as from Ein Gedi. At some point after his death Babatha of Maoza went to the Ein Gedi area, probably to protect her interests in his property (*P. Yadin* 26).

What can we infer from the formal elements of the documents in Babatha's archive? Many are in Greek because that was the official language of the Roman province of Arabia and of the registries where transactions and legal decisions were recorded. Other documents and many subscriptions and signatures are in Aramaic, which was the first language of the Jewish residents of the area. The Greek documents were written by scribes, some not very proficient in Greek grammar, and signed in Greek, Hebrew, or Nabataean.[53] Just a couple of decades after the Roman Province of Arabia was formed in 106 C.E., these documents show, Roman legal forms were already in use. The *parousia* of the governor is in Latin a *conventus*, that is, the official court session in the presence of the governor (*P. Yadin* 14.14, 33). Several documents contain a version of the Latin *stipulatio*, a formal question-and-answer concerning the validity of the transaction (*P. Yadin* 17–18, 20–22 and 37). The scribe who wrote the translation of Babatha's subscription to her inventory and registration of her land (#16) has her swearing to its accuracy by the *tychē* (the spirit, good fortune, protective deity [Latin *genius*]) of Lord Caesar.[54] (Babatha's original Aramaic subscription, which was in the official document submitted to the government, was not included in

---

[53] Babatha's Aramaic marriage contract, however, was written by her husband, Judah, who also wrote other parts of Aramaic documents. See Yigael Yadin, Jonas C. Greenfield, Ada Yardeni, "Babatha's *Ketubba*," *IEJ* 44 (1994), 76.

[54] Kraemer, "The Term 'Jew'," 41–42, cites Latin Jewish inscriptions that use invocations of the Gods such as *Dis Manibus* and *Iunonibus*. Some Jews may have felt comfortable using conventional references to the Gods without implying any commitment to their worship.

her own copy so we do not know what was written for her in Aramaic.) Jews clearly used the prevailing legal forms and institutions to make and litigate contracts with other residents of the province.

Greek norms affected married life, at least to some degree. In two Greek marriage contracts the husband is committed to clothe and feed his wife and children according to Greek custom (*nomos*) (*P. Yadin* 18.51) or Greek custom (*nomos*) and manner (*tropos*) (*P. Yadin* 37.9– 10). On the other hand, in Babatha's own Aramaic marriage contract she is taken as a wife by Judah according to the Law of Moses and the Jews or Judaeans (*yhwd*ʾ*y*).[55] Similarly, an Aramaic marriage contract from Wadi Murabbaʿat, dated 117, has a son of a man named Manasseh take a wife "according to the Law of Moses" (*kĕ-dîn Moše*).[56] The Greek marriage contract uses the phrase "Greek law and custom" of the main-tenance of a wife, that is, providing her with food and clothing, while Babatha's Aramaic contract uses "according to the Law of Moses and the Jews" of the marriage in general.[57] However, in Babatha's contract the maintenance clause immediately follows the phrase "according to the Law of Moses and the Jews" and is clearly governed by the Law of

---

[55]   The contract (*P. Yadin* 10) has been published with commentary in Yadin, Greenfield, Yardeni, "Babatha's *Ketubba*." Just a few phrases and a brief description of the contract are given in the original publication by Yigael Yadin, "Expedition D" *IEJ* 12 (1962), 244–45. Later Mishnaic law in Tractate Ketubot has both similarities and differences with practices in these early second century marriage contracts, showing the variety yet continuity in Jewish practices.

[56]   *Mur* 20 (Fitzmyer, *Manual*, 41, pp. 140–43). The end of the line is missing, so the full phrase may have been "according to the law of Moses and the Jews."

[57]   Hayim Lapin, "Early Rabbinic Civil Law and the Literature of the Second Temple Period," *JSQ* 2 (1995), 171, n. 67 suggests that the equivalent of the Aramaic "according to the law of Moses and the Jews" in the Greek marriage contract (*P. Yadin* 18) is in lines 7 and 39 where the father, Judah son of Elazar, gives his daughter Shelamzion to Judah Cimber "for the partnership of marriage *according to the laws* (*nomous*)." Even if this is the case, "the laws" governing the marriage are amorphous enough or well accepted and understood enough not to require speci-fication.

Moses and the Jews (cf. Exodus 21:10). Both Greek and Aramaic forms seem to have been used interchangeably by Jews around the Dead Sea and perhaps with the same general meaning.[58] Interestingly, we know of no Greek "custom and manner" of maintaining one's family. For example, the Greek marriage contract, *P. Yadin* 18, provides for the support of the wife and children if the husband dies. This provision is not found in Greek law, but in Jewish law. So even if the contract says "according to Greek custom," Jewish customs are being followed by Jews who make contracts in Greek. Most probably, in this and other matters of law the villagers followed prevailing local custom that they called the "Law of Moses" in Hebrew and Aramaic and "Greek custom" in Greek.[59]

The use of Greek and Roman courts does not mean that the Jewish residents of the Dead Sea basin were cut off from Jewish custom and law. Admittedly Babatha and her friends were not influenced by the early rabbis who were promoting an intensely and self-consciously religious, all-encompassing and uniform "halakhic" system. In these documents there is no religious language, beyond the perfunctory and conventional, such as the reference to Caesar's *tychē* in *P. Yadin* 16. The Mishnaic and Talmudic halakhic system with its stress on obedience to divine commandments and its elaborate discussions of what is forbidden and permitted is not operative. Yet similarities among these documents and the Mishnah show that traditional Jewish law, customs, and local practices were operative along with imperial law and that all these social and legal practices and understandings contributed to the highly

---

[58]   The suggestion that the use of Greek in the marriage contracts of the younger generation (Judah's daughter Shelamzion in *P. Yadin* 18 and Salome in *P. Yadin* 37) bespeaks a social trend toward gentile ways is very doubtful. See Naphtali Lewis, Ranon Katzoff and Jonas C. Greenfield, "Papyrus Yadin 18," *IEJ* 37 (1987), 231. The time difference is slight and the interpenetration of Aramaic and Greek in Jewish culture is extensive and long-lived. Many other circumstances could have dictated the language of the marriage contract, or it might have been a matter of indifference.

[59]   For the expression "Greek custom," see Lewis, Katzoff, Greenfield, "Papyrus Yadin 18," 239–41.

articulated Mishnaic synthesis later on. For example, Babatha's Aramaic marriage contract had a provision that, if her husband Judah died, she could continue to live in his house and be supported by his heirs. She could only be sent away if Judah's heirs returned her dowry to her in exchange for the marriage contract.[60] This is one of two competing practices recorded in *m. Ketubot* 4:12. Babatha's Ketubbah contains, not surprisingly, the Judaean rule, in contrast to a different Galilean custom, since Judah came from Ein Gedi (that is, part of Judaea).[61] Other provisions of the marriage documents in Aramaic and Greek also have provisions derived from Jewish law that were later enshrined and discussed in the Mishnah.

What kind of a social world did the people mentioned in these documents inhabit? The documents do not distinguish, exclude, or polemicize against outsiders. The signatories and principals interact easily with whoever lives in their area. The tensions with gentiles, disputes with Jewish or gentile Christians, and avoidance of idolators we see elsewhere in Jewish literature have no effect here. Neither the destruction of the Temple and Jerusalem, the war of fifty or sixty years previously, the apocalyptic hopes of some groups, nor the reconstructive efforts of the early rabbis receives any notice. These admittedly limited and narrowly focused documents reflect the lives of prosperous Jews living in and around the boundaries of the traditional land of Israel in peace with their neighbors, following traditional Jewish and local ways of life, and cooperating with the government without reflection or worry about the theological or religious problems of rabbinic or early Christian literature.

The signatories and subjects of these documents were part of a network of villages and cities in the Province of Arabia and around Ein

---

[60] See Yadin, Greenfield, Yardeni, "Babatha's *Ketubba*," 78–79, lines 14–17.

[61] See Yadin, Greenfield, Yardeni, "Babatha's *Ketubba*," 94. The Galilean custom allows the widow to remain and be maintained in her late husband's house unless she remarried. *y. Ket.* 4:15 (29a), approves of the Galilean practice as honorable and disdains the Judaean as mercenary.

Gedi, one of the traditional toparchies of Judaea.[62] Babatha's husband
Judah had a first wife, Miriam daughter of Beianos of Ein Gedi, and
property in Ein Gedi, but he resided in Maoza when he married
Babatha. After his death Babatha disputed over Judah's property with
his other wife, Miriam (*P. Yadin* 26), by bringing suit in her own home
town, Maoza. In turn, Babatha was sued for some of the property she
had inherited from her late husband Judah by Julia Crispina, acting in
place of Besas, the guardian of Judah's nephews, because Besas was ill
and unable to perform his duties as guardian (*P. Yadin* 25). Marriages
linked various families around the Dead Sea. Shelamzion, Babatha's
step daughter, residing in Maoza with her father and Babatha, was married to Judah Cimber, a man from Ein Gedi, her town of origin. Another
woman from Maoza, Salome Komais, was married to Jesus son of
Menahem from the village of Soffathe in the district of Livias, a city
across the Jordan from Jericho (*P. Yadin* 37). The network of social and
marital relationships in these few documents stretched around the Dead
Sea and spanned Judaea and the new Roman Province of Arabia.

The Babatha Archive tells us some things and leaves us ignorant
about many others but in the end suggests a context for the instructional, apologetic, and polemical literature of early Jews and Christians
in Israel and its neighborhood. Jews lived together with many peoples
under the imperial authorities. Arguments about how Jewish a region
was seem irrelevant in the face of these documents. As we saw above,
independent, self-contained ethnic groups, unrelated to their surroundings, are a scholar's fantasy. The social world of Babatha (and probably
the social worlds of most Jewish communities) supports the modern
sociological analyses of ethnic groups. The social and political world in
which all these people lived was Graeco-Roman and local at the same
time. In the limited cases covered by these documents, Jews married
Jews but lived as residents of their home villages. They did business with

---

[62]   Josephus, *BJ* 3.54–55 lists the toparchies just before the war with Rome. For
other references to them, see E. Schürer, *The History of the Jewish People in the Age
of Jesus Christ*, rev. ed. G. Vermes *et al.* (Edinburgh: Clark, 1973–87) 2, 190–94.

a variety of people using the customary contractual documents that had been adapted to Roman legal procedures and forms. A marriage contract could be in Aramaic or Greek and might include elements of Jewish, Greek and Roman law.[63] The dispute over the maintenance of Babatha's son Jesus is fought out in the Roman law courts according to the Roman rules and customs concerning guardianship.[64] These residents of Ein Gedi and Maoza felt as comfortable doing business in Greek as in Aramaic and invoked Greek custom and Roman law as naturally as Jewish law.[65] Readings of the Mishnah and Talmud that picture Jewish life as separate, independent and self-defining do not accord with what we see here and probably need revision.[66]

---

[63] Lewis, Katzoff, Greenfield, "Papyrus Yadin 18," 236–47. For a study of marriage contracts, see M. A. Friedman, *Jewish Marriage Law in Palestine. A Cairo Geniza Study* (Tel Aviv and New York: Jewish Theological Seminary, 1979–80). A briefer treatment may be found in Léonie J. Archer, *Her Price is Beyond Rubies: The Jewish Woman in Graeco-Roman Palestine* (JSOTSS 60; Sheffield: JSOT Press, 1990). Since *P. Yadin* 18 and 37, the two Greek marriage contracts, have nothing explicitly Jewish about them, A. Wasserstein, "A Marriage Contract from the Province of Arabia Nova: Notes on Papyrus Yadin 18," *JQR* 80 (1989), 105–30 and others have disputed their Jewishness. Ranon Katzoff has responded in "Papyrus Yadin 18 Again: A Rejoinder," *JQR* 82 (1991), 171–76 and elsewhere.

[64] Hannah M. Cotton, "Guardianship of Jesus son of Babatha: Roman and Local Law in the Province of Arabia," *JRS* 83 (1993), 94–108, esp. 102–7. In Roman law a woman could not be a guardian, but a mother could take legal action if her child's guardians were not fulfilling their obligations. Babatha does just this.

[65] Cotton, "Guardianship," 101 notes correctly that the rabbinic system was not operative in the Babatha documents and sets this fact within the general tendency of Jews to use the laws of lands in which they lived.

[66] Gary Porton, *Goyim: Gentiles and Israelites in Mishnah-Tosefta* (BJS 155; Atlanta: Scholars, 1988), and *The Stranger Within Your Gates: Converts and Conversion in Rabbinic Literature* (Chicago Studies in the History of Judaism: Chicago: Chicago University Press, 1994), traces the tensions and paradoxes caused to the Mishnaic system by interactions with Gentiles. The rabbis used a variety of strategies for marginalizing all outsiders in favor of an integral, divinely mandated, well structured Israel. The rabbis' view of Israel in relation to others was an ideal seldom

We do not know how Babatha and her family viewed the matters raised in rabbinic, mystical, hymnic, and apocalyptic literature or what they thought about the empire, Jewish autonomy, the Bible, worship, God, or divine law. We do know that Babatha and some of her friends were dislocated by the war with Rome in 132–35, because Babatha hid her important documents and probably herself in a cave south of Ein Gedi. The Bar Kosiba letters show us that Bar Kosiba appointed governors for Ein Gedi and actively gathered supplies and oversaw civic affairs there during the four years of his rule.[67] Babatha's second husband Judah, as well as her step-daughter and son-in-law, all came from Ein Gedi. Babatha claimed some of Judah's property there in a dispute with his other wife Miriam (*P. Yadin* 26). This probably led in some way to her presence there and eventually to her death as a civilian victim of a Roman military campaign in that area or perhaps as an active supporter of Bar Kosiba. Though we cannot know what these people thought or how Second Temple and early post-destruction Jewish views influenced them, we can surmise that they were the types of people among whom Jewish political and reform movements took shape. The early rabbis and the followers of Jesus addressed by Matthew in the late first century, as well as the rabbis gathered around Rabbi Judah the

---

experienced. It certainly does not describe, but may have been a response to, the kind of web of relationships mirrored in the Dead Sea documents.

[67] Several letters from Bar Kosiba in Hebrew, Aramaic, and Greek are addressed to Jonathan and Masabala, natives of Ein Gedi, who governed there for him. They testify to the difficulty Bar Kosiba had with getting supplies, to the transfer of prisoners and to the indifference of the Ein Gedians including Jonathan and Masabala in some circumstances. Whether Babatha was there by chance, went there as a supporter of Bar Kosiba, or fled hostility in Maoza we do not know. The Bar Kosiba letters have not been finally published. See Y. Yadin, *IEJ* 11 (1961), 38–52 for preliminary publication of some passages and a description. Y. Yadin, *Bar-Kokhba* (London and Jerusalem: Weidenfeld and Nicolson, 1971), chs. 10 and 12 describe the contents of the letters. Fitzmyer, *Manual*, nos. 53–60, has published the Aramaic letters with translations. For a list of all the documents from the Bar Kosiba war, see Millar, *Roman Near East*, App. B., 545–52.

Prince and the Jewish Christian groups active in the late second century did not live in a cultural island of *halākâ* or doctrine but sought to influence their fellow Jews, who lived as part of the Roman empire, their Roman province, their geographical district, and their city or village. The total web of relationships, not just in-group or inter-sectarian points of disagreement and debate, must define the nature of ethnic and religious groups.

Jews and Jewish Christian Groups

Can this extended case study of the social world of the Babatha Archive illuminate the social worlds of other Jewish and Jewish Christian groups in the first two centuries? We have already alluded to the beginnings of the post-70 C.E. Jewish reform movement initiated by a group of sages (*ḥakāmîm*) or rabbis. The early sages are placed in Judaea by talmudic and midrashic stories and their leaders, Rabban Yohanan ben Zakkai and Rabban Gamaliel II, are associated with Yavneh (Iamnia) on the coastal plain between the wars. The historicity of every saying and story is in doubt, and the tradition history and literary contexts of the same materials require meticulous analysis. But, at a minimum, we may surmise that a group of learned survivors of the war of 66–70 C.E., comprising of former Pharisees, priests, scribes, teachers, and perhaps others began to meet together and develop a way of life, an interpretation of the legal and Scriptural tradition and a symbolic understanding of Jewish history and life that could sustain them, and hopefully the people, in the wake of the loss of the Temple, the central city of Jerusalem, and any semblance of Jewish local autonomy. Though traditional literature often presents the rabbis as the authoritative leaders of Israel and their assembly as a replacement for the Jerusalem council (Sanhedrin) right from the beginning in the late first century, critical research has increasingly indicated that the rabbis only gained influence and then power very slowly and unevenly over Jewish communities during the first several centuries of the Common Era.

These early reformers sought to stabilize, adapt, and revivify Jewish life, practice, and thought in the wake of a national disaster. They began to discuss the meanings of biblical and traditional laws, debate opposing interpretations, and hammer out decisions concerning permitted and forbidden foods and actions, practices mandated by Torah (the Pentateuch), and implications of the law not developed explicitly in the Bible and previous teachings. They taught the requirements of tithes, Temple rituals, festival celebration, and priestly purity as if the Temple, Jerusalem and the priesthood still functioned, and they spoke of Israel as if it lived in peace as God's people, while ignoring historical disasters and political constraints.

In light of the developing Mishnah in the early part of the second century, what can we to say about Babatha and Rabbi Aqiba, two Jews who perished during the Bar Kosiba War? Ironically, we have documents written for and sworn to by Babatha but we have no writings from the pen of Aqiba. Minimally, though they were poorer for the deaths of Babatha and Aqiba, Jewish communities continued to thrive. More substantively, Jews continued to live and do business in the Roman world, as Babatha had. However, some of them, like Aqiba, developed and taught and applied a new, intricate, compelling, and engaging mode of living Jewish life with an explicit stress on faithful attention to God's power, presence, and revelation, on the sanctification of every significant aspect of daily life, and on the energetic transmission and appropriation of the law, including the disagreements over and reasons for the law and the interpretations that undergirded the law. Why did the ascendancy of the rabbis take several centuries? Perhaps because sages like Aqiba had to spend generations convincing, instructing, and training village people like Babatha, her husband Judah, her son Jesus, and all their family and associates.

How did this rabbinic way of life work itself out in the late Roman empire? The rabbis and their followers lived among Jews who did not follow their teachings, among gentiles who did not believe in their God, and under a government that was greatly at variance with the ideal Israel found in the Mishnah. This complex social and intellectual situation manifested itself in the way gentiles are treated in the Mishnah and Tosefta. Gary Porton has noted that Gentiles are treated in three ways:

as nations according to biblical law, as a theoretical "other" in the rabbinic system, and as neighbors in normal social interactions.[68] So Gentiles could be treated as idolators who were condemned by Scripture. They could also be perceived simply as non-Jews whose actions had an impact on topics of concern to the Mishnah, such as purity, tithing, sacrifice, or taking an oath. Finally, they were real human beings, neighbors, and business associates with whom Jews interacted on a daily basis. In all these roles "the discussions of the gentiles provided the rabbis with a means of constructing and defining the People Israel as an ethnic unit, so that the rabbis dealt with the non-Israelites in the same manner that all other peoples deal with their neighbors.[69] In Porton's view one of the results of the Mishnah was "the creation of a coherent cultural system that in turn led to a rabbinic definition of the Israelite People as an ethnic group."[70] In comparison with Babatha and her friends, the rabbis envisioned and demanded sharper boundaries and more inner cohesion. Insofar as possible, Jews were to live life according to a code and in a symbolic world proper to Israel and oriented toward God. It is difficult to imagine a rabbi approving of a marriage agreement that used as a norm "Greek custom," as did documents in the Babatha Archive, or willingly resolving a dispute in a Roman court, as Babatha and her neighbors and family did constantly.[71]

The rabbinic way of life offered Jews a distinctive, highly disciplined mode of existence within a larger political unit, the Roman empire. Since the rabbis tamed apocalyptic expectations and did not mount a

---

[68] Porton, *Goyim*, 285–88.

[69] Porton, *Goyim*, 288.

[70] Porton, *Goyim*, 296.

[71] This is not to deny that the rabbinic leaders exercised influence and consulted with the Roman authorities, as shown by Bowersock, "The Greek Moses," in this volume. But the rabbis had an ideal alternative to the Roman system of government and justice that guided their thinking and hopes for the future and their inner community behavior as much as possible.

political program, they probably proposed their code of law, life of learning, and interpretation of Israel's traditions as a response to life in the Roman empire both before and after it was taken over by the Christians. The Mishnah has often been treated as an unworkably ideal and theoretical system of laws, but for reasons that are not clear to the rational modern world, the Mishnah has survived long after Rome, the dominant reality of the Mediterranean world, fell from power. The rabbis reformed and formed an Israel for survival.

The rabbis were not alone in their project of reforming and reinvigorating Jewish life in Israel and the eastern Mediterranean. Thousands of Jews lived in the land and in the diaspora without any particular commitment to any Jewish school of thought and practice. They were an object of attention to a number of teachers and leaders who sought to influence them. As strange as it may seem, the author of the Gospel of Matthew was one of those Jewish teachers seeking to convince his fellow Jews, probably in Galilee or somewhere near there, that they should live Jewish lives according to the teachings of Jesus and that they should acknowledge Jesus as the Messiah and Son of God sent to save them. Although this summary of Matthew's message makes him a Christian in our eyes today, in the late first-century milieu this teaching was most probably understood by him and his fellow Jews as a type of Judaism.[72] Matthew's gospel has more detailed interpretations of Jewish law than the other three New Testament gospels and the author uses arguments and enters into debates found in other Jewish works of the time and in the early layers of the Mishnah. His stories, sayings, narratives, and discussions fit into the legal debates, apocalyptic speculations, and pious stories found in second Temple and late first century Jewish literature.

The Gospel of Matthew has been read as anti-Jewish throughout Christian history. But the gospel itself speaks from within Judaism. When Jesus in the narrative attacks his opponents, the Pharisees, scribes,

---

[72] See Saldarini, *Matthew's Christian-Jewish Community* for this interpretation and detailed arguments.

and chief priests, he does not attack Israel as a whole nor Jews in general, but only those Jewish leaders who oppose him within the Jewish community. Jesus and his opponents in the narrative mirror to some extent the author of Matthew and his opponents in the late first century, some of whom were probably early rabbis.[73] The author of this gospel attacks his fellow Jews from within Israel as did the prophets, but he never rejects Israel as such.[74] The gospel presents the Galilean crowds as interested in Jesus and as potential followers.[75] Many have claimed that at least the gospel's teaching about the status and roles of Jesus Christ put it beyond the boundaries of Judaism. But even in his teaching about Jesus, as Messiah, Son of Man, or Son of God, the author of Matthew never goes beyond the kinds of claims made in first-century Jewish literature for various messianic and angelic mediator and messenger figures.[76] Matthew mobilizes a different set of Jewish traditions from those that the rabbis used, in order to propose to Israel an alternative road to fidelity to God and a stable community life in accordance with God's will. The general goal is the same for the early rabbis and for Matthew, but the particular understandings and the path to the goal are very different.

The social context of the author of Matthew has often been located in Antioch in Syria. However, a setting in Galilee or somewhere contiguous in south Syria, Peraea, Gaulanitis, or along the Mediterranean coast is more likely.[77] This would put Matthew and his group in a city or

---

[73]   See J. Andrew Overman, *Matthew's Gospel and Formative Judaism: The Social World of the Matthean Community* (Minneapolis: Fortress, 1990), for the disputes over authority and over interpretation of the thought world of Judaism found in the gospel. See Saldarini, *Matthew's Christian-Jewish Community*, 85, for aspects of gospel's characterization and plot as transparencies for the author's late first century situation.

[74]   Saldarini, *Matthew's Christian-Jewish Community*, ch. 3.

[75]   Saldarini, *Matthew's Christian-Jewish Community*, ch. 2.

[76]   Saldarini, *Matthew's Christian-Jewish Community*, ch. 7.

[77]   Overman, *Matthew's Gospel*, 158–60. Anthony J. Saldarini, "The Gospel of Matthew and Jewish-Christian Conflict in Galilee," in L. Levine, ed., *Studies on Galilee in Late Antiquity* (New York: Jewish Theological Seminary, 1992), 23–38.

in villages much like those inhabited by Babatha and her family and friends. Thus these early followers of Jesus, along with the early rabbis, would have been part of a social network analogous to that which knit together the Jewish and non-Jewish families who appear in the Babatha archive.

The similarities and differences between Matthew's and Babatha's social worlds are instructive. Matthew's main interest was his fellow Jews. In the Matthean narrative Jesus teaches his countrymen almost exclusively and orders his own followers not to travel among the gentiles or Samaritans but to "the lost sheep of the house of Israel" (10:5–6). Jesus occasionally travels outside predominantly Jewish area to the "district of Tyre and Sidon" (15:21), where he reluctantly performs one cure, and to "the district of the Gadarenes" across the Sea of Galilee, where the inhabitants ask him to leave after an exorcism (8:28–9:1). Otherwise he confines his teaching and wonder-working to the northeast corner of lower Galilee.

Generally speaking, gentiles are on the margins of the gospel's Jewish world and are often characterized pejoratively. The nations (gentiles) worry about material goods rather than trusting in God (6:32). They do not love their enemies (5:47), and they babble at length when they pray (6:7). They are associated with tax collectors, another rejected group (6:46–47; 18:17). This usage is similar to the Greeks' pejorative use of *ethnē* for non-Greeks and for common, ill-mannered rural folk. Matthew, like the rabbis, saw gentiles as "others" who were not properly part of his group's world. The public world of Babatha's legal documents reflects a much more easy and substantial interaction between Jews and non-Jews within the larger world of the Roman empire.

Though the author of the Gospel of Matthew promoted a specific way of living a Jewish life, he was also subtly urging his Jewish group to recruit gentile members to their way of life. The Magi who came to see the newborn Jesus (2:1–12) are contrasted positively with Herod, who seeks to kill Jesus. They are a model for the sincere gentile seeking God. The Roman centurion who requests a cure for his ill servant (8:5–13) is praised for his faith in Jesus and contrasted positively with the Jewish leaders who oppose him. The Canaanite woman who requests a cure for her daughter overcomes Jesus' own reluctance to act with her persistence and faith (15:21–28). Finally, at the very end of the gospel, Jesus appears to his followers after his resurrection and tells them to make disciples of all the nations, baptizing them and teaching them everything Jesus has commanded (28:16–20). Thus the author opens up the boundaries of his Jewish group to other peoples who will accept God and Jesus. It should be emphatically noted that the author of Matthew does not suggest that gentiles are exempt from keeping the law. His teaching on the law firmly requires that all who follow Jesus, Jews and gentiles, obey the law as interpreted by Jesus.[78] This openness to non-Jews is often taken as an indication that the author and his Jewish followers have left Judaism. However, significant interactions of a Jewish group with non-Jews is to be expected in the Roman empire at this time. The profile of ethnic groups sketched out earlier demonstrates that the social relations and boundaries of groups vary greatly and change often. The proximity and interrelations among Jews and non-Jews seen in the Babatha Archive suggest the texture of social relationships within which the author of the Gospel of Matthew worked and thought.

Jewish Christians flourished right through the second century. The Pseudo-Clementine literature of the third and fourth centuries (the Greek *Homilies* and *Recognitions* [the latter extant now only in Latin and Syriac]) contains within it a document from the end of the second century and beginning of the third, about the time the Mishnah was being composed. In the Clementine *Recognitions*, 1.27–71 a Greek didactic narrative seems to derive, for the most part, from around 200 C.E.[79] One hypothesis suggests that this document was originally passed

---

78   Saldarini, *Matthew's Christian-Jewish Community*, 124–26, 156–64.

79   Sources for the Pseudo-Clementine literature are given above in n. 3. This source in *Recognitions* 27–71 has been called the "Ascents of James," probably incorrectly. That this section is different from the rest of the *Recognitions* has been recognized by most scholars for over a century, even as they differed on its interpretation and significance. The most recent and best study, along with a translation

on in the name of Matthew.[80] However, the author of this Jewish Christian document took a different path from the Gospel of Matthew, even though he was familiar with it. The whole narrative in which this source is set is too lengthy and complex to be summarized here. However, in the section in question, the author identifies his "race" as the "Hebrews, who are also called Jews" (*Recog.* 1.32). He reviews history from the creation, unifying it through the activities of the "true prophet" who appeared to Abraham and Moses (32, 34)[81] and finally has appeared as Jesus, who is also the Messiah who will come again (66–71). The author identifies strongly with the land of Israel (30–39), promises, ex post facto, a refuge in the land during the (Bar Kosiba) war to all Jews who are faithful to Jesus (37, 39), and envisions a final kingdom on earth (61), which will presumably be in the land. He disagrees with the usual interpretations of Jewish law, however. Most strikingly, he is against sacrifice, claiming that Moses instituted it only because of Israel's propensity toward idolatry (35–37).[82] His rejection of the Temple and sacrifices may be a covert attack on developing Rabbinic Judaism, which put great emphasis on studying the laws connected with the Temple and sacrifices in order to preserve, if only in mind and voice, the lost center of Jewish cult. The author reviews a number of Jewish sects and offers his own group and its teachings as a cure for this disunity and confusion (53–64). His view of Judaism includes calling the gentiles to follow the law as interpreted through Jesus' teachings.[83] Whether gentiles were to be circumcised is

---

from Latin and Syriac (and Armenian fragments) is F. Stanley Jones, *Jewish Christian Science.* Another useful study is Robert E. Van Voorst, *The Ascents of James: History and Theology of a Jewish-Christian Community* (SBLDS 112: Atlanta: Scholars, 1989).

[80]   See Jones, *Jewish Christian Source,* 154–55.

[81]   The Syriac version says that Moses himself is the true prophet.

[82]   Van Voorst, *Ascents of James,* 166–70 reviews the Jewish and Christian sources that were anti-cultic and constitute the tradition that this author continues.

[83]   One of the reasons for the call of the gentiles is that many Jews have rejected Jesus (41–42; 63.2; 64.2).

unclear,[84] although the document is clearly anti-Pauline.[85] In general, this group kept its Jewish identity even as it embraced a law-observant mission to the gentiles,[86] which stressed the Ten Commandments (35) and defended the origin of Jesus' teaching in the Bible (69).

The author of this Jewish Christian document attempted to hold together the complex, conflicting traditions and interpretations emerging among the early Christian and Jewish communities at the beginning of the third century and to create a community that embraced both Jews and gentiles. He affirmed the demands of the Bible and the continuity of Jewish life and customs even as he accepted and revered Jesus as the true prophet and Messiah sent by God to reform Jewish life and call gentiles to God. This author, with his group, was one of many among Jews in the late Roman empire. His effort to convince his fellow Jews that his message was true was doomed to failure in the face of the Mishnah, which substantially reached its present form in approximately 200–220, the same time as this Jewish Christian document in *Recognitions* 1. The Mishnah, as we have seen, took a radically different path in order to give shape to a Judaism without the Temple in a hostile world. The sages of the Mishnah synthesized Jewish traditions and customs into a coherent, normative body of law that covered, in their interpretation, all aspects of Israel as it was called by God at Sinai. Study of these laws, with full acceptance of the lawgiver and his will, would lead to practice, and practice would constitute the community of Israel as God wished. Laws that could not be put into practice, such as those con-

---

[84] Circumcision is spoken of positively in *Recog.* 1.33. On the other hand, baptism and not circumcision is stressed in this work (e.g., 39). Van Voorst, *Ascents of James*, 174, thinks this group might have required circumcision. Jones, *Jewish Christian Source*, 164–65, argues against the requirement of circumcision.

[85] At the end of the document (70–71) an unnamed hostile enemy appears to attack James verbally and physically on the steps of the Temple, convince the priests and people in Jerusalem to reject Jesus and initiate a persecution of the Jewish followers of Jesus. Allusions to the New Testament documents identify this enemy as Paul.

[86] Van Voorst, *Ascents of James*, 174, 177. See also J. Louis Martyn, *The Gospel of John in Christian History* (New York: Paulist, 1979), ch. 2.

cerned with sacrifices and the Temple, were as important as those that were practicable, because both had been ordained by God and both were thus worthy of effort and mastery. The rejection of sacrifice as a temporary expedient now replaced by some other reality, as we find in the Jewish Christian document of the *Recognitions*, was unthinkable. Sacrifice and the Temple were enshrined in Scripture and Jewish experience; they had to be incorporated into the thought world of this new interpretation of Judaism. The realities of life in the empire and in the diaspora were ignored in the texts because they were of lesser importance compared with the revealed will of God. Study of God's laws and the rabbinic interpretations of them became the core response to Torah. The Messiah and the apocalyptic end to the world, so important in the Gospel of Matthew and the Jewish Christian document because of their focus on Jesus, were moved firmly to the background in the Mishnah, perhaps as a response to the defeats in the wars with Rome or to the Christian affirmation of the Messiahship of Jesus, or both.

The author of the Jewish Christian source offered another road to fidelity to God, one that could unite Jews who would accept Jesus with gentiles who would do the same. This seems farfetched centuries later, after Jews and Christians have gone their separate ways and Christianity has persecuted Judaism. In the villages and cities of the eastern Mediterranean such a life was possible. It was probably farfetched in the light of gentile Christian communities from Asia Minor to Gaul. But in Syria-Palestine, as was noted above, the networks of villages, the interactions of Greek, Roman, and indigenous customs and ways of thought, the international influences on architecture, religion, inscriptions, and legal forms, and a host of other minutiae of life, society, and culture created a rich milieu for the formation and development of groups with diverse and challenging views of God(s), the world, society, politics, cult, and customs. In ways that we understand dimly, the Jews in the villages, the rabbis who eventually influenced and guided them, the Jewish Christians who lost out to them, and the gentile Christians who went on to control the empire all began in the same place and worked out their paths in relationship to one another.

III.

THE URBAN CONTEXT
IN ROMAN PALESTINE

IDENTITY AND THE LATE ANTIQUE CITY: THE CASE OF CAESAREA

Kenneth G. Holum

University of Maryland

MY POINT IN THIS ESSAY is that studying identity—personal, ethnic, and religious—is another way of exploring the transformation of the classical city in late antiquity. For some years now, my effort has been to understand that process of transformation in one particular city, Caesarea Palaestinae in Israel,[1] on the assumption that each of these Roman cities was a unique organism that deserves individual treatment. I take my departure from Saul Lieberman's article "The Martyrs of Caesarea" that appeared in 1945 in a volume dedicated to scholars who recently had fallen victim to barbarous enemy invasion and persecution.[2] In that article Lieberman discusses a passage of Eusebius' *Martyrs of Palestine*

---

[1] A. Raban and K. G. Holum, eds., *Caesarea Maritima: A Retrospective after Two Millennia* (DMOA 21: Leiden: Brill, 1996) (henceforth *Caesarea Retrospective*); also three impressionistic works: K. G. Holum *et al.*, *King Herod's Dream: Caesarea on the Sea* (New York and London: Norton, 1988); J. A. McGuckin, "Caesarea Maritima as Origen Knew It," in R. J. Daly, ed., *Origeniana Quinta, Papers of the 5th International Origen Congress, Boston College, 14–18 August 1989* (Leuven: University Press, 1992), 3–25; and L. Cansdale, "What Became of Herod's Caesarea Maritima," *Patristic and Byzantine Review* 11 (1992), 53–66.

[2] S. Lieberman, "The Martyrs of Caesarea," *Annuaire de l'Institut de Philologie et d'Histoire Orientales et Slaves* 7 (1939–1944), 395–446, *Dédié à la mémoire des orientalistes et des slavisants victimes de l'invasion et de la persécution des barbares.* The dedicant, editor of this comprehensive volume, was the great Belgian Byzantinist Henri Grégoire.

about a miracle that happened at Caesarea just a year or two before
Eusebius wrote his account, in November or December of 309:

> The sky was clear and the atmosphere bright. Then all at once a great
> number of the pillars of the porches of the city let fall as it were drops, like
> tears, and the market-places and streets, though not a single drop had
> fallen from the sky, were sprinkled and moistened with water. And the
> story was on everyone's lips that the stones wept and the earth shed tears
> ... [because] the senseless stones and the impassive earth could not endure
> this foul and cruel deed.[3]

What caused the pillars to weep, Eusebius insists, was a Roman governor who refused decent burial to Christian victims of persecution, and
dogs, birds, and wild beasts thus fed on their corpses before the city
gates. Yet some miracles permit more than one explanation, and the
Christian apologist was apparently not the only one who interpreted
these sympathetic stones. Lieberman proposed that it was on that same
bright day in 309 that the great Jewish sage Abbahu of Caesarea
breathed his last. "When R. Abbahu died," the Talmud of Palestine
relates, "the pillars of Caesarea wept." "Not true!" responded still a third
religious community, one that had apparently suffered no immediate
loss. The kûtîm, or Samaritans, saw nothing miraculous in the weeping
pillars and put forward a more mundane explanation, that "They are
only perspiring."[4]

What struck Lieberman about this episode was the convergence of
independent sources deriving from apparent eyewitness that allowed
him, he thought, to date Abbahu's death almost precisely, to a sunny
day in the late months of 309. Indeed, we all do experience a certain
thrill nowadays when a historian can assert plausibly that an event actually happened, even at a specific time. After the recent excavations, more-

---

[3]   Eusebius, *Mart. Pal.* 9.12, trans. H. J. Lawlor, J. E. L. Oulton, *Eusebius, The
Ecclesiastical History and the Martyrs of Palestine* (London: SPCK, 1954) 1, 375.

[4]   *y. ᶜAbod. Zar.* 3:1 (42c). Cf. Lieberman, "Martyrs," 401, for discussion of the
text and translation, and L. I. Levine, "R. Abbahu of Caesarea," in J. Neusner, ed.,
*Christianity, Judaism and other Greco-Roman Cults: Studies for Morton Smith at
Sixty* (SJLA 12: Leiden: Brill, 1975), 56–76.

over, archaeologists may even point to a few standing columns from a street colonnades at Caesarea, the survivals of porticoes well known from literary sources, that could indeed have "wept" in the days of Eusebius and Abbahu, or exhibited condensation from a heavy morning dew.[5]

There is another side, though, to the parallel Christian and Rabbinic texts, one unexplored by Lieberman, that wins poignancy from our discussions about ethnic and religious communities. This episode of the weeping pillars is manifestly a debate among three such communities. Whatever the facts about this miracle, the *Sitz* of the debate's *Leben* is clearly a city that harbors ethnic and religious communities in rivalry with one another. Indeed the miracle's setting is strikingly urban, amid the streets and markets of Caesarea where the paths of inhabitants from different ethnic and religious groups most frequently converged, with consequent sharing of weeping columns and other puzzling and suggestive public occurrences. Above all, in this setting each community asserts itself, insisting that its special voice be heard, claiming that the very stones of urban buildings reinforced, on the Christian side, the injustice and violence of the persecutors, or, among Jews, the sagacity of a revered community leader. On the Samaritan side, the Talmud records, perhaps unfairly, just the impertinent assertion that mere weeping pillars should not privilege the competition.

It is this last aspect of the "weeping columns" episode, the implicit self-assertion of rival communities within the ancient city, that I should like to emphasize. Other evidence, most of it already familiar, confirms the existence of assertive rival ethnic and religious communities in

---

[5]   E.g., Eusebius *Mart. Pal.* 9.12 speaks of "the columns across the city that supported the public stoas"; *t. ᵓOhol.* 18:13 (ed. Zuckermandel, p. 617), of *sṭā(y)w ha-mizrāḥî*. For the Greek stoa as street colonnade, cf. G. Downey, "The Architectural Significance of the Words 'Stoa' and 'Basilikē' in Classical Literature," *AJA* 41 (1937), 210–12, and for an example of standing columns surviving from Caesarea's street colonnades, see L. I. Levine and E. Netzer, *Excavations at Caesarea Maritima 1975, 1976, 1979, Final Report* (*Qedem* 21: Jerusalem: The Hebrew University, 1986), 183, incl. ill. 157.

Caesarea at the beginning of the fourth century, at the time of the weeping columns. It seems to me that by and large this was a good thing, indeed that the assertiveness of rival communities helps account for the prosperity of Caesarea and similar cities in the fourth century and after. Further, such assertiveness is a public manifestation of community self-confidence, which implies that despite persecution members of ethnic and religious communities experienced sufficient physical and economic security to live rewarding and productive lives. It should be remembered that it was just at this moment that Caesarea, like other Roman cities of Palestine, entered its period of greatest prosperity. Within a century or so after the weeping pillars new fortification walls were built that enclosed more than twice the urban space of the earlier ones.[6] The old aqueducts from the first and second centuries remained in service, and in the fourth century the urban authorities built a new one that vastly increased water flow to the city.[7] In Caesarea's hinterland, as in the rest of the country, the Archaeological Survey of Israel has discovered that more sites—towns, villages, hamlets, and isolated farms—were occupied in the fourth, fifth, and sixth centuries than ever before.[8] Years ago Michael Avi-Yonah adduced Christian emigration to the Holy Land and pious imperial investment to explain this economic and demographic upswing,[9] but at Caesarea it clearly included as well prosperous and assertive ethnic and religious communities.

---

[6]   Most recently C. M. Lehmann, "The Excavation of Caesarea's Byzantine City Wall, 1989," in W. G. Dever, ed., *Preliminary Excavation Reports: Sardis, Bir Umm Fawakhir, Tell el-ᶜUmeiri, The Combined Caesarea Expeditions, and Tell Dothan* (AASOR 52: Ann Arbor, Mich.: The American Schools of Oriental Research, 1994), 121–31.

[7]   Y. Olami and Y. Peleg, "The Water Supply System of Caesarea Maritima," *IEJ* 27 (1977), 127–37; Y. Porath, "Pipelines of the Caesarea Water Supply," ᶜ*Atiqot*, Hebrew Series, 10 (1990), 101–10 (Hebrew, English summary, pp. 19*–20*).

[8]   Y. Ne'eman, *The Archaeological Survey of Israel: Map of Ma'anit (54)* (Jerusalem: Israel Antiquities Authority, 1990).

[9]   M. Avi-Yonah, "The Economics of Byzantine Palestine," *IEJ* 8 (1958), 39–51.

The Christian community, most prominent in the episode of the weeping pillars, will take a back seat in our discussion. It was not a proper ethnic community at all, in Fredrik Barth's classic definition, because it was not biologically self-perpetuating, opening itself to indifferently to men and women of any ethnic background who adopted its "fundamental cultural values."[10] Caesarea's Christian community went back to the Apostolic age.[11] In the later second and third centuries its bishops emerged as metropolitans of Palestine, corresponding with Caesarea's status as metropolitan city of the province and normal headquarters of the Roman governor and administration. Demographically, the Christians remained a small minority, but in the third century the community harbored the theologian Origen of Alexandria and his pupils, nurtured the great librarian Pamphilus and his disciple Eusebius, and attracted rich men like the Ambrose who patronized Origen by providing secretaries, scribes, and female calligraphers.[12] Caesarea's Christians obviously had the internal cohesion and leadership to weather the storm of persecution that the emperors unleashed against the cities of the Empire 303–13, and after the Peace of the Church they emerged in the driver's seat. The process by which Caesarea became Christian eludes us, but clearly its physical, urban manifestation was the

---

[10]   F. Barth, "Introduction," in F. Barth, ed., *Ethnic Groups and Boundaries: The Social Organization of Culture Difference* (Boston: Little, Brown and Company, 1969), 10–11. Barth's definition also includes a common "field of communication and interaction."

[11]   See in general G. Downey, "Caesarea and the Christian Church," in C. T. Fritsch, ed., *Studies in the History of Caesarea Maritima* (Missoula: Scholars Press, 1975), 23–42; L. I. Levine, *Caesarea under Roman Rule* (SJLA 7: Leiden: Brill, 1975), 113–34; and E. Krentz, "Caesarea and Early Christianity," in R. L. Vann, ed., *Caesarea Papers* (Ann Arbor: *Journal of Roman Archaeology Supplementary Series* 5, 1992) (henceforth *Caesarea Papers*), 261–67.

[12]   Eusebius *Hist. Eccl.* 6.18.1, 23.1. Cf. now H. Lapin, "Jewish and Christian Academies in Roman Palestine: Some Preliminary Observations," *Caesarea Retrospective*, 496–512; and D. Runia, "Caesarea Maritima and the Survival of Hellenistic-Jewish Literature," *Caesarea Retrospective*, 476–95.

abandonment and destruction of pagan temples—like the Mithraeum
that Robert Bull excavated in the 1970's, apparently in use at least to the
end of the third century[13]—and their replacement in the city's various
quarters by Christian *martyria* and other buildings. Literary sources
record no fewer than ten holy places and churches that existed at Caesarea
between the fourth century and the Muslim conquest, and there were
probably many more.[14] So far the archaeologists have found only two,[15]
neither identified by dedication, one of which rose on the Temple Platform, dominating city and harbor, where King Herod had built a temple
to Roma and Augustus when he founded the city in the first century
B.C.E. The church is a case of extreme architectural assertiveness. It was a
magnificent octagonal *martyrion*, reveted in marble, similar in design
and scale to the Dome of the Rock.[16]

---

[13]   J. A. Blakely, *Caesarea Maritima: The Pottery and Dating of Vault 1: Horreum,
Mithraeum, and Later Uses* (Lewiston: Edwin Mellen, 1987), 103–4.

[14]   For a listing of attested churches and sources see K. G. Holum, "The End of
Classical Urbanism at Caesarea Maritima, Israel," in R. I. Curtis, ed., *Studia Pom-
peiana & Classica in Honor of Wilhelmina F. Jashemski* (New Rochelle: Caratzas,
1989) 2, 92–93, 99–100, nn. 30–32; also *idem*, "A Newly Discovered Martyr Church
at Caesarea Maritima, Israel," *Akten des XII. internationalen Kongresses für christliche
Archäologie, Bonn, 22.–28. September 1991 (Jahrbuch für Antike und Christentum,
Ergänzungsband,* 20:2: Münster: Aschendorffsche Verlags-buchhandlung, 1995),
849–50.

[15]   First was the octagonal church on the Temple Platform (below), and recently
the Israel Antiquities Authority team brought to light a basilical church and
associated cruciform baptistry above the earlier south entrance to the Herodian
amphitheater; see Y. Porath, "The Evolution of the Urban Plan of Caesarea's
Southwest Zone," *Caesarea Retrospective,* 117, for brief mention and Map 4 in
Caesarea Retrospective, for the location.

[16]   K. G. Holum, A. Raban, *et al.,* "Preliminary Report on the 1989–1990 Seasons,"
Caesarea Papers, 100–8; Holum, "Martyr Church"; also K. G. Holum, "Caesarea,"
in E. M. Meyers, ed., *The Oxford Encyclopedia of Archaeology in the Near East* (New
York and Oxford: Oxford University Press, 1997) 1, 403, for a perspective view,
designed by Anna Iamim, of this church on the Temple Platform. The proposed
dedication to Procopius is hypothetical and problematic.

As Raymond van Dam and others have pointed out,[17] these churches were of course just the physical side of a less tangible social process, the Christianizing of Caesarea's urban society. By the fifth and sixth centuries, the whole power structure had embraced the new religion, including the *boulē*, or municipal senate of wealthy landowners, and the provincial governors headquartered in Caesarea, who always cut a large figure in urban society. According to Procopius of Caesarea, namesake of the city's most famous martyr, any Samaritan "possessed of reason and a sense of propriety" might be expected to abandon his religion and adhere readily to Christianity,[18] and presumably so would a Jew. From the historian's sixth-century perspective, in Caesarea society Christianity had become a mark of good urban manners or basic civility.

Yet despite prejudice one could also prosper as a Jew, both before Christianization and after. The Jewish community likewise had ancient roots, dating back to the founding of the city and beyond, for Jews had inhabited Straton's Tower, the town that preceded Caesarea on the same site, and formed a large minority in Herod's foundation. From the eve of the First Revolt until about the end of the second century there was a hiatus, when relatively few Jews still lived at Caesarea, and then, in the third and fourth centuries, the Jewish community really blossomed.[19] We have no very good idea either of the total population of Caesarea and its territory, perhaps 25,000 within the "Byzantine" forti-

---

[17]   R. Van Dam, "From Paganism to Christianity at Late Antique Gaza," *Viator* 16 (1982), 1–20.

[18]   Procopius *Hist. Arc.* 11.25.

[19]   Levine, *Caesarea*, 61–106; cf. also several of the same author's essays, "Abbahu"; "The Jewish Community at Caesarea in Late Antiquity," *Caesarea Papers*, 268–73; "Caesarea's Synagogues and Some Historical Implications," in A. Biran, J. Aviram, eds., *Biblical Archaeology Today, 1990, Proceedings of the Second International Congress on Biblical Archaeology, Jerusalem, June–July 1990* (Jerusalem: Israel Exploration Society; Israel Academy of Sciences and Humanities, 1993), 666–78; and "Synagogue Officials: The Evidence from Caesarea and Its Implications for Palestine and the Diaspora," *Caesarea Retrospective*, 392–400.

fications, and twice that in Caesarea's subject lands or "territory,"[20] or of the strength of the Jewish community, but we do learn from the Talmud of Palestine that about 350 it took the Jewish and the gentile (pagan and Christian) populations together to equal the Samaritan.[21] There were therefore anywhere from 5,000–15,000 Jews in Caesarea and its subject lands, of whom more than one-third will have lived in the city.[22] There were certainly Jewish farmers,[23] though I know of no specific evidence for Jewish landowners, and Jews lived in the towns, villages, and hamlets of Caesarea's territory. Recently Leah Di Segni published a limestone slab found near the ancient town of Kefar Shuni or Maioumas northeast of Caesarea displaying a prominent but crudely carved menorah, a Greek inscription: "God is One! Help Judah the Elder!" and a date that likely equals 408/9 or so. Di Segni suggests reasonably that this inscription was fixed to the wall of a Jewish synagogue,[24] so

---

[20]   Cf. M. Broshi, "The Population of Western Palestine in the Roman-Byzantine Period," *BASOR* 236 (1980), 1–10. Broshi's estimate of 400 inhabitants per hectare on three-fourths of Byzantine Caesarea's urban space, 95 hectares, would give a total of about 28,500 within the Byzantine fortifications, but I reduce this because more than one-fourth of Caesarea's urban space was devoted to streets, markets, and public facilities like the hippodrome. In the same article Broshi adopts an estimate that urban population was one-third of the total, so Caesarea's territory, depending on its (uncertain) extent, may have contained upward of 50,000 inhabitants.

[21]   *y. Dem.* 2:1 (22c); Lieberman, "Martyrs," 402; Levine, *Caesarea*, 106, 227, n. 3.

[22]   Assuming about 35,000 Samaritans and a significantly large minority of Jews. The prominence of merchants, craftsmen, and tradesmen in the rabbinic evidence (below), and relative silence about Jewish farmers and landowners, indicates that the majority were city dwellers.

[23]   Hence the agricultural laws discussed in E. Habas, "The Halachic Status of Caesarea as Reflected in the Talmudic Literature," *Caesarea Retrospective*, 454–68.

[24]   L. Di Segni, "A Jewish Greek Inscription from the Vicinity of Caesarea Maritima," ʿ*Atiqot* 22 (1993), 133–36; cf. D. Barag, "The Dated Jewish Inscription from Binyamina Reconsidered," ʿ*Atiqot* 25 (1994), 179–81; and Di Segni, "The Date of the Binyamina Inscription and the Question of Byzantine Dora," ʿ*Atiqot* 25

it represents a Jewish community in one of Caesarea's subject towns, as does a Jewish epitaph published years ago from the same vicinity.[25] The urban Jewish community comprised men and women of various pursuits and economic levels. From rabbinic literature and inscriptions we know of potters,[26] a weaver of Babylonian-style textiles(?),[27] shopkeepers,[28] an apprentice baker,[29] fish merchants,[30] barbers,[31] a goldsmith,[32] a Jewish pantomime who performed in Caesarea's theater,[33] and a man who from poverty hired himself to a *ludus* to be trained as a gladiator.[34] The wealthy included the rabbis, several of whom were merchants. R. Abba, contemporary of R. Abbahu, dealt in silk.[35] One third-century Jew, probably from Caesarea, was a *palatinus*, a member of the governor's staff.[36]

(1994), 183–86, debating the date. Di Segni has the upper hand. Cf. C. M. Lehmann and K. G. Holum, *The Greek and Latin Inscriptions of Caesarea Maritima* (forthcoming) (henceforth *Inscr.*), 137.

[25] *Inscr.* 182.

[26] *y. B. Meṣ.* 6:8 (11a).

[27] *Inscr.* 184. The usual interpretation of this epigraphical *babylōnarios* as a weaver is speculative, but at any rate he was likely a craftsman.

[28] *y. B. Qam.* 6:8 (5c).

[29] *Qoh. Rab.* 1:23.

[30] *y. Šebi.* 7:4 (37c); *y. Ter.* 10:3 (47a).

[31] *y. Taʿan.* 4:9 (69b).

[32] Cf. below, n. 36.

[33] *y. Taʿan.* 1:4 (64a), cf. Zeev Weiss, "The Jews and the Games in Roman Caesarea," *Caesarea Retrospective*, 447.

[34] *y. Giṭ.* 4:9 (46b), cf. *b. Giṭ.* 46b–47a; esp. Weiss, "Jews and the Games," *Caesarea Retrospective*, 451–52.

[35] *b. Beṣa* 38a-b, cf. Levine, *Roman Rule*, 91.

[36] This was Julian, brother of Rabbi Paregorios, son of Leontios "of the goldsmiths," all mentioned in a tomb inscription, M. Schwabe and B. Lifshitz, *Beth Sheʿarim, Vol. 2: The Greek Inscriptions* (Jerusalem: Massada Press, 1974), 61. Levine, *Roman Rule*, 70, suggests that the family was from Caesarea, where there

The evidence shows that Jews used a variety of strategies for asserting personal and group identity. The Jews were endogamous and thus ethnic in the strict sense. Among the Caesarea community was Aste, identified as a proselyte, who was thus born pagan, or more likely Christian, but underwent conversion according to Jewish law and became a Jew before marriage to her husband. We conclude from their joint epitaph that he lay with her in the same tomb.[37] Some have suggested a Jewish cemetery outside the Byzantine wall between the great hippodrome and the present Dan Hotel.[38] The 32 certain and probable Jewish epitaphs found in that vicinity and elsewhere at the site are all in Greek, inscribed on small marble slabs a few centimeters thick, presumably once affixed to built tombs.[39] Greek was the language of the broader community, and the form of tomb was common to Jews and Christians at Caesarea, but a Jewish cemetery would be a marker of group identity. The onomasticon represented in epitaphs contains no names that were not also pagan or Christian but does feature a large component of biblical names, like Jacob and Leah, and others that were Greek versions of Hebrew names, like the common Paregorios (including Aste's husband) translating Menachem.[40] More or less certain assertions of personal Jewishness are ethnic markers carved on the stones, the shofar, incense shovel, and menorah, along with the Hebrew word *salom*, "peace," or *šālôm ʿal yiśrāʾēl*, "peace upon Israel."

Further, Jewish barbers closed for business on the feast of the ninth day of Ab, and merchants frequently built *sûkkôt* into the front of their

---

was a Rabbi Paregorios, and where *palatini* were most common.

[37] *Inscr.* 165.

[38] E.g. B. Lifshitz, "La nécropole juive de Césarée," *RB* 71 (1964), 384–87, linking *m. ʾOhol.* 17:49, which mentions a Jewish cemetery east of Caesarea, with the findspots of several Jewish epitaphs.

[39] *Inscr.* 165–96. Since Samaritans shared ethnic markers like names and iconography with the Jews, some of these tombstones could equally be Samaritan (below).

[40] On Jewish gravestones and their onomasticon cf. Lehmann and Holum,

shops,[41] reminding other Caesareans that Jews adhered to a different calendar of festivals from the official pagan or Christian one of Caesarea. As for architecture, few non-Jewish passers-by would have failed to notice a *bêt midrāšâ* a rabbinic "house of learning," located in downtown Caesarea and opening onto the *agora*.[42] So far archaeologists have identified only one synagogue in the city, located right on the coast in the northwestern part of the city, where the encroaching sea destroyed most of it before anyone noticed. What survives of the architectural vocabulary is mosaic pavements with common decorative motifs and late Corinthian capitals decorated with the menorah.[43] Not even complete foundations survive, but it would be interesting to know how this building struck passersby. Presumably this urban synagogue did not assert itself as boldly in a large Christian city as the magnificent white limestone synagogue in the village Capernaum, where it rose in bold contrast to the black basalt dwelling quarters surrounding it, and to the rather meager Church of St. Peter just a few feet away.[44]

Speaking the same Greek language, using the same architectural vocabulary, Caesarea's Jews appear to have well-embedded in urban society as in the economy. Like other city dwellers, they frequented the urban baths. R. Abbahu, a man of striking physique and personal beauty as well as learning, rescued two of his attendants when the hypocaust of a bath collapsed beneath them. Clinging to a pillar, he was able by sheer strength to draw them out of the flaming abyss.[45] Frequent

---

Inscr., Introduction.

[41]   *y. Taʿan.* 4:9 (69b); *y. B. Qam.* 6:8 (5c); Levine, *Roman Rule*, 69.

[42]   *b. Ḥul.* 86b, cf. Levine, *Roman Rule*, 103; Lapin, "Jewish and Christian Academies," *Caesarea Retrospective*, 496–512, esp. 509–10 on the physical setting of the *bêt midrāš*.

[43]   For what is known of this building and bibliography, see M. Avi-Yonah, "Caesarea," *NEAEHL* 1, 278–80; and, for the location, *Caesarea Retrospective*, Map 4.

[44]   For brief description and bibliography, S. Loffreda, "Capernaum," *NEAEHL* 1, 291–96.

rabbinic scoldings reflect the popularity of the hippodrome, amphitheater, and theater among Jews as well as among pagans and Christians.[46]
But when they attended the theater, Caesarea's Jews apparently found
themselves to be victims of derision. Lee I. Levine, and now Zeev Weiss,
have recognized a theatrical mime in one of R. Abbahu's sermons:

> "They that sit in the gate talk of me" (Psalm 69:13). This [said R. Abbahu]
> refers to the nations of the world who sit in theaters and circuses. They
> then take a camel into their theaters, put their shirts upon it, and ask one
> another, "Why is it mourning?" to which they reply, "The Jews observe
> the law of the sabbatical year and have no vegetables, so they eat this
> camel's thorns, and that is why it is in mourning ..."[47]

Texts like this remind the modern observer that however comfortable
Jews were in Caesarean society, in order to prosper they required protection from a majority society and state that were fundamentally hostile.
Within the community, as Levine explains, rich men came to the aid of
the less fortunate in the communal function known as *parnāsîm*, virtually heads or patrons of the community.[48] R. Abbahu acted as *parnās*
when he gave money to release that would-be gladiator (above). An
inscription from the synagogue records the benefactions of Beryllos
arkhisynagōgos and *phrontistēs*.[49] If we interpret *phrontistēs* as the functional equivalent of *parnās*, perhaps the dichotomy between the Greek/
diaspora terminology for leadership in the Jewish communities and the
rabbinic one is not as great as Levine has recently suggested.[50] Vis-à-vis
the broader society, wealthy and learned men could also come to the aid
of Jews in difficulty. We remember R. Abbahu again, appearing at
Caesarea in the court of the governor, where his prestige was so great that
the women of the court sang his praises when he arrived:

---

[45]   *b. Ket.* 62a, cf. Levine, "Rabbi Abbahu," 63.

[46]   Weiss, "Jews and the Games," *Caesarea Retrospective*, 443–53.

[47]   *Lam. Rab.* Proem. 17 (ed. Buber 7b); Levine, "Rabbi Abbahu," 59–60; Weiss,
"Jews and the Games," *Caesarea Retrospective*, 446.

[48]   Levine, *Roman Rule*, 92–93.

[49]   *Inscr.* 79.

Leader of his people, spokesman of his nation, a glowing lamp, blessed be your coming in peace.[51]

Such a man had the influence to protect Jews in a hostile environment.

We need to remember, though, that when under stress Jews could also resort to violence and rioting. There is a little-remembered text of the fifth-century ecclesiastical historian Theodore Anagnostes that records an event dated about 439, during the reign of Theodosius II and his sister Pulcheria, to judge only from its position among the fragments:

> The Jews of Palestine, especially from Caesarea, rioted and killed some Christians. When the emperors heard of it, they ordered the governors to exact the penalty for these crimes, but the governors accepted bribes, and the guilty escaped punishment. Thus the Empress Pulcheria, dominating her brother, relieved the governors of their posts and confiscated half of their property.[52]

One suspects that what looked like bribery to the imperial court was closer to the exercise of patronage by influential communal leaders like R. Abbahu. The cooperative governors were naturally nearer at hand than the court in Constantinople, where the emperor's enthusiastic sister was in charge, and faced the task of keeping order in a society of mixed ethnic and religious communities.

The Samaritans, children of Israel who considered God's holy mount to be not Zion but Gerizim in Samaria, resembled the Jews. In the later second and third centuries they had apparently expanded from their traditional home in Samaria to the coastal cities. Like Jews, Samaritans were endogamous and thus a proper ethnic community, and like Jews they were well-embedded in the society and economy of Caesarea.[53] We know much less about the Samaritans because they did

---

[50]   Levine, "Synagogue Officials," *Caesarea Retrospective*, 392–400.

[51]   *b. Sanh.* 14a; *b. Ket.* 17a; Levine, "Rabbi Abbahu," 66–69.

[52]   Theodore Anagnostes *Hist. Eccl.* 336 (ed. G. C. Hansen) *GCS* [unnumbered volume], 96, dated by its position at the beginning of the fragments.

[53]   See in general A. D. Crown, ed., *The Samaritans* (Tübingen, J. C. B. Mohr, 1989); and for Caesarea specifically Levine, *Roman Rule*, 107–12.

not develop a rabbinic class or leave behind a rabbinic literature. Biblical names were frequent, like Joseph b. Shutelah and the priest Aharon b. Zohar attested as heads of the community in the fourth century.[54] There were indeed shopkeepers and craftsmen among the Samaritans. Di Segni has recently published an inscription from Mount Gerizim of a Samaritan from Caesarea named Zosimus, the thriving keeper of a cookshop, who made a pilgrimage to the Holy Mountain to offer three solidi on behalf of his sister.[55] As in the case of Caesarea's Jews, there is no evidence of Samaritans in Caesarea's *boulē* or in municipal posts like *ekdikos* and *patēr tēs poleōs*, but they did enter imperial service in large numbers. The Talmud of Palestine records that the *taxis*, or office, of the civil governor at Caesarea about 300 C.E. consisted mostly of Samaritans.[56] One Samaritan, Faustinus, a native of Palestine, perhaps advanced to the proconsulship at Caesarea after 536, but he had embraced Christianity.[57] Conversion or assimilation to the dominant religion and community was apparently easier for Samaritans than for Jews. R. Abbahu, whom we remember died in 309, had treated them as gentiles,[58] and from a different perspective Procopius affirms that any in the city who had good sense and regard for propriety converted to Christianity when

---

[54] *Samaritan Chronicle* 9.15, ed. J. M. Cohen, *A Samaritan Chronicle, A Source-Critical Analysis of the Life and Times of the Great Samaritan Reformer, Baba Rabbah* (SPB 30: Leiden: Brill, 1981), 21 (text) and 74 (translation); cf. Levine, *Roman Rule*, 228, n. 22.

[55] L. Di Segni, "The Church of Mary Theotokos on Mount Gerizim: The Inscriptions," in G. C. Bottini, L. Di Segni, and E. Alliata, eds., *Christian Archaeology in the Holy Land* (Studium Biblicum Franciscanum 36: Jerusalem: Franciscan Printing Press, 1990), 347–48.

[56] *y. ʿAbod. Zar.* 1:2 (39c); Lieberman, "Martyrs," 405–9.

[57] Procopius *Hist. Arc.* 27.26–31, cf. J. R. Martindale, *The Prosopography of the Later Roman Empire, Vol. 3: A.D. 527–631* (Cambridge: Cambridge University Press, 1992), 478–79, s.v. "Faustinus."

[58] *y. ʿAbod. Zar.* 5:44 (44d); *b. Ḥul.* 6a; cf. Liebermann, "Martyrs," 402–9; Levine, *Roman Rule*, 109–12.

pressured by imperial legislation.[59] There must have been Samaritan synagogues within the city. From them may have come the "God is one" inscriptions found at the site, e.g., *heis theos boēthi Marinō,* "God is one, let him help Marinos." Leah Di Segni has demonstrated that the use of this formula is in Palestine most commonly associated with Samaritans.[60] If so, they surely represent an assertion of individual and group identity.

But the weight of the Samaritan community lay in Caesarea's countryside. If indeed nearly half of Caesarea's total estimated population of 75,000 were Samaritans, we should locate most of the 35,000 or so in the towns, villages, hamlets, and isolated farms of the territory and not more than a few thousand within the city. A man as prominent as Faustinus, for example, must have owned land, but the great majority were peasant farmers who tilled the land of Christian proprietors. That is the point of Procopius' lament that when the Samaritan rebellion of 529–30 had been crushed "the best land in the world," the fields of his native Caesarea, "was denuded of its farmers."[61] Here the historian clearly wrote from the perspective of the urbanized Christian landholding class from which he emerged. Rabbinic sources confirm a strong Samaritan presence in a number of towns and villages that ought to be situated in Caesarea's territory, including Burgatha south along the coast, Narbatta to the east, and Kefar Shuni or Maioumas to the northeast, in all of which there were also Jews.[62] It is possible that the territory of Caesarea extended as far eastward as Kefar ʿAra, where a burial cave was excavated in 1962–63 that must have been used mainly or exclusively by Samaritans.[63] It contained the well known Samaritan lamps. These are generally mold-made lamps of the third–fifth centuries with a

---

[59] Above, n. 18.

[60] *Inscr.* 138–40, cf. L. Di Segni, "Εἷς θεός in Palestinian Inscriptions," *SCI* 13 (1994), 94–115.

[61] Procopius *Hist. Arc.* 11.29.

[62] Levine, *Roman Rule,* 107–8.

[63] V. Sussman, "A Burial Cave at Kefar ʿAra," *ʿAtiqot* 11 (1976), 92–101.

round body and a wide, short nozzle, decorated with a typical ladder design and sometimes a menorah on the nozzle.[64] When molded the discus was left closed, perhaps to guarantee ritual purity, and one broke through it to fill the reservoir with oil. A lamp of this type found within Caesarea with an inscription on the in Samaritan script quoting Deuteronomy 33:26: $^{)}$ên kā-$^{)}$ēl yĕšurûn, "There is none like the God of Jeshurun."[65] This is surely a marker or assertion of personal identity, like the substantial and growing group of Samaritan amulets and rings that have come to light in Caesarea, its territory, and other places in Israel's coastal plain.[66]

Like the Jews, Samaritans had wealthy and influential community leaders who could represent their interests before the governors or other powerbrokers, and even more than the Jews they had the numbers and toughness to assert themselves when violence was required. We must remember that these were mainly a rural, laboring population that developed powerful physiques and the ability to use not only hoes and mattocks but military weapons. We hear of Samaritan *banditti* plaguing Christian pilgrims,[67] and when the monophysite monks of Palestine rebelled against the Empire following the Council of Chalcedon (451), the emperor Marcian had both "Roman" and "Samaritan" troops at his disposal, who savaged and cut down the monks.[68] Obviously, the state

---

[64]   V. Sussman, "Samaritan Lamps of the Third-Fourth Centuries A.D.," *IEJ* 28 (1978), 238–50; also *eadem*, "Caesarea Illuminated by Its Lamps," *Caesarea Retrospective*, 354–56.

[65]   I. Ben-Zvi, "A Lamp with a Samaritan Inscription," *IEJ* 11 (1961), 139–42.

[66]   A. Hamburger, "A Greco-Samaritan Amulet from Caesarea," *IEJ* 9 (1959), 435; R. Reich, "Two Samaritan Rings from Gelilot (El-Jalil), near Herzliyya," ^{c}*Atiqot* 25 (1994), 135–38.

[67]   *Itinerarium Antonii*, ed. Geyer, *CSEL* 39, 164; John Moschus *Pratum Spirituale* 165, *PG* 87.3, 3032.

[68]   [Zacharias Rhetor] 3.5, trans. Brooks, *CSCO*, series 3, vol. 5, 109, reporting that Dorotheus, the local commander, *Et Romanis ac Samaritanis mandavit, eosque feriebant et occidabant ....*

would tamper with the integrity of this ethnic community at its extreme peril.

But this appears to be just what the state did. The Samaritan rebellions of the fifth and sixth centuries are a well-known story, analyzed from various perspectives by Michael Avi-Yonah, by the Marxist scholar Sabine Winkler, by myself, and more recently by Leah Di Segni.[69] The pattern of violence established itself in 484, according to Procopius of Caesarea, at Neapolis in Samaria.[70] A Samaritan gang attacked Christians at worship there, cut off the fingers from the bishop's hand, and insulted the eucharist. John Malalas makes this out not as rioting or random violence but as open rebellion. According to him, the Samaritans selected a "brigand chief" (*lēstarkhos*) named Justasas and "crowned him" (*estepsan*). Justasas then marched with his Samaritan followers from the highlands of Samaria to the coastal plain and seized Caesarea, where he burned the Church of St. Procopius and held chariot races in the hippodrome. With assistance from local police, the *dux Palaestinae* recovered Caesarea, captured and executed Justasas, and dispatched his severed head "with the diadem" (*meta tou diadēmatos*) to the emperor Zeno. Zeno punished the rebels by depriving them of Mount Gerizim, ordering their synagogue there destroyed, and consecrating a church to the Theotokos in its place. Malalas adds that he issued a law excluding Samaritans from imperial service and confiscating the estates of wealthy Samaritans.[71]

---

[69] M. Avi-Yonah, "The Samaritan Revolts Against the Byzantine Empire" [Hebrew], *EI* 4 (1956), 127–32; S. Winkler, "Die Samariter in den Jahren 529/30," *Klio* 43–45 (1965), 434–57; K. G. Holum, "Caesarea and the Samaritans," in R. L. Hohlfelder, ed., *City, Town and Countryside in the Early Byzantine Era* (East European Monographs 120: Boulder and New York: Columbia University Press, 1982), 65–73; L. Di Segni, "Metropolis and Provincia in Byzantine Palestine," *Caesarea Retrospective*, 577–79, 586, and the contribution of Di Segni in this volume.

[70] Procopius *Aed.* 5.7.5–9.

[71] John Malalas *Chronographia* 15, ed. L. Dindorf (*CSHB* 13: Bonn, 1831), 382–83.

In my article, published more than a decade ago, I argued that this was rebellion and usurpation in the classical sense, a view clinched for me by report that Justasas, crowned with the diadem in the manner of a Roman emperor, then conducted races in the hippodrome, seat of the imperial governor. Very recently, Leah Di Segni has argued that this was not a rebellion but "a riot, or a series of riots," as Procopius indicates, while much of the Malalas account is just a doublet of the real rebellion of 529/30.[72] If there was a pogrom it was "unpremeditated" and came from "the excitement of the races." In my view, though, the events of ca. 484, as Malalas describes them, do not correspond in particulars with those of 529/30 (below), and there is thus no good reason to reject his plausible account. At any rate, if "rioters" had the discipline to put forward a strong leader, their rioting might have begun to look very dangerous to the Roman state. However we sort out the sources, from the perspective of ethnicity this was an extreme case of community self-assertion.

In the next generation, it appears to me, the episode was repeated. In 527 the emperor Justinian, acting in the spirit of Pulcheria and her brother, issued several edicts confirming various disabilities of Samaritans and Jews and forbidding them in addition to possess real estate. In 529 an edict against the Samaritans alone ordered destruction of their synagogues.[73] Enforcement of this legislation, according to Procopius, was the occasion of the second rebellion that broke out in 529.[74] Samaritans rose again in Neapolis, seized back Gerizim, and once again "crowned" a "brigand chief," this one named Julian. Once again the Samaritan leader held chariot races in the hippodrome, but this time in the hippodrome of Neapolis itself.[75] Once again the *dux Palaestinae* was

---

[72]   See Di Segni, "Metropolis and Provincia," *Caesarea Retrospective*, 586, n. 64, and in this volume.

[73]   *Cod. Iust.* 1.5.12–14, 17.

[74]   Procopius *Hist. Arc.* 11.24.

[75]   John Malalas *Chronographia* 15, *CSHB*, 446.

needed to suppress the rebellion, and this time assistance came not only from other Roman generals but from the federate Ghassanid Arabs under their phylarch Arethas. Once again the victors executed the Samaritan leader and dispatched his severed head to Constantinople "with its diadem." This time, however, a contemporary and local source, Cyril of Scythopolis, records concisely what occurred: "Raising a tyranny, the Samaritans crowned for themselves (*estepsan*) a certain Julian, a man of their own ethnicity (*synethnon autōn*), as *basileus*."[76] Basileus in this author normally means "sovereign" or "emperor," and to "raise a tyranny" (*tyrannēsantes*) was to challenge the legitimate emperor's rule. Thus the state's response was ferocious, and Samaritan casualties were extremely heavy. Malalas reports 20,000 dead, Procopius 100,000. Malalas claims that 50,000 fled to the Persians and that the Arab phylarch received 20,000 enslaved Samaritans, young men and women, as a reward, to be sold abroad in the Persian Empire.[77]

The third "revolt" in 555 does appear to have been just a riot. Presumably the Samaritans no longer represented a major military threat. Together with the Jews, they rose against Caesarea and burned its churches—by which, of course, the Christian power structure asserted its superiority over the ethnic groups. When the provincial governor Stephanus resisted, they slaughtered him in his *praitōrion* and destroyed his property. The Emperor Justinian sent Amantius, the *comes Orientis*, to investigate the affair, and he sentenced the guilty, as appropriate, to confiscation, imprisonment, or beheading.[78]

---

[76] Cyr. Scyth. *V. Sab.* 70, ed. E. Schwartz (*Texte und Untersuchungen zur Geschichte der altchristlichen Literatur* 49 ii: Leipzig: J. C. Hinrichs Verlag, 1939), 172.

[77] Procopius *Hist. Arc.* 11.24–30, *Aed.* 5.7.17; John Malalas *Chronographia* 15, *CSHB*, 445–47; Choricius of Gaza *Laus Arati et Stephani* 1019, *Laus Summi* 11–15, ed. R. Foerster and E. Richtsteig (Leipzig: Teubner, 1929), 51–54, 72–73; Cyril of Scythopolis *V. Sab.* 70, ed. Schwartz, 171–74.

[78] John Malalas *Chronographia* 15, *CSHB*, 487–88; Theophanes *Chronographia* a. M. 6048, ed. C. de Boor (Leipzig: Teubner, 1883), 1, 230.

Adopting the perspective of personal and group identity, we can promote current debate on the fate of the ancient city. In the case of Caesarea, it was once accepted doctrine that the Persian and Muslim conquests in the seventh century caused enough physical destruction to bring the ancient city to an end, but this view is no longer tenable.[79] Neither literary nor archaeological evidence for this destruction appears to exist, and other explanations are required for the apparent significant drop in population and the abandonment of urban space. The plague pandemic that first struck the coastal cities of Palestine in 541 and 542 might be adduced as an explanation, but specific evidence does not exist about the number of plague deaths at Caesarea or the economic and social results.[80] What is clear to me from the evidence discussed here is the force of Procopius' lament that "now the most beautiful land in the whole world is bereft of farmers."[81] What we know of the demography confirms how large a disaster the fifth- and sixth-century rebellions and riots were for the city of Caesarea. The damage is compounded if, as seems likely, the Jews largely shared the Samaritans' fate.[82] Physical annihilation and deporting of restive groups were only part of the prob-

---

[79]   K. G. Holum, "Archeological Evidence for the Fall of Byzantine Caesarea," *BASOR* 286 (1992), 73–85.

[80]   P. Allen, "The Justinianic Plague," *Byzantion* 49 (1979), 5–20; and especially L. I. Conrad, "The Plague in the Early Medieval Near East" (Ph.D. dissertation, Princeton University, 1981), 83–119, also 357–414, 474–82 for the plague's impact on cities, and more recently *idem*, "Die Pest und ihr soziales Umfeld im Nahen Osten des frühen Mittelalters," *Der Islam* 73 (1996), 81–112.

[81]   Archaeological evidence may confirm the destruction of Samaritan life in numerous villages and farms of the northern Sharon Plain and other regions of Samaritan settlement in the later fifth and early sixth centuries. See S. Dar, "Additional Archaeological Evidence of the Samaritan Rebellions in the Byzantine Period," *New Samaritan Studies*, A. D. Crown and L. Davey, eds. (Studies in Judaica 5: Sidney: Mandelbaum Trust and the University of Sidney, 1995), 157–68. Unfortunately, the evidence presented so far is imprecisely dated and of questionable relevance.

[82]   Jewish involvement with the Samaritans is specifically attested only in the rioting of 555.

lem. As we have seen, the Samaritans, and likely the Jews, forfeited synagogues, part of their means of community self-assertion. Surviving Jews
and Samaritans lacked the security and communal self-confidence to
flourish and contribute as shopkeepers and craftsmen to the city's prosperity. Above all, the Christian landowners who formed Caesarea's
bouleutic class and were the upholders of urban life forfeited much of
their economic well-being. The embedded ethnic communities that
account for much of Caesarea's economic upswing in the third and
fourth centuries, by the sixth and early seventh were alienated and uprooted.

In 640 or 641, according to Islamic tradition, a Jew named Joseph,
another member of Caesarea's ethnic Jewish community who carried a
biblical name, led a party of Arabs, after seven years of unsuccessful
siege, into the city. The route he knew and they did not was a concealed
water channel in which the water reached a man's waist—surely the
low-level aqueduct, surviving in good condition, that penetrates the
Byzantine fortifications on the city's northern quarter.[83] If my interpretation is correct, and the story is not a legend, Joseph was more than a
symbol.[84] He was the very last Jew of Roman Caesarea to assert his ethnic
identity.

---

[83] al-Balādhurī *Futuḥ al-buldān* 141–42, translated in P. Hitti, *The Origins of the
Islamic State* (Columbia University Studies in History, Economics and Public Law
68: New York: Columbia University Press, 1916), 217–18; cf. Olami and Peleg,
"Water Supply System," 135–37.

[84] On the symbolism of numerical data in this passage, cf. L. I. Conrad, "The
Conquest of Arwad: A Source-Critical Study in the Historiography of the Early
Medieval Near East," in A. Cameron, L. I. Conrad, eds., *The Byzantine and Early
Islamic Near East, vol. 1: Problems in the Literary Source Material* (Princeton: The
Darwin Press, Inc., 1992), 356–58.

Some Reflections on the Archaeological Finds from the Domestic Quarter on the Acropolis of Sepphoris

Leonard V. Rutgers

University of Utrecht

THE AREA COMMONLY REFERRED TO as "Lower Galilee" has long attracted the attention of students of rabbinic literature and New Testament scholars alike. It is all the more paradoxical to note, therefore, that even today we know relatively little about the archaeology of this region during the Roman period. The entry "Galilee" in the *New Encyclopedia of Archaeological Excavations in the Holy Land* is symptomatic of the general absence of reliable information. After reviewing recent archaeological discoveries in Upper Galilee, M. Aviam, the author of this entry, is forced to limit his discussion of the archaeology of Lower Galilee largely to an analysis of early Christian material remains. Lacking the necessary excavation reports, Aviam cannot but draw a sketchy picture of what went on in Lower Galilee before the late antique period, that is, during a period in which the area was becoming the heartland of rabbinic Judaism, at a time that it also witnessed the birth and rise of Christianity.[1]

Given the lacunose character of our knowledge on these matters, it should hardly come as a surprise to note that the excavations in Sepphoris—an important administrative center in the very heart of Lower Galilee—have already attracted a great deal of attention. New Testament scholars, foremost among them R. Batey and, more importantly, R. Horsley, have been particularly eager to come to grips with these new

---

[1] Mordechai Aviam, "Galilee. The Hellenistic to Byzantine Periods," *NEAEHL*, 453–58.

discoveries.[2] The challenge posed by the archaeological discoveries at Sepphoris to students of Jewish history has not gone unnoticed either, especially because the excavated remains promise to throw an entirely new light on issues that have recently become important in this particular field of study. Such issues include the question of the religious and cultural makeup of the population in the Galilee during the Hellenistic, Roman, and Byzantine periods, the development of rabbinic Judaism within the context of Jewish and non-Jewish contemporary society, and, more generally speaking, the question of how Roman-period Judaism is to be defined.[3]

In this essay I would like to address two questions that are as straight-forward as they are difficult to answer. (1) Can the architectural remains and artifacts discovered in the domestic quarter of Sepphoris be used to identify its inhabitants, and if so, how? (2) What presuppositions under-lie the work of scholars who have written about these materials thus far? My point of departure is the archaeological materials discovered in a domestic complex known to the excavators as area 84.1, which is located on top of the acropolis of Sepphoris, not far from the citadel.

At first sight, such an approach might seem methodologically objec-tionable. After all, one may justifiably wonder whether archaeological materials originating from one large house alone provide us with suffi-

---

[2]   Richard A. Batey, *Jesus and the Forgotten City: New Light on Sepphoris and the Urban World of Jesus* (Grand Rapids: Baker Book House, 1991); Richard A. Horsley, *Galilee: History, People, Politics* (Valley Forge: Trinity Press International, 1995). On Batey, see Stuart S. Miller, "Sepphoris, the Well Remembered City," *BA* 55 (1992), 74–83; Eric M. Meyers, "The Challenge of Hellenism for Early Judaism and Christianity," *BA* 55 (1992), 84–91; and several papers in the *Society of Biblical Literature 1994 Seminar Papers* (Atlanta: Scholars Press, 1994).

[3]   The more significant studies include, in addition to Horsely, *Galilee*, A. Oppenheimer, *The 'Am Ha-aretz* (Leiden: Brill, 1977); Sean Freyne, *Galilee from Alexander the Great to Hadrian, 323 B.C.E. to 135 C.E.* (Wilmington: Glazier, 1980); M. Goodman, *State and Society in Roman Galilee, A.D. 132–212* (Towota: Rowman and Allanheld, 1983) and the essays collected in Lee I. Levine, ed., *The Galilee in Late Antiquity* (New York and Jerusalem: Jewish Theological Seminary, 1992).

cient evidence to reach conclusions of a more general nature. There are two good reasons why I have nevertheless opted for the approach just indicated. First, a comparison of the finds from area 84.1 with those discovered in the 1930s by a team from the University of Michigan who worked in the same general area suggest that, in terms of architectural appearance and material culture, the domestic complex of 84.1 cannot be considered an isolated example. Rather, it may represent a typical house at this part of the site.[4] Second, under the house, in the huge cisterns that were used as dumps at a later stage in the history of this domestic unit, an abundance of artifacts has been preserved. In fact, such enormous amounts of archaeological material have survived there that they represent a true cross-section of everything that was to be had in terms of material culture in the Galilee during the middle and late Roman period, that is, during the period from 135 to 363 C.E.[5]

Area 84.1: A Short Description of the Archaeological Remains

The building history of the area known as 84.1 can be briefly reconstructed as follows.[6] In the early Roman period, a house consisting of several rooms arranged around a courtyard, was constructed along a road leading up to the acropolis. Although little stratigraphic evidence testifying to this early period survives, the house, which was in constant use until its destruction by an earthquake in 363 C.E., and which probably consisted of two stories, was provided with cisterns and *miqwā'ôt* or ritual baths at this time. The fragmentary nature of the artifacts discov-

---

[4] Leroy Waterman, *Preliminary Report on the University of Michigan Excavations at Sepphoris, Palestine, in 1931* (Ann Arbor: University of Michigan, 1937), esp. 31–34; James F. Strange, "Six Campaigns at Sepphoris: The University of South Florida Excavations, 1983–1989," in Levine, *Galilee,* 339–55.

[5] The periodization used is based on Dennis E. Groh, "Jews and Christians in Late Roman Palestine. Towards a New Chronology," *BA* 51 (1988), 80–96.

[6] For preliminary reports on area 84.1, see "Notes and News" in *IEJ* 35 (1985), 296; 37 (1987), 275–76; 40 (1990), 219–20; 44 (1994), 247; 45 (1995), 69–71 (general plan and reconstruction).

ered in them indicates that during the middle Roman period most of these cisterns fell into disuse and were turned into dumps. This happened after an enormous water reservoir to the southeast of the town had been carved out of the rock and carefully plastered. The *miqwā'ôt* suffered a similar fate, for they too went out of use and were filled up during the middle and later Roman periods. Although there is evidence for activity in this part of the site during the Byzantine period, perhaps in the form of a glass-producing workshop, the house does not seem to have been reoccupied in its entirety in the period following the earthquake of 363 C.E.

Insofar as the artifacts excavated in this complex are concerned, it is possible to discern a direct relationship between the state of preservation and the places from which individual artifacts were recovered. In the cisterns, conditions for preservation were clearly superior to those above ground. It is in these cisterns that much of the evidence survives that permits us to start theorizing about the artistic, religious, and economic makeup of Lower Galilee in relation to the rest of Roman Palestine.

Area 84.1 in Light of Archaeological Remains Discovered in Other Parts of Roman Palestine

It is well known that only in the case of Upper Galilee have attempts been made to fit the archaeological materials discovered there into a larger geographical and historical context. As a result of the work of Meyers in particular, we now know, among other things, that Upper Galilee was an area that was distinctively Jewish. We also know, however, that the economic focus of the villages there was mainly on the Phoenician coast and not—as one would perhaps expect—on nearby areas such as Lower Galilee or the Golan, where the density of Jewish settlement was considerably higher.[7] Although some of Meyers's sug-

---

[7]   Eric M. Meyers, "Galilean Regionalism as a Factor in Historical Reconstruction," *BASOR* 221 (1976), 93–101; *idem,* "The Cultural Setting of the Galilee: The

gestions have been criticized recently, most of these criticisms turn out not to be valid.[8] In my view, the picture as Meyers originally drew it still holds.

When we now turn to Lower Galilee, we encounter a situation that is radically different. When we look at both the architecture of the house of area 84.1 in Sepphoris and at some of the artifacts discovered in it, we cannot but notice that this house bears an unmistakable resemblance to some of the pre-70 mansions discovered by N. Avigad during his excavations in the Upper City of Jerusalem.[9] Perhaps most striking is the presence of *miqwāʾôt*, which are arranged very similarly to the ones discovered in Jerusalem, in the entrance areas of the house, among other places.

It is true that with their lavishly decorated walls and carefully arranged floors the houses in Jerusalem make, at first sight, a much more opulent impression than do their Sepphorean counterparts. Such an impression, however, is misleading. In various rooms that together make up the house discovered in area 84.1, and also in some of the cisterns, fragments of wall painting were discovered that were decorated with geometrical designs. Evidence of floral designs has also been preserved. What is important about these fragments of wall paintings, however, is that, more often than not, they were found together with fragments of marble revetment plaques as well as fragments of molded stucco. In one case, a fragment of a Corinthian capital was found in association with the wall painting fragments. Taken together, such

---

Case of Regionalism and Early Judaism," *ANRW* 2.19.1 (1979), 686–702; *idem*, "Byzantine Towns of the Galilee," in Robert L. Hohlfelder, ed., *City, Town and Countryside in the Early Byzantine Era* (Boulder: East European Monographs, 120, 1982), 115–29; *idem*, "Galilean Regionalism: A Reappraisal," in William S. Green, *Approaches to Ancient Judaism* (*BJS* 32: Atlanta: Scholars Press, 1985), 115–31.

[8] Ruth Vale, "Literary Sources in Archaeological Description: The Case of Galilee, Galilees and Galileans," *JSJ* 18 (1987), 209–26, with graphs that are not reliable.

[9] N. Avigad, *Discovering Jerusalem* (Jerusalem: Shikmona, 1980), 81–82.

remains suggest that more sophisticated forms of domestic architecture were not confined to Jerusalem alone.

Several other finds further complement this picture. For example, white tesserae have been found in various rooms. These finds are in too fragmentary a state to permit reconstruction of how the tessellated floors of our Sepphorean house would have originally looked. Yet the presence of these small mosaic cubes in and by itself suggests that in their domestic architecture the inhabitants of Sepphoris—or at least some of them—did not really distinguish themselves from well-to-do Jerusalemites, who adapted, in their domestic architecture, to trends generally characteristic of the Hellenistic Near East.

That the commonalities between Jerusalemite and Sepphorean material culture were considerable also follows, finally, from the presence of white stone vessels, most of which have been preserved in a rather fragmentary state. Forming a distinctive class of artifacts that we have come to understand better only recently as a result of the excavations in Jerusalem, these vessels were discovered in Sepphoris in considerable quantities, mainly in the cisterns and virtually always in early and middle Roman layers. Thus, chronologically, the Sepphorean examples conform to what is generally known about these vessels, namely that they became popular in the first century and that they went out of use again in the course of the second century C.E. The stone vessels are probably "imported" items insofar as they derive from the Jerusalem area, where they might have originated in quarries such as the Hizma cave to the north of the city.[10]

---

[10]   The most complete survey of these vessels may be found in Roland Deines, *Jüdische Steingefäße und pharisäische Frommigkeit: Ein archäologisch-historischer Beitrag zum Verständnis von Joh 2,6 und der jüdischen Reinheitshalacha zur Zeit Jesu* (WUNT 2. Reihe, 52: Tübingen: J. C. B. Mohr, 1993). Also important is Jane M. Cahil, "Chalk Vessel Assemblages of the Persian/Hellenistic and Early Roman Periods," in Alon de Groot and Donald T. Ariel, eds., *Excavations at the City of David 1978–1985 Directed by Yigal Shiloh*. Vol. III. *Stratigraphical, Environmental, and Other Reports*. Qedem 33 (Jerusalem: Ahva Press, 1992), 190–272. In a recent article, R. Deines and M. Hengel, "E.P. Sanders' 'Common Judaism', Jesus, and the

Given such discoveries, one should be careful not to overestimate the Jerusalem connection. After all, most of the artifacts used in Seppho-ris on a daily basis were produced locally. This follows from the fact that, for example, the majority of the pottery uncovered in the domestic quarter came from Kefar Hananiah and Shikhin.[11]

From the coins, it can be observed that there is little or no evidence for a direct connection with Tyre, as was the case in Upper Galilee. Thus, although export patterns appear to have differed significantly from those documented for Upper Galilee, the Sepphoreans seem by and large to have made use of what was commonly available in Lower Galilee. This becomes particularly evident when we turn to Roman discus lamps, the lamp type found most frequently in our excavations. In fact, a preliminary comparison of the lamp profile at Sepphoris in area 84.1 with the one attested at Dor reveals striking similarities in terms of the iconographic repertoire evidenced at both sites.[12]

It should be obvious that such finds should not be taken to mean that the economic universe of Sepphoris was exclusively regional in its orientation for Sepphoris continued to be an urban center of some note well into late antiquity. In the late Roman period, from the fourth century onwards, we thus find evidence for imports from outside the

---

Pharisees," *JTS* 46 (1995), 1–70, interpret these vessels as an example of a typical Pharisaic form of piety. This is disputable, but for lack of space I cannot deal with this issue here.

[11]   See, in general, David Adan-Bayewitz, *Common Pottery in Roman Galilee. A Study of Local Trade* (Ramat Gan: Bar-Ilan University Press, 1993); James F. Strange, "Excavations at Sepphoris: The Location and Identification of Shikhin. Part II," *IEJ* 45 (1995), 171–87.

[12]   E. Stern, *Dor: Ruler of the Seas* (Jerusalem: Israel Exploration Society, 1994), 304–7, figs. 211–15, plate VIII. Note that we know hardly anything about lamp production in Roman Palestine; see the brief remarks of David Adan-Bayewitz, "A Lamp Mould From Sepphoris and the Location of Workshops for Lamp and Common Pottery Manufacture in Northern Palestine," in *The Roman and Byzantine Near East: Some Recent Archaeological Research* (*Journal of Roman Archaeology Supplementary Series* No. 14: Ann Arbor, 1995), 177–81.

country. Such imports include several types of late Roman wares and mortaria. Although on the acropolis of Sepphoris terra sigillata wares do not occur in the same abundant numbers as at other Galilean sites such as Capernaum,[13] their presence nevertheless suggests that in this respect, Sepphoris participated in a trend that is well attested through-out the Galilee in late antiquity, namely a sizeable increase in foreign trade starting in the fourth century C.E.[14] Some of the mosaics found in Sepphoris, such as the famous Dionysus mosaic, have to be understood in a similar light. These mosaics find their closest stylistic parallels in the mosaics preserved in the archaeological museums of Shahba (ancient Philippopolis) and Suweida, both in the Syrian Hauran. This likewise indicates that in terms of artistic production Sepphoris participated in a material culture that linked it to the larger world of late antiquity.

The archaeological remains discussed thus far permit us to draw the following preliminary conclusion. During the Roman period, people living on the acropolis of Sepphoris were the inhabitants of a Roman provincial town whose cultural horizon was far wider than the orienta-tion of the town's economy would at first sight suggest, given that the economy appears to have been based primarily on the area directly surrounding it. While the inhabitants of Sepphoris obviously had ties with Jerusalem, such contacts were clearly not the only supra-regional ones they developed. In fact, in Late Antiquity, Sepphoris's commercial

---

[13] Stanislao Loffreda, *Cafarnao*. II. *La ceramica* (SBF Collectio Maior 19: Jerusalem: Franciscan Printing Press, 1974). Note that not all the terra sigillata pottery from Italian excavations in Capernaum has been published yet. See also M. Peleg, "Domestic Pottery," in Vassilios Tzaferis, *Excavations at Capernaum Vol. 1, 1978–1982* (Winona Lake: Eisenbrauns, 1989), 31–32.

[14] Hans-Peter Kühnen, "Kirche, Landwirtschaft und Flüchtlingssilber. Zur wirtschaftlichen Entwicklung Palästinas in der Spätantike," *ZDPV* 110 (1994), 36–50, esp. 42–44. For the provenance of mortaria, see now Jeffrey A. Blakeley *et al.*, "Roman Mortaria and Basins from a Sequence at Caesarea: Fabrics and Sources," in Robert L. Vann, ed., *Caesarea Papers. Straton's Tower, Herod's Harbour, and Roman and Byzantine Caesarea* (*Journal of Roman Archaeology Supplementary Series* No. 5: Ann Arbor, 1992), 194–213.

network went far beyond the borders of the Galilee, and even of Palestine. Thus, for Sepphoreans there was nothing unusual about trading with their non-Jewish neighbors in general, and with those to the north and the northeast in particular.

Interpreting the Evidence from Area 84.1

One of the reasons that it is so difficult to interpret the data from Sepphoris is that our knowledge of what Jewish, pagan, and early Christian daily life in the area looked like depends to a large extent on literary sources that are often very hard to interpret in ways that are historically convincing or methodologically defensible.[15] A second reason that interpretation of the archaeological finds from Sepphoris is such a difficult undertaking is that our knowledge of what happened in the Galilee during the Persian and Hellenistic periods is all too limited—a statement that holds true especially where the archaeology of the area is concerned. Thus, it is hard to measure the impact of the conquest of this area by the Maccabees, or to determine the development of customs and beliefs that have their origins in Israelite times.[16] What we do know is that during the Roman period the rural population of the Galilee can no longer be considered to have consisted solely of ʿammê hā-ʾāreṣ, or country bumpkins, as an earlier generation of scholars believed. The reason for this is that the ʿammê hā-ʾāreṣ are largely an invention of the redactors of the various types of rabbinic literature, people whose ideological agenda cannot directly be equated with the realities of daily life in later Roman Palestine.[17] Yet such an otherwise important insight

---

[15]   For a recent analysis of the problem, insofar as rabbinic literature is concerned, see H. Lapin, *Early Rabbinic Civil Law and the Social History of Roman Galilee: A Study of Mishnah Tractate Babaʾ Meṣiʿaʾ* (*BJS* 307: Atlanta: Scholars Press, 1995).

[16]   S. Schwartz, "The 'Judaism' of Samaria and Galilee in Josephus's Version of the Letter of the Letter of Demetrius I to Jonathan (*Antiquities* 13.48–57)," *HTR* 82 (1989), 377–91; Horsley, *Galilee*, 19–20.

[17]   Oppenheimer, *'Am Ha-aretz*; Lawrence H. Schiffman, "Was There a Galilean Halakhah," in Levine, *Galilee*, 143–56.

hardly helps us to understand which factors did in fact characterize Jewish life in the Galilee in late Hellenistic and early Roman times.

Criticizing the work of earlier scholars such as Sean Freyne, Richard Horsley has recently suggested that in the pre-70 period, contacts between Galilee and Judaea, or rather between Galilee and the Temple in Jerusalem, were not very intense.[18] Horsley also identifies the inhabitants of our house in Sepphoris as Judaeans.[19] Although he never says why he believes this to be the case, one may conjecture that Horsley's conclusion is based on the presence of ritual baths and on the discovery of the stone vessels referred to earlier. Are Horsley's suggestions convincing?

Horsley's line of reasoning is implicitly based on the assumption that Jewish life in the Galilee was so fundamentally different from that in Jerusalem that Galilean Jews *could* not have produced domestic units of the kind that we find in Sepphoris. To put it differently, Horsley has reached this conclusion because he reads the archaeological finds in light of the (sparse) literary remains. One may wonder, however, whether there are reasons justifying such an approach. Should one not try to evaluate the archaeological evidence first, before one attempts to fit it into a picture that is primarily based on an analysis of (literary) sources —sources that can hardly be said to provide us with an ideologically neutral, let alone "objective," access to the past?

Similarly, Horsley's quantitative approach, which stresses that few Galileans can be shown to have actually gone to the Temple in Jerusalem during the three major holidays when such pilgrimages were required, leads to interesting observations. Ultimately, however, this approach is not very satisfying, for it fails to address the question of how the contacts between the Galilee and the Jerusalem Temple originated in the first place, and it also prevents one from exploring the concomitant question of what the nature of these contacts was.

---

[18]   Horsley, *Galilee*, 144–47.

[19]   Horsley, *Galilee*, 166.

Taking such considerations into account, it is possible to propose a reconstruction that differs in significant respects from the one suggested by Horsley. Rather than interpreting the evidence from Sepphoris as an example of Jerusalemite piety imposed on the local population, the evidence allows us to suppose that Galilean Jewry evolved not in complete isolation, but rather in ways that were comparable to the manner in which Judaism took shape in Judaea. The *miqwāʾôt* are a case in point. Excavations in the village of Qedumim have confirmed what was already known on the basis of rabbinic literature, namely that even groups such as the Samaritans—that is, groups that had almost entirely severed their ties from Judaism—nevertheless developed the notion of ritual immersion on the basis of biblical texts that do not properly speak of such immersions at all.[20] Would it not make sense, therefore, to suppose that the Jewish population of the Galilee was, like their co-religionists in Judaea and their Samaritan neighbors, capable of developing such a notion, rather than supposing that the ritual baths in Sepphoris are evidence of successful attempts to "colonize" on the part of the Jerusalem establishment?

Along similar lines, rabbinic literature and inscriptions refer repeatedly to priestly families in the Galilee that were resident in sizeable numbers in Sepphoris as well as in the nearby Bet Natufa valley.[21] Even if one concedes that such traditions are later inventions that do not in any way reflect the relationship between the Galilee and Jerusalem during the pre-70 period, it is surely significant that Galileans did go to the Temple, apparently of their own will. Again, should we take the existence of such contacts merely as evidence of the political power the

---

[20]   Cf. *t. Miqw.* 6:1, according to which the ritual baths of the Samaritans are pure. For the excavated materials, see Y. Magen, "The Ritual Baths (Miqva'ot) at Qedumim and the Observance of Ritual Purity Among the Samaritans," in F. Manns and E. Alliata, eds., *Early Christianity in Context. Monuments and Documents* (SBF Collectio Maior 38: Jerusalem: Franciscan Printing Press, 1993), 181–92.

[21]   Lee I. Levine, *The Rabbinic Class of Roman Palestine in Late Antiquity* (Jerusalem and New York: Yad Izhak Ben-Zvi and Jewish Theological Seminary of America, 1989), 171.

Jerusalem establishment was able to exert, or should we not rather allow for a more informal type of relationship—a relationship based on a sense of Jewish communal feeling, national solidarity, and agreement on the importance of certain religious practices and beliefs?

Despite the strong similarities between the archaeological data in Jerusalem and area 84.1 in Sepphoris, I see, in short, no good reason to regard the archaeological materials from Sepphoris *a priori* as evidence for settlers from Judaea rather than as a manifestation of *Jewish* life in a *Galilean* town. In my view, the archaeological evidence from the domestic quarter in Sepphoris documents in the first place how similar Jewish daily life in the Galilee was to that in Jerusalem, that is, for some inhabitants of this town at least, during the early and middle Roman periods.

Unfortunately, such observations do not solve all our problems, primarily because they do not account for some of the other artifacts that were excavated in this supposedly Jewish house—artifacts that seem entirely out of place in such a house. To start with the late Roman period: as has been pointed out before, it was during this period that the *miqwā'ôt* went out of use and were filled up and turned into dumps. Although this conforms to what is known about the use of *miqwā'ôt* (or rather about the discontinuation of their use) in late Roman Palestine in general, no good explanations for this phenomenon have yet been put forward.[22] Should the "disappearance" of *miqwā'ôt* in Sepphoris be seen as evidence for a fundamental change in Jewish perceptions of purity? Or should the sealing up of *miqwā'ôt* on Sepphoris' acropolis be regarded as a reflection of a still more fundamental change, namely a takeover of our house by owners who were no longer Jewish?

---

[22]   In the same general area, *miqwā'ôt* go out of use, see, for example, Liora K. Horwitz *et al.*, "Subsistence and Environment on Mount Carmel in the Roman-Byzantine Periods: The Evidence from Kh. Sumaqa," *IEJ* 40 (1990), 292; Y. Hirschfeld and R. Birger-Calderon, "Early Roman Estates near Caesarea," *IEJ* 41 (1991), 88. See in general, R. Reich, *Miqwa'ot (Jewish Ritual Baths) in Eretz Israel in the Second Temple and the Mishnah and Talmud Periods* [Hebrew] (diss. Hebrew University, 1990).

No less puzzling in this respect is the fact that from this period onwards we find isolated evidence for the presence of pig bones (*sus scrofa*) at the site. Traditionally, the presence of such bones in Galilean settlements has been explained as an indicator for the rise of Christianity.[23] In light of what we know about Jewish food taboos—perhaps most graphically illustrated by Peter's vision in Jaffa as related in Acts 11:5–6—and considering the strikingly uniform archaeozoological profile of sites in the Land of Israel from the Bronze Age onwards, such a conclusion seems inevitable.[24] Is this really so?

In a passage in *Leviticus Rabba*, also preserved in the Jerusalem Talmud, reference is made to a butcher in Sepphoris who "caused Israel to eat the flesh of the *něbēlâ* and *těrēpâ*," that is of animals killed improperly (from a Jewish perspective) and of animals suffering from imperfections.[25] Such traditions suggest quite strongly that some Jews (for whatever reason) did not care excessively about the purity prescriptions of the rabbis. They also suggest that such Jews did not observe the purity rules that, from biblical times onward, had served as an essential element to set Israel apart from the nations. Put differently, pig bones alone cannot automatically be used to posit the presence of Christians in area 84.1. in Sepphoris, or, for that matter, anywhere else in Roman Galilee. Before reaching such a conclusion, one would have to account for Jews of the type just referred to. One would also have to make clear how such Jews are to be distinguished archaeologically from Christians.

The question of how to account for certain data and how to interpret these convincingly becomes even more problematic, however, when we turn from the late Roman to the early and middle Roman materials

---

[23] Horwitz *et al.* "Subsistence and Environment," 298. Eric M. Meyers *et al.*, "Sepphoris (Sippori) 1994," *IEJ* 45 (1995), 71 speak in reference to Sepphoris of "an ethnic reconfiguration."

[24] For a review of osteological remains from various sites in Israel, see the survey of Walter Houston, *Purity and Monotheism: Clean and Unclean Animals in Biblical Law* (*JSOT Supplement Series* 140: Sheffield: JSOT Press, 1993), 124–80.

[25] *Lev. Rab.* 5:6 (ed. Margaliot, 119); *y. Ter.* 8:5 (45c).

from Sepphoris. The iconography of some of the discus lamps, and especially those bearing erotic representations, has attracted much attention, and rightfully so. These lamps seem out of place in a house in which most of the other finds suggest that observation of Jewish law was the single most important element characterizing the existence of its inhabitants. Because of all the excitement generated by these finds, one is easily tempted not to take into consideration the following three important points.

First, according to my estimates, which are based on weight, discus lamps showing a figural decoration of some sort represent only 6.4% of the entire corpus of lamps from area 84.1.[26] Second, the majority of these decorated lamps comes from the cisterns, into which they had been dumped. This makes it rather difficult to say anything about their usage in the daily life of the household. And third, in other places, as, for example, in the Jewish Monteverde catacomb in Rome, Jews are known to have used lamps decorated with a wide variety of iconographic motifs, including themes that are undeniably of pagan derivation.[27] Such considerations bring us to the larger question of how all the different archaeological materials can be brought into a coherent whole.

Further Reflections

The interpretation of the archaeological evidence from Sepphoris depends in the first place on the manner in which we define the terms used to interpret this evidence. In this case, it depends on how we define Judaism in late antiquity. Scholars working on Jewish materials from the Diaspora in particular have started to speak about Judaisms in the plural. However, since most scholars using this expression generally do not define it by saying how one of their types of Judaism differs from the next, it is far from clear how speaking about Judaisms in the plural

---

[26] E.g., Horsley, *Galilee*, 104, who inappropriately speaks of "hundreds of discus lamps decorated with pagan symbols in Jewish residential areas."

[27] Leonard V. Rutgers, *The Jews in Late Ancient Rome. Evidence of Cultural Interaction in the Roman Diaspora* (Leiden: Brill, 1995), 85–88, with further references.

could be helpful or, more fundamentally, why such a typology should be appropriate at all. A more attractive option is perhaps available in the notion of "Common Judaism" as used by E. P. Sanders in his work on the different Jewish groups of first century Roman Palestine.[28] As we increasingly realize that the expression "rabbinic Judaism" is misleading, insofar as it denotes only a fairly small group of like-minded people (who quite often held widely diverging views on one and the same topic[29]), the expression "Common Judaism" may also be helpful when studying Jewish society during the late antique period.

Common Judaism can be defined as the Judaism of the majority of the population, that is, of people who observed the more basic elements of Jewish religious life such as the sabbath, circumcision, and so forth, but who may not have been familiar or even interested in the more complex details of biblical and rabbinic *halakhah*. In the particular case of Sepphoris this would mean that we can account for at least some of the data that at first sight seem inexplicable. For the inhabitants of area 84.1 purity was a major issue, but presumably they did not consider themselves less Jewish because they also availed themselves of oil lamps displaying an iconography that some rabbinic authorities would instantly have disapproved of.

Although it is beyond the scope of this essay to develop this notion any further, I would like to stress that the approach I am proposing here does not solve all problems, essentially because we find ourselves in a catch-22 situation. For example, did the butcher in Sepphoris who sold non-kosher meat or the person who dumped the pig bones in area 84.1 still consider themselves to be Jews? This, despite the fact that the rabbis did not think this to be the case, for they note, with a sense of satisfac-

---

[28]   E. P. Sanders, *Judaism: Practice and Belief, 63 B.C.E.–66 C.E.* (London and Philadelphia: SMC and Trinity Press International, 1992), 11–12 and *passim*.

[29]   E.g., David Weiss Halivni, *Midrash, Mishnah, and Gemara: The Jewish Predilection for Justified Law* (Cambridge, Mass.: Harvard University, 1986); C. Hezser, "Social Fragmentation, Plurality of Opinion, and Nonobservance of Halakhah: Rabbis and Community in Late Roman Palestine," *JSQ* 1 (1993–94), 234–51.

tion, that the butcher died prematurely when he fell off the roof. They actually might have, but the problem is that rabbinic literature cannot give us that information. The archaeological remains too, suggestive as they are, ultimately remain inconclusive in this respect.

That the notion of "Common Judaism" cannot solve our problem either may be clear, for the strength of this notion is also its main weakness: common Judaism usefully allows for the inclusion of people who would otherwise not be considered Jewish at all. Being all-inclusive, this notion fails to specify, however, how far people can go and still be considered Jews. Similarly, this notion is too unspecific in that it cannot accommodate the possibility of various groups' having different, but still exclusivist notions of what constitutes common Judaism.

Conclusion

Much of what has been written on the Galilee in general, and on Sepphoris in particular, is based on the assumption that as scholars we all essentially use the same definitions. In this essay I have tried to indicate that this might not always be the case. Phrases such as "Christianity brought a gradual change in the population, but the Jewish community remained strong"[30] are problematic as long as we have not clearly defined how, in daily life, Jews differed from pagans, or Christians, let alone from Jewish Christians. Confronted with the problem of having to interpret finds that do not fit into our analytical categories, we should start questioning some of the assumptions underlying our use of these categories. In addition, we need to state explicitly how much and what type of evidence is sufficient to reach far-reaching conclusions such as "Sepphoris remained predominantly Jewish throughout its existence," or "Jewish-Christianity was not a factor in Sepphoris."[31] Finally, I also

---

[30]   Ehud Netzer and Zeev Weiss, "New Evidence for Late-Roman and Byzantine Sepphoris," in *Roman and Byzantine Near East*, 164.

[31]   E.g., Ehud Netzer and Zeev Weiss, "Sepphoris (Sippori) 1991–1992," *IEJ* 43 (1993), 195 (Jewish); Stuart S. Miller, "The *Minim* of Sepphoris Reconsidered," *HTR* 86 (1993), 377–402 (Jewish Christianity).

believe that if we want to tackle some of the problems I have alluded to, we need to address these problems in a more comprehensive fashion than has been the case hitherto. Thus, the question of the pig bones in Sepphoris cannot be solved satisfactorily as long as we do not also address the larger question of why in the fourth century (if not earlier) concerns for ritual purity seem to change, as evidenced by both rabbinic literature *and* the archaeological record. Similarly, we also need to look at factors that affected the region as a whole, economically, politically, and culturally. One such factor that has hardly been dealt with is the presence of a sizeable Roman military force at Legio-Kfar Otnay.[32]

The importance of the archaeological materials discovered in Sepphoris by the different teams working at this site can hardly be over-estimated. Yet, if we do not pay attention to questions of methodology and theory while in the process of publishing these remains, our reconstructions will fail to convince anyone.

---

[32] Few scholars have paid attention to this issue, see Eric M. Meyers, "Aspects of Roman Sepphoris in the Light of Recent Archaeology," in F. Manns and E. Alliata, eds., *Early Christianity in Context*, 32–33. And see, in general, Ze'ev Safrai, *The Economy of Roman Palestine* (London: Routledge, 1994), 339–49.

THE FATE OF PAGAN CULT PLACES IN PALESTINE:
THE ARCHAEOLOGICAL EVIDENCE WITH EMPHASIS ON BET SHEAN

Yoram Tsafrir

The Hebrew University

A. The Fate of Pagan Cult Places

The major thrust of the Christianization of Palestine took place in the fourth century C.E.[1] Although we do not know the ratio between pagans, Jews, Samaritans, and Christians around the year 300, it seems reasonable to assume that the majority of the population was pagan at that time. There were no clear borders between the settlement areas of Jews, Samaritans, pagans and Christians, and there was some overlap between these religious elements as well as towns of mixed population. Still, we do know that, after the suppression of the Bar Kokhba revolt, Jewish settlements were concentrated mainly in Galilee and in the marginal areas of the Judaean hills, and the Samaritans inhabited the Samarian hills. Pagans lived in Judaea, the coastal plain, and Transjordan and in all the large cities (except perhaps the Jewish city of Tiberias).

At the end of the fourth century we find a different picture. The Christian triumph following the conquest of the East by Constantine

---

[1] For the settlements of ethnic and religious elements in Palestine, see M. Avi-Yonah, *The Land of Israel,* rev. ed. (Grand Rapids: Baker Book House, 1979); Y. Tsafrir, L. Di Segni, and J. Green, *Tabula Imperii Romani: Iudaea. Palaestina* (Jerusalem: Israel Academy, 1994). On the methodological problems, see recently, Y. Tsafrir, "Some Notes on the Settlements and Demography of Palestine in the Byzantine Period: The Archaeological Evidence," J. D. Seger, ed., *Retrieving the Past: Essays on Archaeological Research and Methodology in Honor of Gus W. Van Beek* (Winona Lake: Eisenbrauns, 1996), 269–83.

started a rapid process of Christianization. By around the year 400 the
Christians formed a majority in Palestine. From both texts and archaeological evidence we learn that many churches were first built in the
fourth century.[2] At the same time we note an increase in population and
the number and size of settlements—towns, villages and farms all over
the country. Jews and Samaritans resisted the Christian pressure and
rejected the process of Christianization, but with little success; Christianity gradually gained power at the expense of the Jews and the Samaritans. In the two maps of Jewish synagogues and of Christian churches
in western Palestine edited by L. Di Segni and the author,[3] we counted
archaeological remains of more than 390 churches in some 335 settlements and about 118 synagogues, of which ten are Samaritan. This ratio
reflects, more or less, the demographic situation in Palestine in the
Byzantine period.

The struggle for the faith between Christianity and the other, older
religions was sometimes accompanied by the use of force and violence.
It is surprising, therefore that archaeology points to only a single case of
a Jewish synagogue whose site was taken over by a Christian church.
This was at Jerash (ancient Gerasa) in Arabia, where the synagogue was
destroyed and a church was built on top of its ruins in 531 C.E., as the
dedicatory inscription of the church shows.[4] Although we do not know
the specific circumstances of the demolition of the synagogue and the
building of a church above it is hard to believe that the Jews voluntarily
gave up their rights to the site, and apparently we find here clear archae-

---

[2]   See in particular J. W. Crowfoot, *Early Churches in Palestine* (London: British
Academy, 1941); A. Ovadiah, *Corpus of the Byzantine Churches in the Holy Land*
(Bonn: Peter Hanstein Verlag GMBH, 1970); A. Ovadiah and C. G. De Silva,
"Supplementum to the Corpus of the Byzantine Churches in the Holy Land,"
Levant 13 (1981), 199–202; 14 (1982), 122–70; 16 (1984), 129–65.

[3]   In Tsafrir, Di Segni, and Green, *Tabula Imperii Romani*.

[4]   For the synagogue and church of Jerash, see J. W. Crowfoot, "The Christian
Churches," in C. H. Kraeling, *Gerasa: City of the Decapolis* (New Haven: Yale
University Press, 1938), 234–41; F. M. Biebel, "Mosaics," *ibid.* 318–24.

ological evidence of Christian confiscation of a Jewish cult center. A reasonable explanation may be found in the fact that the synagogue was located on the highest hill in the city. However, this case seems to be exceptional; many other synagogues continued to exist through the sixth, seventh and eighth centuries all over the country.

The attitude of the Byzantine regime and the church toward the Samaritans, at least in the region of Samaria, seems to have been less tolerant. The Samaritan cult place (and probably the main Samaritan synagogue) on Mount Gerizim, on the site of the former Samaritan Temple, which had been destroyed already by the Hasmoneans at the end of the second century B.C.E., was confiscated by the Emperor Zeno in 484 C.E. A monumental octagonal church dedicated to the Mother of God was built on the site in the center of a fortified precinct.[5] This act was part of the political and religious struggle between the Samaritans and the Christians, which lasted through the second half of the fifth and first part of the sixth century.

However, there seems to be a great difference between Christian attitudes toward the Jews and Samaritans, with whom some kind of *modus vivendi* was sought, and toward the pagans. The fate of pagan cult places was therefore totally unlike that of synagogues: from the Christian point of view; paganism had no place in Palestine. The abandonment of paganism was faster in some cities or regions than in others, but in no place in Palestine or Arabia can we recognize the survival of pagan communities later than the first half of the fifth century.[6]

---

[5]   Procopius of Caesarea, *Aed.* 5.7; Y. Magen, "The Church of Mary Theotokos on Mount Gerizim," in G. C. Bottini, L. Di Segni, and E. Alliata, eds., *Christian Archaeology in the Holy Land: New Discoveries* (Jerusalem: Franciscan Printing Press, 1990), 333–42; *idem,* "Mount Gerizim and the Samaritans," in F. Manns and E. Alliata, eds., *Early Christianity in Context: Monuments and Documents* (Jerusalem: Franciscan Printing Press, 1993), 91–148.

[6]   The definition of "paganism" is in itself rather vague. See for example in A. Kazhdan and A. M. Talbot, *ODB,* 1551–52, *s.v.* "Paganism." The authors point to three main streams of paganism in the Late Roman Empire: political, intellectual, and cultic. It is clear that "intellectual" paganism, in other words the survival of the

Although the trend toward the abandonment of paganism was clear
and irreversible, the pace of Christianization varied from place to place
in the various provinces of the East and the West. One can continue to
find some pagan expressions throughout the fifth, sixth, and even
seventh centuries.[7] In Palestine, we know that a kind of Arabian paganism existed on the southern and eastern fringes of the settled country,
especially in the Negev, Sinai and eastern Transjordan, and perhaps
even in the rough terrain of Mount Hermon.[8] However, in the main areas
of the settled country the change was clear. Pagan cults were strictly
prohibited and temples were destroyed. The question is how, and especially when, this procedure took place.

There is no doubt that the end of paganism occurred mostly during
the fourth century.[9] As a starting point for our study we may use the two
most crucial events that demonstrate the destruction of Roman temples
and their replacement by churches. The first, which took place in the
days of Constantine in the first third of the fourth century, was the
discovery of Jesus' tomb and the building of the Church of the Holy

---

classical heritage and tradition, had a much longer duration than the "official" cult
of pagan gods (see below). The survival of pagan cult and habits in everyday life, in
such forms as magic or astrology, or the use of amulets, continues not only
throughout the medieval period but even into our own time, both among circles of
believers in the monotheistic religions as "popular religion," and among non-
religious circles. Our article refrains from approaching such questions and making
value judgments but concentrates on the fate of "official" pagan cult places.

[7]   See, for example, F. Trombley, "Religious Transition in Sixth Century Syria,"
Byzantinische Forschungen 20 (1994), 153–95; P. Chuvin, *A Chronicle of the Last
Pagans*, trans. B. Archer (Cambridge Mass. and London: Harvard University Press,
1990).

[8]   For the Mt. Hermon area, see recently S. Dar, *Settlement and Cult Sites on
Mount Hermon, Israel* (Oxford: BAR International Series 589, 1993).

[9]   For the religious changes and the decline of paganism in the fourth century, see
among others, J. Geffken, *The Last Days of Greco-Roman Paganism*, trans. S. Mac-
Cormac (Amsterdam, New York and Oxford: New Holland Publishing Company,
1978); A. Momigliano, *The Conflict between Paganism and Christianity in the
Fourth Century* (Oxford: Clarendon Press, 1963).

Sepulchre in Jerusalem.[10] In Jerusalem, says Eusebius, the pagans built a temple in order to conceal the tomb of Christ. The impure and evil remains of the pagan shrine of the "demon Aphrodite" were removed in order to clean the area and purify the site for the building of the Church of the Holy Sepulchre. The procedure of cleaning the area was very solemn: not only was the temple destroyed but also the earth fill of the podium on which it stood was taken away. The question of authenticity of the Holy Sepulchre must remain open, and it cannot be proved that the venerated place of the *anastasis* is indeed Jesus' tomb. The question became the subject of a major dispute in the nineteenth century among Christian devotees after the discovery of the Garden Tomb north of the Old City walls by the Anglican General Gordon,[11] and continues to be contested by critical scholars of the present generation.[12] Still, neither

---

[10]   Eusebius, *Vita Constantini* 3.25–54. On the historical circumstances, see E. D. Hunt, *Holy Land Pilgrimage in the Later Roman Empire AD 312–460* (Oxford: Clarendon Press, 1982), 6–49. For the topographical and archaeological evidence, see in particular H. Vincent and F. M. Abel, *Jérusalem* II, *Jérusalem nouvelle* (Paris: J. Gabalda, 1914–26), 40–300; C. Coüasnon, *The Church of the Holy Sepulchre, Jerusalem* (London: The British Academy, 1974); V. Corbo, *Il Santo Sepolcro di Gerusalemme* I–III (Jerusalem: Franciscan Printing Press, 1981). For a short up-to-date summary see J. Patrich, "The Church of the Holy Sepulchre in the Light of Excavations and Restoration," in Y. Tsafrir, ed., *Ancient Churches Revealed* (Jerusalem: Israel Exploration Society, 1993), 101–17. See also recently on the urban, sociological, and cultural significance of building the church in fourth-century Jerusalem, A. J. Wharton, *Refiguring the Post Classical City: Dura Europos, Jerash, Jerusalem, and Ravenna* (Cambridge, New York and Melbourne: Oxford University Press, 1995), 85–100.

[11]   See a description of the new theory and its impact on the research of Jerusalem since the last quarter of the 19th century in J. Simons, *Jerusalem in the Old Testament* (Leiden: Brill, 1952), 282–343.

[12]   See in particular J. E. Taylor, *Christian and Holy Places: The Myth of the Jewish-Christian Origins* (Oxford: Clarendon Press, 1992) 113–42. See also the critical structural analysis of the ancient walls, rockcuts, and installations on the site of the Holy Sepulchre, including the Hill of Golgotha and Jesus' Tomb: S. Gibson and J. E. Taylor, *Beneath the Church of the Holy Sepulchre, Jerusalem, The Archaeology and Early History of Traditional Golgotha* (Palestine Exploration Fund Monograph

the claim that the tomb was authentic nor that the site was remembered and commemorated by Christians during the long period following the destruction of Jerusalem by Titus, through the building of Aelia Capitolina by Hadrian, can be disproved. On the contrary, it is hard to believe that the Christians relinquished the identification of their most holy place and let it disappear from their memory, even if it was buried under Roman monuments. There is strong evidence for the existence of a Jewish congregation in Aelia Capitolina;[13] thus the presence of a small Christian community is very likely, and there is literary evidence that supports the possibility of the authenticity of the tomb.[14]

The second famous case took place in Gaza, in the southern coastal plain, at the end of the fourth century. The story is told by the deacon Mark, in his biography of the bishop Porphyrius.[15] Porphyrius, who was appointed as bishop of Gaza at 396, found himself the head of a small community of a few hundred Christians in a rich pagan city.[16]

Series Maior, 1: London: Palestine Exploration Fund, 1994). See also A. J. Wharton, *Refiguring*, esp. 90–91. Against the Christian narrative as presented by Eusebius, according to which the site of Jesus' tomb was deliberately covered by Hadrian underneath the podium of the temple of the demon Aphrodite, Wharton suggests another "analytical" narrative. Constantine chose an appropriate place for building the main Christian complex of Jerusalem and an ancient Jewish tomb that was discovered in the site was interpreted as the tomb of Jesus.

[13] S. Safrai, "The Holy Congregation of Jerusalem," *Scripta Hierosolymitana* 23 (1972), 62–78.

[14] See the meticulous research on the *aedicula* of Jesus' tomb in the Rotunda of the Church of the Holy Sepulchre and its ancient documentation by M. Biddle, "The Tomb of Christ: Sources, Methods and a New Approach," in K. Painter, ed., *Churches Built in Ancient Times* (London: Society of Antiquaries of London, 1994), 73–147, esp. 93–105.

[15] Marc le Diacre, *Vie de Porphyre évêque de Gaza*, H. Gregoire and M. A. Kugener, eds. (Paris: Société d'édition "Les belles lettres," 1930); P. Peeters, "La vie géorgienne de saint Porphyre de Gaza," *Analecta Bollandiana* 59 (1941), 65–216; G. Downey, *Gaza in the Early Sixth Century* (Norman: University of Oklahoma Press, 1963), esp. 14–32.

[16] One must be cautious in using the numbers of inhabitants of Gaza given in the report and especially the ratio between Christians and pagans. It is reasonable that

The pagan aristocracy of Gaza, a solid class of taxpayers, was protected by the Emperor Arcadius, but Porphyrius gained the support of Eudoxia the *Augusta* and returned to Gaza accompanied by imperial support and the aid of the provincial troops. Officially, the law backed Porphyrius: a series of severe laws against pagan rites and the practice of paganism both in public and private had been issued in the time of Theodosius I, following on anti-pagan legislation in place since the days of Constantine.[17]

The story is rich in literary mannerisms but there is no reason to doubt its historical core.[18] The temples of Gaza were abandoned, the last and most important among them the temple of Marnas, the local deity of the city of Gaza, who had gained much fame and prestige. The temple was burned to ashes, its site was cleared down to the bedrock and new stones were hewn and carried to the site by the entire Christian population in order to build a new church on the very place where the temple had previously been situated. Jerome, too, mentions this event in his commentary to Isaiah, connecting the destruction of the temple of Gaza with that of Sarapis' great temple in Alexandria, a temple even more prestigious than the Marneion.[19] The two, says Jerome, had been the last pagan strongholds, and their destruction marked the total victory of Christianity in the East.

---

the deacon Mark, the biographer of Porphyrius, might have played down Porphyrius, the power of the Christians and enlarged the number of pagans in order to magnify Porphyrius' achievements. However, there can be no doubt that pagans were a great majority in Gaza, while Maioumas (Constantia), i.e., the port town of Gaza, was Christian.

[17] See, for example, *Cod. Theod.* 9.16.1–12. See, in general, R. MacMullen, *Christianizing the Roman Empire (A.D. 100–400)* (New Haven and London: Yale University Press, 1984); Chuvin, *Chronicle.*

[18] But see in contrast, MacMullen, *Christianizing,* 86–87, following Peeters (n. 15 above), who minimize the historicity of the text and accept it as a later (late-fifth or sixth-century) text of Syrian origin from which we can learn only the main facts and the general ideas typical of the Christian mind.

[19] Jerome, *In Esaiam,* 17.2–3 (*CCSL* 73, 268).

The destruction of the temple of Gaza was followed by a solemn ceremony of purification of the site in order to enable the building of a new church on the same spot. This church was dedicated to the empress Eudoxia and is perhaps the one that we see in the depiction of Gaza on the Madaba Map.[20] The stones of the temple, once holy and revered, were installed as paving stones in the city's streets, trodden on and despised by men, women, and animals.

The foundation of churches on sites of ruined temples in Jerusalem and Gaza was exceptional. In Palestine Christians usually refrained from settling in such sites, which were viewed as the places of demons and called for a solemn procedure of purification. Both exceptions can be explained by the very special circumstances. In Jerusalem the building of the church was inevitable because of the discovery of the Holy Sepulchre underneath the platform of the temple. In Gaza the decision was taken to suppress the spirit of the stubborn worshippers of Marnas, "the last pagans," by the construction of the church on the very spot of the Marneion.

Theoretically, there were several options for the Christian treatment of the site and remains of the abandoned temples (including building materials, statues and art objects). The Christian practice indeed shows a great variety, which depended on the circumstances of each individual case.[21] The most immediate and understandable response would have been to occupy the abandoned pagan place, whether completely or partially ruined and build a church within the same building, or on top of it, while using the *spolia* of the former monument. By doing so the Christians not only saved much effort and expense and gained a central location within the city for their own temple; they also demonstrated their great triumph over the defeated

---

[20]   M. Avi-Yonah, *The Madaba Mosaic Map* (Jerusalem: Israel Exploration Society, 1954), 74 (mistakenly printed Eudocia).

[21]   See in particular H. Saradi-Mendelovici, "Christian Attitudes toward Pagan Monuments in Late Antiquity and Their Legacy in Later Byzantine Centuries," *DOP* 44 (1990), 47–61.

paganism. Such acts must have had enormous impact on the entire population and did indeed take place, but mostly at a rather later date, especially in the sixth century or later. Very famous examples are the conversion of the Parthenon in Athens under Justinian, the temple of Concordia in Agrigento, also in the sixth century, and the temple of Aphrodite in Aphrodisias in the late fifth century. The condition for performing such an act of outright confiscation was confidence on the part of the Christian authorities that the conversion of the pagan place into a Christian church would cause no harm to the new occupants and evoke no sympathy for the pagan cause. Such confidence might result from the span of time through which the temple was standing in ruins without harming the Christians, who in the meantime had reached a position of strength and conceived paganism as an "immature" episode in the past with no hope of revival. At this point citizens of the classical cities could reap the benefits of using the old buildings and enjoy the aesthetic values of the lavish monuments.

The concept of the builders of the Church of the Holy Sepulchre and the Eudoxiana in Gaza was different. The practice at these places included the complete destruction of the temples, clearing the site down to bedrock and building new churches by using virgin stones, or at least *spolia* of neutral origin. The texts give us a clear understanding that the sites of temples, as well as the building materials, were polluted by demons. It was not just the mere impurity of the site that repelled the Christians, but mostly their fear of the demonic powers of the gods, which they believed still resided in the sites of the temples. Such a conclusion emerges from the texts of Eusebius and Mark and from numerous other sources, especially biographies of monks who struggled with demons in Egypt and in Palestine. Favorite dwelling places for the demons were caves, ancient tombs[22] (in Egypt they were probably painted with images of the ancient Egyptian gods), and ruined settle-

---

[22]   For Egypt see, for example, the vivid descriptions of the battles with the devil and demons in Athanasius, *Vita Antonii, passim.*

ments.[23] It is very reasonable to believe that the ruined pagan temples were viewed as residences of demons, places that wise people would do well to avoid.

On the other hand, it has become clear, as we will see below, that in most cases some use was made of parts of the ruined temples, and it is likely that building stones from the ruined temples were reused, albeit for profane projects such as paving the streets in front of the church of Gaza. This type of use, as well as the variety of the solutions, is shown in the archaeological findings in Palestine and Arabia. An interesting case is currently being unearthed in Caesarea Maritima. The main temple of the city (Herod's temple?), which was located on the hill at the center of the city, was completely dismantled to the level of the foundations, probably not later than 400 C.E. A new lavish octagonal church (dedicated to Procopius the martyr?) was built at the beginning of the sixth century on the site of the ruined temple, perhaps even using some of the building blocks of the temple.[24] It is clear that the builders of the church liked the central position (and the free space) of the former temple. The site of the temple seems to have been in ruins for about a century between the destruction of the temple and the building of the church. Only around 500 C.E. did Christians dare to make use of the dominant place and the free space of the former temple at the center of the city.

---

[23] For example the description of the ruins of ancient Hyrcania (Byzantine Castellion) that was seized by demons in Cyril of Scythopolis, *Vita Sabae* 27, ed. E. Schwartz (*Texte und Untersuchungen zur Geschichte der altchristlichen Literatur* 49 ii; Leipzig: J.C. Hinrichs Verlag, 1939), 110. Only the strong power of Sabas, who used the holy oil of the cross and stayed there alone for the forty days of the fast, purified the site.

[24] For the results of the excavations of the temple I owe thanks to K. Holum, who also shared with me his conclusions about the chronology of the finds. For the church and the results of the early seasons of excavation, see K. G. Holum *et al.* "Preliminary Report on the 1989–1990 Seasons," R. L. Vann, ed., *Casarea Papers, Strato's Tower, Herod's Harbour, and Roman and Byzantine Caesarea* (*Journal of Roman Archaeology*, Supplement 5, 1992), 100–8.

Most of the temples in Palestine have been found in an advanced state of ruin, and thus the study of the process of their abandonment is impossible unless a meticulous excavation is carried out. Still, there are several monuments, mostly in today's Jordan and Syria, which have been preserved to a considerable height, permitting us to explore some aspects of their abandonment. The most explicit example is the temple of Artemis in Gerasa.[25] We have no information concerning the exact date of abandonment, but it most probably took place sometime in the late fourth century. The archaeological evidence shows clearly that the site of the temple was abandoned and remained unused until a very late stage of its existence in the late Byzantine period and especially in early Islamic times, when a potter's workshop was installed in the place.

Most instructive is the state of the ruins as preserved even today. The *cella* and especially the *adyton*, the shrine of the goddess Artemis, were destroyed and desecrated. At the same time the *pronaos* in front of the temple and parts of the *pteron* around it were saved, displaying the grandeur of the city up to our own times. These decorative parts were retained by the Christian citizens of Gerasa. It is clear that the citizens refused to destroy one of the most grandiose monuments of their city and give up its glorious architecture. The solution was to differentiate the *naos*, i.e., the *cella* and the *adyton* of the temple from the "functional" portico. The magnificent facade was viewed as an ornamental member and not as a religious institution.

As mentioned above, the Christians in Jerash refrained from using the temple of Artemis itself, even for profane purposes, until a rather late period. On the other hand they built a church in the *propylaion* of the temple of Artemis, probably around 565 C.E.[26] The *propylaion* was a

---

[25] C. Fisher, "The Temple of Artemis," in Kraeling, ed., *Gerasa*, 125–38; F. Zayadine, "The Jerash Project for Excavation and Restoration," in F. Zayadine, ed., *Jerash Archaeological Project 1981–1983* I (Amman: The Department of Antiquities, 1986), 10–11; R. Pierobon, "Sanctuary of Artemis: Soundings in the Temple-Terrace, 1978–1980," *Mesopotamia* 18–19 (1983–84), 85–109; R. Parapetti, "Scavi e restauri Italiani nel santuario del Artemide," *Syria* 66 (1989), 1–39.

[26] J. W. Crowfoot, "The Propylaea Church," in Kraeling, ed., *ibid.* 227–34.

part of the ceremonial *via sacra* that led in Roman times to the temple, but not in itself a place of pagan cult. Thus there was no offense or danger in reusing the site as a church. A similar situation probably occurred in the temple of Zeus in Jerash and several other places, where columns and decorated facades remain standing even today, while the *cella* is ruined. Examples are found in Kedesh in Galilee; and Kanawat, Atil, and others in Southern Syria. Apparently contradictory evidence has been found south of the Artemis temple. Remains of a molded plinth of a monumental building were found underneath the level of the "cathedral" church, dated to the late fourth century, and it is clear that the remains of this building were erased by the builders of the church. The excavators identified this monument as a small temple, perhaps dedicated to Dionysus.[27] However, the identification of this plinth as a part of a temple is, at present, very hypothetical.

B. The Evidence from Bet Shean (Scythopolis)

The fate of the temples has been of special interest to us during our excavation of Bet Shean (Scythopolis).[28] The main challenge in connec-

---

[27] J. W. Crowfoot, *Churches at Jerash* (London: British School of Archaeology, 1930), 7; *idem*, in Kraeling, ed., *Gerasa*, 201. For recent excavations on the site, see B. Brenk, C. Jäggi, and H.-R. Meier, "The Buildings under the 'Cathedral' of Gerasa: The Second Interim Report on the Jerash Cathedral Project," *ADAJ* 39 (1995), 211–20.

[28] For the recent excavations of the Hebrew University team at Bet Shean see the preliminary reports: G. Foerster and Y. Tsafrir, "The Bet Shean Project: B. Center of Bet Shean—North; C. The Amphitheater and Its Surroundings," *ESI* 6 (1987–88), 25–43; "The Bet Shean Project—1988: Hebrew University Expedition," *ESI* 7–8 (1988–89), 15–22; Y. Tsafrir and G. Foerster, "Bet Shean Excavation Project—1988–1989," *ESI* 9 (1989–1990), 120–28; G. Foerster and Y. Tsafrir, "The Bet Shean Excavation Project (1989–1991): City Center (North); Excavations of the Hebrew University Expedition," *ESI* 11 (1992), 3–32; also Y. Tsafrir and G. Foerster, "The Hebrew University Excavations at Beth-Shean, 1980–1994" [Hebrew], *Qadmoniot* 107–8 (1994), 93–116; and Y. Tsafrir and G. Foerster, "Urbanism at Scythopolis-Bet Shean in the Fourth-Seventh Centuries," *DOP* 51 (1997), 85–146. For the Israel Antiquities Authority excavations, see G. Mazor, "The Bet Shean Project: A. City Center of Bet Shean—South," *ESI* 6 (1987–88), 10–24; "The Bet Shean Project—

tion with the desertion of pagan cult places in the early Byzantine period (a fact that nobody denies) is the quest for a more accurate dating of the process. We have already mentioned the historical texts, mainly the legal texts of the Theodosian Code. In general, the answer is clear: the destruction of pagan cult places occurred mostly in the second half of the fourth century and no later than the first half of the fifth century. One can point to the laws against pagan sacrifices that were issued by Theodosius I, 379–395 C.E., especially after 391.[29] However, we had hoped that meticulous archaeological excavation and stratigraphic analysis would provide some solid dates for the desertion of individual temples. Previous excavations had presented only little evidence. Very naturally, the main efforts of researchers have commonly been dedicated to the identification of the buildings, together with their deities, and their liturgical and architectural character, rather than the question of their end. We tried to respond to this challenge in our excavation at Bet Shean but found the task more difficult than we expected.

Christianity was embraced in Scythopolis before the conquest of the East by Constantine. Procopius, a native of Jerusalem who was a reader, translator and exorcist in the Christian community of Scythopolis, suffered martyrdom in Caesarea in 303 C.E.[30] Patrophilus, the bishop of Scythopolis, was one of the most prominent leaders of Christianity in the East in the mid-fourth century. He was an Arian, and the great majority of the Christian congregation of Scythopolis supported Arianism at that time.[31] This fact is confirmed by the writing of Epiphanius, a

---

1988: Department of Antiquities Expedition," *ESI* 7–8 (1988–89), 22–32; R. Bar-Nathan and G. Mazor, "The Bet Shean Excavation Project (1989–1991): City Center South and Tel Iẓtaba: Excavations of the Antiquities Authority Expedition," *ESI* 11 (1992), 33–51; also G. Mazor and R. Bar-Nathan, "Scythopolis—Capital of *Palaestina Secunda*" [Hebrew], *Qadmoniot* 107–8 (1994), 117–37; *idem*, "The Bet Shean Excavations Project—1992–1994, Israel Antiquities Authority Excavations" [Hebrew], *HA* 105 (1996), 1–33, English version in *ESI* (forthcoming).

[29] See n. 17 above.

[30] Eusebius, *Mart. Pal.* 1.1–2.

[31] For Patrophilus, see G. Fedalto, *Hierarchia Ecclesiastica Orientalis II, Series*

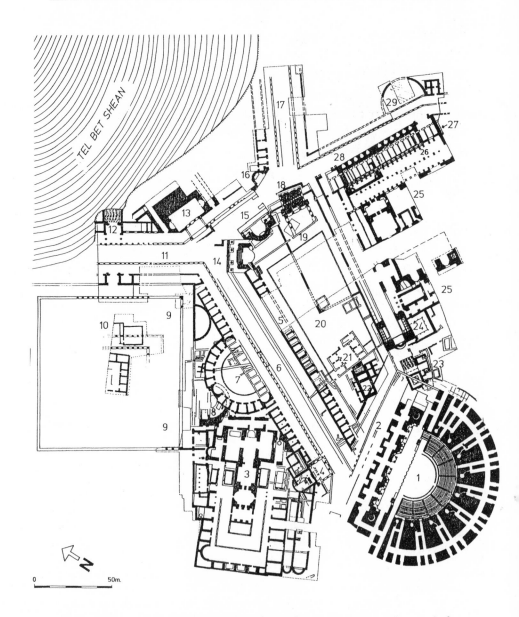

City Center of Bet Shean-Scythopolis in the Roman-Byzantine Period
(Excavations of the Hebrew University and the Israel Antiquities Authority)

Palestinian monk and author, who in 367 became the bishop of Salamis in Cyprus.[32] Epiphanius writes that the city was totally occupied by Arians, except for the *comes* Joseph, a converted Jew from the region of Tiberias, who found shelter in Scythopolis after retiring. Another Orthodox Christian in the Arian city was the bishop Eusebius of Verccelae, who was expelled to Scythopolis and stayed there for a short period in harsh conditions.[33] From reading only the Christian sources one might conclude that most of the citizens of Bet Shean were already Christian in the middle of the fourth century. This is, of course, a misconception, since many citizens still adhered to pagan religions. The process of Christianization took somewhat longer, and lasted a few more decades than Epiphanius acknowledges.[34]

Roman Scythopolis displayed the Hellenistic-Roman culture in its prime. An inscription found on the pedestal of the statue of the Emperor

---

Episcoparum Ecclesiarum Christianorum Orientalium (Padova: Edizione Messaggero, 1988), 1032.

[32] Epiphanius, *Panar.*, 30.4–12. See also the discussion by Z. Rubin, "Joseph the Comes and the Attempts to Convert the Galilee to Christianity in the Fourth Century C.E." [Hebrew], *Cathedra* 26 (1982), 105–16.

[33] Eusebius of Verccelae, *Epistula* 2.8 (*PL* 12, cols. 947–54); Rubin, "Joseph the Comes," 113–16.

[34] Compare to Ammianus Marcellinus, *Rerum Gestarum Libri*, 19.12.8, who at the same time describes Scythopolis role as a center but does not mention Christians at all.

◄——————— 1. Theater. 2. Portico in front of theater. 3. Western bathhouse. 4. *Propylon* in Palladius Street. 5. Shops of Roman and Byzantine period. 6. Palladius Street. 7. Semicircular plaza (the *sigma*). 8. Odeon. 9. Colonnades and reconstructed area of the Roman *temenos*(?). 10. Byzantine public building, over dismantled Roman colonnades. 11. Northern Street. 12. *Propylon* and stairway to tell. 13. *Propylon* between the temple esplanade and the tell. 14. Temple with round *cella*. 15. Nymphaeum. 16. Monument of Antonius. 17. Valley Street. 18. Central monument. 19. Roman basilica, and above it porticoes of the "Byzantine Agora." 20. "Byzantine Agora." 21. Umayyad ceramic workshop. 22. Roman Temple. 23. Roman cult structures. 24. Public latrine. 25. Eastern bathhouse. 26. Roman portico and decorative pool (later Silvanus Hall). 27. Umayyad shops on top of Roman decorative pool. 28. Silvanus Street. 29. Semicircular plaza.

Marcus Aurelius defined Scythopolis as a Greek city of Coele-Syria, probably pointing to its status as a member of the former league of ten cities or the Decapolis, the flagship of Hellenistic culture in the region.[35] We have evidence that the upper classes maintained their sympathy and admiration for this cultural heritage and the classical tradition even through the Byzantine period. A conclusion we may draw, therefore, is that Scythopolis was one of the last cities to give up paganism, and that the abandonment of temples in Scythopolis indicates a further stage of the Christianization of the country.

Five Greco-Roman pagan cult places have hitherto been detected in the city of Bet Shean-Scythopolis: the temple of Zeus Akraios on the tell; a cult place near the theater; a temple northeast of the theater in the area of the later Byzantine agora; a temple on the saddle between the valley of Nahal Harod and its tributary, Nahal Amal (if we correctly identify the remains as connected with a temple; only parts of the *temenos* of the latter have been discovered); and the temple with the round *cella* in the city center. Four of the five temples were excavated during recent years with great care, and thus we had high hopes for clear answers as to the chronology of the abandonment and destruction of the temples. In general terms, these hopes have been fulfilled and we are able to point to the process of destruction in the fourth and no later than the early-fifth centuries. However, the most important *desideratum*, the definition of narrower limits, if not an exact date, for the act of the abandonment of the temple has proved elusive. The following short survey will describe this situation.

The first temple to be discovered, in the 1920s was the temple of Zeus Akraios on the tell, or the acropolis.[36] Only the foundations were found,

---

[35]   G. Foerster and Y. Tsafrir, "Nysa Scythopolis—A New Inscription and the Titles of the City on Its Coins," *INJ* 9 (1986), 93–116.

[36]   A. Rowe, *The Topography and History of Beth-Shan* I (Philadelphia: University of Pennsylvania Press, 1930), 43–45. For the identification of the temple as the temple of Zeus Akraios, see Y. Tsafrir, "Further Evidence for the Cult of Zeus Akraios," *IEJ* 39 (1989), 76–78.

apart from several drums and capitals of the columns. The excavators did not leave detailed information about their finds and their exact location, and the physical remains were completely removed in order to enable further excavation of the site. It was a rather large building, and the drums belong to very thick columns, 1.25–1.30 m in diameter, enabling a reconstruction of some 10 m for the height of the columns. The walls of the temple were dismantled in antiquity in order to make room for the building of a church on the site. The church, circular in plan, covered part of the foundation of the temple.[37] No useful information as to the date of the abandonment of the temple and the destruction of the walls (perhaps as preparatory work for the building of the church) is given in the laconic report. However, both the plan and the architectural details of the church point to a date in the sixth or late-fifth century, probably a rather long period after the temple had been demolished.

The cult area near the theater was excavated by the team of the Israel Antiquities Authority.[38] The site consisted of a small but lavish central building on a podium reached by a monumental stairway and a series of altars, pools, and fountains. It seems that this complex, which already existed in the first century C.E. and was remodeled during the second and third centuries, went out of use during the fourth century. Although nothing remained of the upper structures, the lower parts, including the foundations, and the pools and altars on the lower terraces, seem to have been carefully covered by earth (although the carved steps were uprooted, probably for secondary use in other places). It is not impossible that the cult area went out of use during the modification in the use of this area, when the new wing of the eastern bathhouse was built nearby, and one must be very cautious in using these data as evidence for the dating the end of the pagan cult places of Scythopolis.

---

[37] The partial superposition of the Church on the western part (the *pronaos?*) of the temple is shown in the ground plan published by A. Rowe, *The Four Canaanite Temples* (Philadelphia: University of Pennsylvania Press, 1940), pl. II.

[38] Number 23 on the general plan. G. Mazor and R. Bar-Nathan, *HA* 105 (1996), 8–10.

Another temple was found by the Israel Antiquities Authority team in the vicinity of the theater a short distance west of the former cult place. This rectangular, classically-shaped temple of rather small dimensions was completely dismantled.[39] No information about the temple has yet been published; thus we cannot discuss its destruction. However, it is clear that sometime after its destruction a new commercial square, named by us the "Byzantine Agora," was built in this place. We tend to date the building of the new square to the mid-fifth century; thus this date may serve as a *terminus ante quem* for the abandonment of the temple. However, it should be remembered that the date of the foundation of the agora is still under discussion and that the hiatus between the abandonment of the temple and the building of the "Byzantine Agora" is unknown.

The fourth temple to be discussed has not yet been found, but is reconstructed by us in the large square found on the saddle between the valleys of Nahal Harod and Nahal Amal.[40] At this spot, west of the Northern Street and north of Palladius Street, segments of rows of monumental columns have been uncovered. They seem to create a peristyle square, the dimensions of which are probably more than 150×150 m. Other, shorter lines of columns were detected within this area. A monumental gate leads to this area from the Northern Street. The complex is built in orientation with the Northern Street, with the Roman street that we believe preceded Palladius Street, and with the temple with the circular *cella* described below. This monumental complex may have been a huge forum with a basilica and other civic monuments, but the arrangement of the buildings is not typical for a civic center and thus such an interpretation remains unlikely. A more plausible suggestion is the identification of the complex as the *temenos* of the main temple of Scythopolis (perhaps connected with Dionysus, the traditional founder and patron god of Scythopolis?), analogous to the *temenos* of Artemis in Gerasa-Jerash.

---

[39]   Number 22 in the general plan.

[40]   Numbers 9–10 in the general plan.

A radical change in the character and function of this area took place in the Byzantine period. The complex lost its monumental character and the Roman precinct was converted into a public building of civil character. One possible interpretation, as we may learn from a dedicatory inscription found in the vicinity, is that the area housed a hostel or inn, an *apantetērion* (if our completion is correct). However, the complex was of some importance, as we realize from a lintel found nearby bearing an inscription adorned with a cross: *hyper tōn Augustōn* "For the *Augusti*," probably referring to a Byzantine emperor and empress. The colonnade of the peristyle was almost completely dismantled; the blocks of the stylobate were taken for reuse in another building, while the column drums, the bases, and capitals were left near the site, buried under the level of the later building.

This new building of the Byzantine period was paved with mosaics. A mosaic inscription: *eiselthatai hygienontes* "enter with good health," may point to a bath or even a public lavatory, the remains of which were found in the area. The walls of the Byzantine building were also later dismantled and the stones were taken for reuse in one of the nearby monuments in the Early Islamic period. The analysis of the material found in the foundation trenches of the Byzantine edifice has not yet been completed; thus we cannot yet give a more accurate date for the construction of the Byzantine building than a general range of time between the mid-fifth and the early-sixth century. By establishing such a general *terminus ante quem* for the reuse of the stones of the Roman *temenos* in the new Byzantine building, we have not greatly advanced our goal.

The last temple to be discussed is the one with the round *cella*, the first discovered in the excavated city center at the foot of the acropolis.[41] Fortunately the stratigraphic analysis of this building and the adjacent monuments, especially the *nymphaeum*, yielded a much more accurate *terminus ante quem* for the desertion of the temple than in the other

---

[41]   Number 14 in the general plan. Foerster and Tsafrir, *ESI* 6 (1987–88), 26–27; 7–8 (1988–89), 18–19; Tsafrir and Foerster, *ESI* 9 (1989–90), 121–22.

cases. The facade of the temple created an architectural front together with the *nymphaeum* and the central columnar monument. A processional road or *via sacra* led from it, through a monumental *propylon*, to the acropolis, probably to the temple of Zeus, or to another monumental part of the complex below the slopes of the tell. The temple was built in the first century C.E. but the present remains belong to a later phase in the second century. A pedestal of a statue of Marcus Aurelius[42] with two altars was installed in front of its facade, probably displaying the cult of the ruler. The exact plan and reconstruction of the temple are not completely clear. It was built on a podium, leaning on nicely built vaults that were connected to the main *cella* by a narrow spiral stairway. The *cella* was rounded but we do not know if the external shape was also circular (like, for example, the famous "Venus temple" in Baalbek) or of a regular rectangular shape. The facade, or *pronaos*, consisted of four monumental monolithic columns made of limestone (the length of each shaft was ca. 9.50 m). Together with the pedestals, bases, and large Corinthian capitals we can reconstruct a facade crowned by a "broken" gable, the apex of which was some 13 m above ground level.

There is no doubt that the temple was destroyed and dismantled by Christians down to the level of its floor. No building earlier than the very late Byzantine or the Early Islamic period was found above the ruins of the *cella*. On the other hand, it is clear that the *pronaos* was preserved throughout the Byzantine period. Two of its columns continued to stand and beautify the Christian city of Scythopolis, and later the little early-Islamic town of Baysan, until they collapsed in the major earthquake of January 749. The Christian differentiation between the *cella*, the impure body of the temple, which was desecrated, and the harmless decorative facade was maintained in Scythopolis, as it was in Jerash, Kanawat, and other places mentioned above.

The question of dating the desecration and destruction of the temple by Christians must be answered by examining the history of the

---

[42] See n. 35 above.

neighboring *nymphaeum*.[43] This lavish Roman building was damaged, probably in the earthquake of 363, and was rebuilt by the governor Artemidorus. The name and titles of the governor (*arkon*), a high official of the rank *peribleptos* and *megaloprepestatos komes*, as well as the identification of the monument as a *nymphaeum*, appear in the monumental inscription that was discovered in the tumble of the earthquake of 749. Unfortunately, Artemidorus found it unnecessary to add the date of his reconstruction, but the crosses that adorn the inscription point to a date no earlier than the mid-fourth century. Fortunately two other inscriptions of the same governor were found at the site. One, also adorned with a cross, is incised on a pedestal of a statue. It says: "Artemidorus set up a golden (statue of) Eudoxia, the queen of all earth, visible from every place in the country." The language of the inscription is archaic and the last phrase, *periskeptō en khōrō* is a quotation from the *Odyssey*. The inscription belongs to the days of the empress Eudoxia, who became an *Augusta* in 400 and died in 404.[44] We may therefore date the inscription to about 400 C.E.

The aqueduct that brought water to the newly built *nymphaeum* passed through the area of the temple in a way that permits no doubt that the temple was already in ruins. The year 400, or at the latest 404, is therefore a *terminus ante quem* for the destruction of the temple. This is, as far as I know, the first stratigraphic evidence for the desecration of a temple no later than the very end of the fourth century or the very first years of the fifth century.

The result of this investigation is in accord with our general knowledge, as described in the first section of this article. When we look for a suitable date in the second half of the fourth century and no later than 404 for the abandonment of the temple, we arrive at the days of Theo-

---

[43] Foerster and Tsafrir, *ESI* 6 (1987–88), 32–35; *ESI* 7–8 (1988–89), 22; Tsafrir and Foerster, *ESI* 9 (1989–90), 126–28; Foerster and Tsafrir, *ESI* 11 (1993), 25–32.

[44] For Eudoxia, see K. G. Holum, *Theodosian Empresses: Women and Imperial Dominion in Late Antiquity* (Berkeley: University of California Press, 1982), esp. 48–78.

dosius I, who in 391 issued laws prohibiting pagan cults. It seems likely that the abandonment of the pagan temple in Scythopolis took place in the days of this emperor, between 379 and 395, or perhaps a little earlier or slightly later.

I have already mentioned the *via sacra*, used for religious processions between our temple and the acropolis, or another building at the slopes of the acropolis. As a consequence of the abandonment of the temple, this area too changed its function. At the end of the fourth century or in the early fifth century the area of the *propylon* of this road was occupied by a system of channels and pools. These installations blocked the gate of the *propylon* and changed the character of the area from a part of the sacred complex to an area of utilitarian use and industrial activity.

This article has dealt with the contribution of archaeology to the search for the end of pagan cult places. It has become clear that only meticulous stratigraphic, ceramic, and epigraphic study will bring us to a solid conclusion. The impression is that the temples and sacrifices came to an end no later than the end of the fourth century. Other aspects of paganism, such as statues, even of gods and mythological heroes, and pagan images in mosaics, survived even as late as the sixth century.[45] This, of course, calls for further discussion. However, the use of the formal pagan temples in Scythopolis most probably ended before the end of the fourth century or slightly later.

---

[45]   See discussion in Tsafrir and Foerster, "Urbanism."

GRECO-ROMAN INFLUENCES ON THE ART AND ARCHITECTURE OF THE JEWISH CITY IN ROMAN PALESTINE

Zeev Weiss
The Hebrew University

ARCHAEOLOGY plays an important role in shedding light on the relationship between Jews and Gentiles in Roman Palestine during the first centuries of the common era. Archaeological finds reveal that Jewish society was not isolated during this period, but rather was influenced, in many ways, by the ambient Greco-Roman culture.[1] This was not restricted to a particular sphere, but manifested itself in different fields, from the world of the living to the resting place of the dead, in language, daily life, and customs. An architectural and artistic analysis of the remains of the two major Jewish cities of the Galilee, namely, Sepphoris and Tiberias, also clearly demonstrate this widespread influence.[2] The

---

[1] This can be clearly seen, for example, in the Jewish cemeteries excavated in the Galilee. See: Z. Weiss, "Hellenistic Influences on Jewish Burial Customs in the Galilee during the Mishnaic and Talmudic Period" [Hebrew], *EI* 26 (1996), 356–64. For general discussions on Hellenistic influences upon Jewish society, see S. Lieberman, *Greek and Hellenism in Jewish Palestine* [Hebrew] (Jerusalem: Bialik, 1962). This influence gradually increased during the Mishnaic and Talmudic periods and reached its peak during fifth and sixth centuries C.E., see M. D. Herr, "Hellenistic Influences in the Jewish City in Eretz Israel in the Fourth and Sixth Centuries C.E." [Hebrew], *Cathedra* 8 (1978), 90–94; *idem*, "External Influences in the World of the Sages of Palestine—Acceptance and Rejection" [Hebrew], in Y. Kaplan, M. Stern, eds., *Acculturation and Assimilation, Continuity and Change in the Culture of Israel and the Nations* (Jerusalem: Merkaz Zalman Shazar, 1989), 83–106.

[2] For Sepphoris see S. Safrai, "The Jewish Community in the Galilee and Golan in the Third and Fourth Centuries" [Hebrew], in *Eretz Israel from the Destruction of*

layout of these cities, their facilities, and art forms indicate that they were constructed according to the Roman tradition, and their public buildings were quite similar to those in other, pagan, cities. This conclusion is based on the examination of three complementary areas: city planning, art and architecture, and the role of games and spectacles, which, as we shall see, also penetrated into the realm of Jewish life.

Tiberias and Sepphoris were both designed according to the Roman model of urban infrastructure, as also known from the pagan cities of ancient Palestine. This plan is based on a street grid extending throughout the city. Some of these streets in Sepphoris connected the older part of the city with the new urban areas—a phenomenon similar to that

---

the Second Temple to the Muslim Conquest, ed. Z. Baras, *et al.* (Jerusalem: Yad Izhak ben Zvi, 1982), 145–58; S. S. Miller, *Studies in the History and Tradition of Sepphoris* (Leiden: Brill, 1984); Y. Neeman, *Sepphoris in the Period of the Second Temple, the Mishna and Talmud* [Hebrew] (Jerusalem: Shem, 1993); Z. Weiss, "Sepphoris," *NEAEHL*, 4, 1324–28; *idem*, "Sepphoris during the Roman and Byzantine Periods in Light of Archaeological Finds" [Hebrew], in *Proceedings of the Eleventh World Congress of Jewish Studies* (Jerusalem: Ha-igud ha-olami le-madae ha-Yahadut, 1994), 47–53; E. Netzer, Z. Weiss, *Zippori* (Jerusalem: Israel Exploration Society, 1994); *idem*, "New Evidence for Late-Roman and Byzantine Sepphoris," in J. H. Humphrey, ed., *The Roman and Byzantine Near East* (Ann Arbor: *Journal of Roman Archaeology* Supplementary Series 14, 1995), 162–76; Z. Weiss and E. Netzer, "Archaeological Finds from the Byzantine Period at Sepphoris" [Hebrew] *Michmanim* 8 (1995), 75–85; R. M. Nagy *et al.* eds., *Sepphoris in Galilee: Crosscurrents of Culture* (Raleigh: North Carolina Museum of Art, 1996). For Tiberias see M. Avi-Yonah, "The Foundation of Tiberias" *IEJ* 1 (1950–51), 160–69; R. R. Kimelman, *Rabbi Yohanan of Tiberias: Aspects of the Social and Religious History of the Third Century Palestine* (diss., Yale University, 1977); L. I. Levine, "Rabbi Simeon bar Yohai, Bones of the Dead and the Purification of Tiberias—History and Tradition" [Hebrew], *Cathedra* 22 (1982), 9–42; Y. Hirschfeld, ed., *Tiberias from Its Foundation to the Muslim Conquest* (*Idan* 11: Jerusalem: Yad Izhak ben Tzvi, 1988); *idem*, "Excavations at Tiberias Reveal Remains of Church and Possibly Theater," *BA* 54 (1991), 170–71; *idem*, *A Guide to Antiquity Sites in Tiberias* [Hebrew] (Jerusalem: Israel Antiquities Authority, 1992); *idem*, "Tiberias," *NEAEHL*, 4, 1464–70; Y. Z. Eliav, *Sites, Institutions and Daily Life in Tiberias during the Talmudic Period* [Hebrew] (*Mi'tuv T'veria* 10: Jerusalem: Ha-merkāz lĕ-ḥēqer tĕberyâ, 1995).

noted in Gerasa or Bostra, for example.[3] The main streets in Tiberias and Sepphoris, as in the other cities of Roman Palestine, were flanked by colonnaded sidewalks and shops (Fig. 1).[4] Their central part was paved with rectangular slabs of hard limestone, which were laid in rows across their width at a slight angle to the sidewalks. Limestone stylobates, supporting rows of columns, separated the streets proper from the sidewalks that were usually paved with mosaics decorated with simple geometrical designs. The pavement in Tiberias was made of basalt stones laid similarly across the street and the columns were of granite. The colonnaded streets or *plateiai* (the Greek term used by the rabbis[5]) served as the urban city market, the focus of economic life in the Roman city.[6] According to the Talmudic literature, both Tiberis and Sepphoris had two market places (*šĕwāqîm*), an upper and a lower one.[7] The topographic evidence at Sepphoris, which was built partly on the summit of the hill and partly on the fairly level area to the east of it,

---

[3]   On city planning and the character of the main thoroughfares in the Roman city, see W. L. MacDonald, *The Architecture of the Roman Empire, II: An Urban Appraisal* (New Haven: Yale, 1986), 5–31. For a general discussion on the finds from Roman Palestine emphasizing the colonnaded streets, see A. Segal, "Roman Cities in the Province of Arabia," *Journal of the Society of Architectural Historians* 40/2 (1981), 108–21; *idem, Monumental Architecture in Roman Palestine and Provincia Arabia* [Hebrew] (Haifa: University of Haifa, 1995), 15–60. For a detailed discussion of the colonnaded streets at Gerasa, see R. Parapetti, "Architectural and Urban Space in Roman Gerasa," *Mesopotamia* 18 (1983–84), 37–74.

[4]   Netzer, Weiss, *Zippori*, 40–42; Z. Weiss, E. Netzer, "Sepphoris in the Roman Period," in Nagy *et al.*, eds., *Sepphoris*, 31–33. Hirschfeld, *Guide*, 18.

[5]   See for example: *t. Šabb.* 10.1 (ed. Lieberman, 2, 41). Stores selling all sorts of goods were located alongside the main thoroughfare, see *Gen. Rab.* 84:5 (ed. Theodor-Albeck, 1005).

[6]   J. J. Coulton, *The Architectural Development of the Greek Stoa* (Oxford: Clarendon, 1976), 177–80. On the economic services provided by the cities of Roman Palestine, see Z. Safrai, *The Economy of Roman Palestine* (London: Routledge, 1994), 34–39.

[7]   For Sepphoris: *b. Yoma* 11a; *b. ʿErub.* 54b. For Tiberias, see *Cant. Rab.* 27:3.

FIGURE 1
One of the main colonnaded streets in Sepphoris
(photo: G. Laron)

clearly corresponds to the situation emerging from the Talmudic sources. The lower market (*šûq taḥtôn*) can thus be identified with the colonnaded streets extending through the level area at the bottom of the hill together with the *forum* (see below), whereas the upper market (*šûq* ᶜ*elyôn*) consisted of the stores built on the summit, of which some have been excavated lately.[8] In the city's market the *agoranomos* held court and this is where he controlled the weights and measures of the merchants, traders, and craftsmen.[9] A colonnaded street is most probably depicted on one side of a lead weight found in Sepphoris. The other side bears a Greek inscription indicating that its weight is accurate, as determined by of two *agoranomoi*, Simon the son of Aianos and Iustus his son.[10]

Several public buildings were constructed along the main thoroughfares of Tiberias and Sepphoris. At Sepphoris, a large structure located in the center of the Roman city next to the intersection of the two colonnaded streets is under excavation by a team from the University of South Florida.[11] This edifice, approximately 70 × 95 m, features a high

---

[8]   The identification of the different markets at Tiberias is not so clear. On the basis of the citation from *Cant. Rab.* 1:27:3, S. Klein suggested that the lower market of Tiberias be identified as the area close to the shore of Sea of Galilee, whereas the upper market is to its southwest, see S. Klein, *Galilee* [Hebrew] (Jerusalem: Mossad Harav Kook, 1945), 99–100. Using the same source but interpreting it differently, Eliav suggested that the upper market be identified as northern part of the city, whereas the lower one should be on its southern side; see Eliav, *Sites*, 17–18.

[9]   For the duties of the *agoranomos* in the Greco-Roman city, see A. H. M. Jones, *The Greek City from Alexander to Justinian* (Oxford: Oxford University, 1966), 215–17.

[10]   Netzer, Weiss, *Zippori*, 41; E. M. Meyers, E. Netzer and C. L. Meyers, "Sepphoris—'Ornament of all Galilee'," *BA* 49 (1986), 16–17. Some Jewish *agoranomoi* from Tiberias are also known by name; see S. Kedar, "Two Early Weights of Herod Antipas and Agrippa II and the Early History of Tiberias," *INJ* 9 (1986–87), 29–35. On the *agoranomus* in Talmudic literature see D. Sperber, "On the Office of the Agoranomus in Roman Palestine," *ZDMG* 127 (1977), 227–43.

[11]   J. F. Strange *et al.*, "Zippori," *ESI* 13 (1993), 29–30; *idem*, "The Eastern Basilical Building at Sepphoris," in R. Nagy *et al.*, eds., *Sepphoris*, 117–21. If the identifi-

standard of architecture. It consists of a central courtyard surrounded by rooms of various sizes that are paved with decorated mosaics. Although the excavators tend to regard this structure as a basilical hall, my view, which is based on the published material, is that it is preferable to identify the building as a *forum* (*agora*).

Two Roman bathhouses were located on either side of the main colonnaded street in Sepphoris.[12] The eastern one, dated to the late first or early second century C.E., is smaller. It included a long, narrow hot room (*caldarium*), flanked by a few rooms, one of which contained a stepped pool. The western bathhouse, dated to the third or fourth century C.E., is a larger building (27 × 26 m). It was planned in the best Roman tradition, with two perpendicular axes of symmetry. The bath had three *caldaria*, one of which was octagonal, a *tepidarium*, two *frigidaria* with small pools, and other rooms, all surrounding a central courtyard. Many of the rooms had mosaic floors featuring geometric patterns. The eastern bathhouse was later demolished. A large building adorned with colorful mosaics and identified as a municipal basilica was constructed above its ruins and other earlier structures during the early Byzantine period.[13] It was named the Nile Festival building because the

---

cation of the building as a *forum* or *agora* is accepted, it might be part of the lower market mentioned by the rabbis.

[12]   Netzer, Weiss, Zippori, 43; Weiss, Netzer, "Sepphoris in the Roman Period," 34. On the origin of the Roman bathhouse and its development, see F. K. Yegül, *Baths and Bathing in Classical Antiquity* (Cambridge: MIT Press, 1992), esp. 48–91. For the bathhouses in the eastern provinces, see I. Nielsen, *Thermae et Balnea* (Aarhus: Aarhus University, 1990) 1, 95–118; F. K. Yegül, "The Roman Baths at Isthmia in Their Mediterranean Context," in T. E. Gregory, ed., *The Corinthia in the Roman Period* (Ann Arbor: *Journal of Roman Archaeology*, Supplementary Series no. 8, 1993), 95–113. For the evidence in Roman Palestine, see M. Gichon, "Roman Bath-Houses in Eretz-Israel" [Hebrew], *Qadmoniot* 11 (1978), 37–59. Roman bathhouses were also used by the Jewish population in ancient Palestine; see Y. Z. Eliav, "Did the Jews at First Abstain from Using the Roman Bath-House?" [Hebrew], *Cathedra* 75 (1995), 3–35.

[13]   Netzer, Weiss, "New Evidence," 166–71

mosaic floor in one of its rooms depicts scenes of the Nile festival celebrated in Egypt. This building, which covers an area 55 × 50 m, has a
basilical hall in its center, surrounded on all sides by corridors and other
rooms. To the east of the main hall was probably an inner courtyard
around which rooms were built.

One of the public bathhouses in Tiberias, the *dēmosion* (a Greek
loanword used by the rabbis), was uncovered east of the colonnaded
street (Fig. 2).[14] It is 42 × 31 m in size and has two wings. The western

FIGURE 2
A room in the bathhouse uncovered in Tiberias east of the colonnaded street
(photo: Zeev Weiss)

---

[14]   Hirschfeld, *Guide*, 14–17. For the term, see, for example, *y. Peʾa* 8:9 (21b);
y. Šabb. 1:1 (3a); *y. Sanh.* 7:19 (25d). For the use of the term *dêmôsîôn* in Talmudic
literature, see M. Jastrow, *A Dictionary of the Targumim, the Talmud Babli and
Yerushalmi, and the Midrashic Literature* (London: Luzac, 1886–1903; rpt. New
York, 1950), 300, *s.v. dîmôsîn*; A. Kohut, *Arukh Completum* (Vienna, 1878–92)

wing contains hot rooms (*caldaria*), pools, and other spaces for bathing purposes, whereas the eastern one has an *apodyterium* and various sizable rooms for social gatherings. Another public building, identified as a covered market, adjacent to the city's main thoroughfare, was unearthed near this bathhouse.[15] The building has one large hall with several rows of piers extending across its width, originally built to support the superstructure.

Buildings for entertainment, which will be dealt with below in connection with cultural life, also existed in the Jewish cities of Roman Palestine, much as they did in any other city of the time.[16] A medium-sized theater compound within the urban infrastructure was found at Sepphoris.[17] The theater, which has been dated to the early second

---

3 84–85; S. Krauss, *Talmudische Archäologie* (Leipzig, 1910) 1, 224. The bathhouse depicted in the topographical mosaic from Antioch is named *dēmosi<o>n*, see D. Levi, *Antioch Mosaic Pavements* (Princeton: Princeton University, 1947) 1, 330. For a discussion on the demosion of Tiberias in Talmudic literature, see Eliav, *Sites*, 22–32.

[15]   Hirschfeld, *Guide*, 12.

[16]   For studies on buildings for entertainment in Roman Palestine and their construction see A. Segal, *Theaters in Roman Palestine and Provincia Arabia* (Leiden: Brill, 1995), 1–34; Z. Weiss, "Roman Leisure Culture and its Influence upon the Jewish Population in the Land of Israel" [Hebrew], *Qadmoniot* 28 (1995), 2–19; *idem*, "Buildings for Entertainment," in Daniel Sperber, *The Cities of Roman Palestine* (Oxford University Press, in press).

[17]   It was once customary to date the building of the theater discovered by Leroy Waterman in 1930 on the hill's northern slope to the Herodian period, although it was debated whether it was built by Herod himself or by his son Herod Antipas; see S. Yeivin, "Historical and Archaeological Notes," in L. Waterman, ed., *Preliminary Report of the University of Michigan Excavations at Sepphoris* (Ann Arbor: University of Michigan, 1937), 29–30; see also A. Segal, "Theaters in Eretz Israel in the Roman Period," in A. Kasher *et al.*, eds., *Greece and Rome in Eretz Israel* (Jerusalem: Yad Izhak ben Zvi, 1989), 532. Several soundings conducted by the Joint Sepphoris Project and the Hebrew University team clearly indicate that the theater was built toward the end of the first century or the beginning of the second century C.E.; see Netzer, Weiss, *Zippori*, 19.

century, has a diameter of 74 m and contains seating for 4,500. It was planned and constructed according to the Roman conventions that influenced many other theaters built in ancient Palestine (Fig. 3). According to Josephus, Tiberias had a stadium that was located on the outskirts of the city.[18] Although we lack any information regarding the exact location or plan of this stadium,[19] it was presumably built by

FIGURE 3
Sepphoris: General view of the Theater
(photo: G. Laron)

---

[18]   *BJ* 2.618; 3.539–40; *Vit.* 92; 331.

[19]   On the basis of the historical sources, it seems that the building was located on the periphery of the city or even beyond its limits; see M. Schwabe, "The History of Tiberias" [Hebrew] in M. Schwabe, J. Gutman, eds., *In Memoriam Iohannis Lewy* (Jerusalem: Magnes, 1949), 238–41. This is in contrast to Avi-Yonah's opinion that the stadium should be located within the city: M. Avi-Yonah, *Carta's Atlas of the Period of the Second Temple, the Mishnah and the Talmud Period* (Jerusalem: Carta, 1966), 92. According to Harris, the stadium should be located to the south of the

Herod Antipas, who founded the city as the capital of Galilee.[20] The stadium is mentioned once again in the third century C.E., thus indicating that it continued to function for a considerable period of time.[21] Tiberias also had a theater, which has been partially excavated (Fig. 4). It is dated to the third century and is located along to the city's main thoroughfare.[22] Literary sources and numismatic finds reveal that both Tiberias and Sepphoris had additional public buildings befitting a Roman city, such as a council house (the *boulē*) or a pagan temple, although no remains of such structures have been found to date.[23] The numismatic

---

city, next to the lake shore (H. A. Harris, *Greek Athletics and the Jews* [Cardiff: University of Wales Press, 1976], 42). Lämmer, however, locates the building to the north of the city (M. Lämmer, "Griechische Wettkämpfe in Galiläa unter der Herrschaft des Herodes Antipas," *Kölner Beiträge zur Sportwissenschaft* 5 [1976], 49).

[20]   Avi-Yonah, "The Foundation of Tiberias," *IEJ* 1 (1950–51), 164; E. M. Smallwood, The Jews under Roman Rule, (Leiden: Brill, 1981), 183–84; Lämmer, "Griechische Wettkämpfe," 37–67.

[21]   *y. ʿErub.* 5:1 (22b), and see also: S. Liebermann, "Emendations on the Jerushalmi (c)" [Hebrew], *Tarbiz* 3 (1932), 207–9.

[22]   Hirschfeld, *Guide*, 19–20; *idem*, "Excavations at Tiberias Reveal Remains of Church and Possibly Theater," *BA* 54 (1991), 170–71. The excavator dates the theater to the third century C.E., without specifying the exact period of its construction. Although one should await the completion of the excavation and the publication of the results, an earlier date, perhaps similar to that at Sepphoris, can be anticipated.

[23]   The *boulē* of Tiberias is mentioned in several sources; see *y. ʿAbod. Zar.* 3:13 (43b). It had a synagogue of its own: *y. Šeq.* 7:3 (50c); *y. Taʿan.* 1:2 (64b). With regard to Sepphoris, the Palestinian Talmud mentions the *bouleutai* approaching R. Judah the Patriarch together with others in the *salutatio*: *y. Šabb.* 12:3 (13a); *y. Hor.* 3:7 (48c), and see also R. Kimmelman, "The Conflict between the Priestly Oligarchy and the Sages in the Talmudic Period (An Explication of PT *Shabbat* 12:3, 13c = *Horayot* 3:5, 48c)" [Hebrew], *Zion* 48 (1983), 135–43; L. I. Levine, *The Rabbinic Class of Roman Palestine in Late Antiquity* (Jerusalem: Jewish Theological Seminary and Yad Izhak ben Zvi, 1989), 167–68. On the *boulē* in Talmudic sources, see A. Gulak, "*Bwly* and *Isṭrṭygy*," [Hebrew], *Tarbiz* 11 (1940), 119–22; G. Alon, "The Strategoi in the Cities of Palestine during the Roman Period," *Tarbiz* 14 (1943), 145–55.

FIGURE 4
Tiberias: section of a theater's outer circle wall
(courtesy of Y. Hirschfeld)

evidence leads one to assume that in both cities there were tetrastyle temples with Syrian or regular gables.[24]

Several of the private dwellings in these cities were built with great elegance. South of the theater at Sepphoris, the Joint Sepphoris Project

---

[24]   Y. Meshorer, *City Coins of Eretz Israel and the Decapolis in the Roman Period* (Jerusalem: Israel Museum, 1984), 34. For the coins of Sepphoris, see also Meshorer, *City Coins*, 37 and *idem*, "Sepphoris and Rome," in O. Morkholm, *et al.*, eds., *Greek Numismatics and Archaeology: Essays in Honor of Margaret Thompson* (Belgium: Cultura, 1979), 159–71. A temple in honor of Hadrian was erected in Tiberias but according to Epiphanius its construction was not completed, see Epiph., *Adv. Haeres.* 30.12. See also Z. Rubin, "Joseph the Comes and the Attempts to Convert the Galilee to Christianity in the Fourth Century" [Hebrew], *Cathedra* 26 (1982), 105–16, esp. 110–13.

uncovered a private home, dated to the early third century C.E., with a peristyle courtyard in its center. This elaborate structure apparently had two stories aside from a basement below its southern part. The main room, a *triclinium* (the Roman dining hall), was located north of the courtyard. Some of the walls within this building were decorated with frescoes, and its various rooms were paved with mosaics. The most important of the floors, the Dionysiac mosaic (see below), was uncovered in the *triclinium*.[25] Several other structures with a similar layout were revealed in Sepphoris. One of them was excavated in the western part of the hill's summit.[26] An additional two, which have been partially excavated, are found in lower Sepphoris. One is located to the north of the market building, and the other is located along the main colonnaded street, at the bottom of the hill.[27] Buildings of this type were also erected in Tiberias. On the basis of recent excavations, it seems that the building in Tiberias formerly identified as a public basilica is none other than an elaborate private building of the Sepphoris type, erected in mid-fourth century C.E. Its core consisted of a basilical hall with a peristyle courtyard to its west, flanked on three sides by various rooms.[28] Another

---

[25]   Netzer, Weiss, *Zippori*, 30–33.

[26]   This building was initially excavated by Leroy Waterman who considered it to be an early church, but the late Michael Avi-Yonah correctly criticized this conclusion and identified it as a Roman mansion; see Waterman, *Preliminary Report*, 4–6; M. Avi-Yonah, "Sepphoris," *Encyclopedia of Archaeological Excavations in the Holy Land* (Jerusalem: Israel Exploration Society and Massada Press, 1975–78), 4, 1053–54. This conclusion is corroborated by the finds of the South Florida University team who re-excavated the building; see J. F. Strange, "Six Campaigns at Sepphoris: The University of South Florida Excavations, 1983–1989," in L. I. Levine, ed., *The Galilee in Late Antiquity* (New York and Jerusalem: Jewish Theological Seminary, 1992), 344–51.

[27]   Z. Weiss, E. Netzer, "The Hebrew University Excavations at Sepphoris, 1992–1996" [Hebrew] *Qadmoniot* 30 (1997), 9–10.

[28]   A. Druks, S. Tamari, "Tiberias" [Hebrew], *HA* 10 (1964), 16; *idem*, "Tiberias" [Hebrew], *HA* 12 (1964), 16. For a new interpretation based on further excavations, see Y. Hirschfeld, "Tiberias" [Hebrew], *HA* 104 (1995), 34–36.

structure uncovered in Tiberias several years ago, which was tentatively identified by the excavator as a *bêt midrāš* (study hall), is possibly the peristyle courtyard of a private home with a plan similar to that of the buildings revealed in Sepphoris.[29] These buildings, which have many parallels throughout the Roman world (e.g., in Antioch, northern Syria, and several North African cities), reflect private architecture at its best during the second and third centuries C.E., as it was adopted in the Jewish cities of the Galilee.[30]

The periphery of the Jewish cities of Roman Palestine was also similar to that of pagan cities in the region. A gate with a projecting rounded

FIGURE 5
General view of the two round tower gates in Tiberias
(courtesy of G. Foerster)

29   Hirschfeld, *Guide*, 26–27. For the interpretation of the building as a private home, see Z. Weiss, "The Architectural Background of a Private Building in Tiberias" [Hebrew], ʿAtiqot (in press).

30   R. Stillwell, "Houses of Antioch," *DOP* 15 (1967), 47–57; Y. Thebert, "Private Life and Domestic Architecture in Roman Africa," in P. Veyne, ed., *A History of Private Life: From Pagan Rome to Byzantine* (Cambridge: Belknap, 1987), 353–409.

tower on either side of the main entrance was uncovered south of Tiberias (Fig. 5).[31] The gate itself is located a short distance from the city's infrastructure, indicating the limits of the city. This city gate can possibly be identified with the *pîlê* (*pûlê*) *dĕ-ṭîberyâ*, mentioned repeatedly in rabbinic sources.[32] A similar structure was revealed in nearby Gadara.[33]

The burial grounds of the Jewish cities were not concentrated in one place, but, as in any Roman city, were scattered around their outskirts.[34] The tombs, especially the mausolea, were built near the main road leading to and from the city, as in Tiberias, where, according to Resh Laqish, the *napšā* *dĕ-siriqîn* ("mausoleum of Sirikios") was located along the road leading west, toward nearby Bet Maon.[35] A similar layout has been

---

[31]   G. Foerster, "The Excavations at Tiberias" [Hebrew], *Qadmoniot* 10 (1977), 87–91; Hirschfeld, *Guide*, 21.

[32]   Although *pûlê/pîlê dĕ-ṭîberyâ* is mentioned repeatedly in rabbinic sources, it is not clear whether this refers to a single gate or to other structures that could have been located in the city; see *Tanḥ B., Wa-yĕḥî*, 6 (107b); *Tanḥ, Šôpṭîm* 10; *Deut. Rab.* 29 (ed. Lieberman, 33); *y. Ned.* 7:6 (40c). For a discussion on the term *pylē* in relation to the city gates of Tiberias see Y. Z. Eliav, "'Pule'—'Puma'—'Sfat Medinah' and a Halakha Concerning Bath-Houses" [Hebrew], *Sidra* 11 (1995), 10–13.

[33]   T. Weber, R. G. Khouri, *Umm Qais: Gadara of the Decapolis* (Amman: Al Kutba, 1989), 29–30; T. Weber, A. Hoffmann, "Gadara of the Decapolis, Preliminary Report of the 1989 Season at Umm Qeis," *ADAJ* 34 (1990), 324–25. T. Weber, "Gadara of the Decapolis: Tiberias Gate, Qanawat al-Far'oun and Beit Rusan: Achievements in Excavation and Restoration at Umm Qais," in S. Kerner, ed., *The Near East in Antiquity* (Amman: Al Kutba, 1911) 2, 123–26. Other gates of different types have been excavated in Roman Palestine, see for example: G. Mazor, R. Bar-Natan, "The Beth Shean Excavation Project—1992–1994 IAA Expedition" [Hebrew], *HA* 105 (1996), 24–25; and see also Segal, *Monumental Architecture*, 89–108. For general information on gates in the cities of the Roman empire see MacDonald, *Architecture* II, 75–77, 82–86.

[34]   Z. Weiss, "The Location of Jewish Cemeteries in the Galilee in the Mishnaic and Talmudic Periods" [Hebrew], in I. Singer, ed., *Graves and Burial Practices in Israel in the Ancient Period* (Jerusalem: Yad Izhak ben Zvi, 1994), 230–40.

[35]   *y. ʿErub.* 5:1 (22b) and S. Liebermann, *Hayerushalmi Kiphshuto* (Jerusalem: Darom, 1934), 292–93; see also Schwabe, "The History of Tiberias," 241–43.

noted in other Roman cities in ancient Palestine, such as Gadara, Gerasa, and Neapolis.[36]

The similarities between the Jewish and non-Jewish cities of ancient Palestine were not confined to city planning and architecture but also found expression in their artistic forms. Several of the public and private buildings in both cities were decorated with colorful mosaics that included depictions of both humans and animals. To date, a few mosaics have been revealed in the Roman bathhouse that was built in the center of the city of Tiberias. These mosaics are decorated with geometric designs and some of them also featured vegetal motifs, animals, and birds.[37] A mosaic of simple design was also exposed in the building that we have already suggested should be identified as a domicile.[38]

The extent of the excavations conducted to date at Sepphoris and the number of mosaics discovered there far exceed those of Tiberias, but in our opinion this artistic medium was put to equal use in both of these cities. Some of the domiciles from the Roman and Byzantine periods in Sepphoris were decorated with colorful mosaics, of which two are particularly noteworthy for their rich figurative designs.[39] The earlier one was uncovered in the *triclinium* of a Roman mansion that

---

[36] For Gadara see Weber, Hoffmann, "Gadara of the Decapolis: Preliminary Report of the 1989 Season at Umm Qeis," 324–25; S. Kerner, A. Hoffmann, "Gadara—Umm Qeis, Preliminary Reports on the 1991–1992 Seasons," *ADAJ* 37 (1993), 360–63. For Gerasa, see C. L. Kraeling, *Gerasa, City of the Decapolis* (New Haven: Yale University, 1938), 549; M. Smadeh, A. Michèle Rasson, J. Seigne, "Fouille sauvetage dans la necropole nord-ouest de Jerash," *ADAJ* 36 (1992), 261–79; J. Seigne, T. Morin, "Preliminary Report on a Mausoleum at the Turn of the BC/AD Century at Jerash," *ADAJ* 39 (1995), 175–91. For Neapolis, see Y. Magen, *The History and the Archaeology of Shechem (Neapolis) during the First to Fourth Centuries A.D.* [Hebrew] (diss., Hebrew University, 1989), 99–100, 245, 269.

[37] R. Talgam, "Mosaic Floors in Tiberias" [Hebrew], in Hirschfeld, ed., *Tiberias from Its Foundation*, 125–31.

[38] Hirschfeld, *Guide*, 26–27; and see above n. 29.

[39] Other domiciles at Sepphoris also had mosaics of a simple kind. Some of the homes in Sepphoris were also decorated with mosaics featuring geometric designs, sometimes even populated with vegetal motifs or animals, see, for example, Water-

was exposed on the summit of the hill. The decorated part of this floor is T-shaped, a common arrangement in other *triclinia*, due to the placement of the couches in the Roman dining room. The floor, which is dated to the early third century C.E., features various scenes from the Dionysiac myth and cult.[40] The richness of detail, the number of the depictions, and especially the combination of myth and the actual performance of the Dionysian cult in one floor, single out this pavement, not only from among the mosaics of Sepphoris, but also from Roman art in general.[41] Another similarly arranged mosaic was discovered in the *triclinium* of a domicile excavated to the west of the main colonnaded street in Sepphoris. This mosaic, which is dated to the end of the third century C.E., contains four panels. Orpheus, the divine musician, is depicted in the large central panel, soothing with his music the animals that have gathered around him (Fig. 6). The other panels feature various themes connected with daily life in the Roman household.[42] T-shaped mosaics with such a clear arrangement ornamented

---

man, *Preliminary Report*, 5; Netzer, Weiss, *Zippori*, 42–43; *idem*, "Sepphoris, 1992–1996," 11, 14.

[40] Netzer, Weiss, *Zippori*, 34–39; Z. Weiss, R. Talgam, "The Dionysiac Mosaic Floor from Sepphoris," in *IV Coloquio Internacional Sobre Mosaico Antiguo—Palencia Mérida (Octubre 1990)* (Palencia: Asociacion Espanola del Mosaico, 1994), 231–37.

[41] Dionysian themes similar to those found in the Sepphoris mosaic decorated private houses in the Roman East, e.g., in Gerasa, Antioch, Nea Paphos, and elsewhere, see H. Joyce, "A Mosaic from Gerasa in Orange, Texas, and Berlin," *MDAIR* 87 (1980), 307–25; I. Kriseleit, *Antike Mosaiken* (Berlin: Staatliche Museen zu Berlin, 1985), 19–21; Levi, *Antioch Mosaic Pavements*, 21–24, 40–45, 156–63; W. A. Daszewski, *Dionysos der Erlöser* (Mainz am Rhein: P. von Zabern, 1985), 21–45; C. Kondoleon, *Domestic and Divine: Roman Mosaics in the House of Dionysos* (Ithaca: Cornell University, 1995), 191–269; H. G. Gotte, "Alpheios in Syrien—Zu einem Mosaik in Tartus," *DaM* 5 (1991), 71–72. Such depictions also appear in many houses of Roman North Africa, see K. M. D. Dunbabin, *The Mosaics of Roman North Africa* (Oxford: Clarendon Press, 1978), 173–87.

[42] Depictions of Orpheus are also to be found in other Roman sites, see D. Michaelides, "A New Orpheus Mosaic in Cyprus," in V. Karageorghis, ed., *Acts of*

FIGURE 6
*Orpheus the Divine Musician depicted in a mosaic
installed in the* triclinium *of a private house uncovered in lower Sepphoris*
(photo: G. Laron)

the *International Archaeological Symposium "Cyprus between the Orient and the
Occident"* (Nicosia: Department of Antiquities, Cyprus, 1986), 473–87; A. Ovadiah,
S. Mucznik, "Orpheus in Roman and Early Byzantine Art," N. Kenaan, ed., *Assaph:
Studies in Art History* (Tel Aviv: Tel Aviv University, 1980) 1, 43–56; I. Jesnick, "The
Mannerist Depiction in Orpheus Mosaics," in *IV Coloquio Internacional Sobre
Mosaico Antiguo*, 333–42. This theme continued to be popular during the Byzan-
tine period: see P. H. Vincent "Une mosaïque byzantine a Jérusalem," *RB* 10 (1901),
436–44; A. Ovadiah, S. Mucznik, "The Jerusalem Orpheus—A Pagan or a Christian
Figure?" [Hebrew] in A. Oppenheimer, *et al., Jerusalem in the Second Temple Period*
(Jerusalem: Yad Izhak Ben Zvi, 1980), 415–33. The theme also appears in early Jewish
art, for example in the synagogue mosaic pavement from Gaza dated to the early
sixth century C.E., which contains the figure of King David portrayed as Orpheus,
see A. Ovadiah, "The Synagogue at Gaza," in L. I. Levine, ed., *Ancient Synagogues
Revealed* (Jerusalem: Israel Exploration Society, 1981), 129–32; R. Ovadiah, A.
Ovadiah, *Hellenistic, Roman and Early Byzantine Mosaic Pavements in Israel* (Rome:
"L'Erma" di Bretschneider, 1987), 60–61; see also: M. Barsch, "The David Mosaic
of Gaza," in N. Kenaan, ed., *Assaph*, 1–41.

the *triclinia* of sumptuous homes in the Roman world,[43] a few examples of which have been found in Roman Palestine.[44] The designs selected for the decoration of the triclinia in Sepphoris as well as in other localities are based mainly on Greek mythology.[45]

Colorful mosaics also adorned the floors of certain public buildings erected in Sepphoris during the Roman and Byzantine periods. Some of the rooms of the basilical hall or market building discussed above were decorated with both figurative and geometrical mosaics, some of which are particularly rich. Among the designs revealed there are depictions of a city and Nilotic landscape and acanthus medallions populated by plants, animals, and various instruments.[46] Colorful mosaics with various geometrical and floral designs have been uncovered in some of the

---

[43]   Several T-shaped *triclinium* mosaics have been excavated, for example, at Antioch in Syria, Nea Paphos in Cyprus, and Port Magnus, Tébessa, and El-Djem in North Africa, see, for Antioch: Levi, *Antioch Mosaic Pavements* 1, 15–25, 91–99, 119–26, 200–1; Stillwell, "Houses of Antioch," 47–57; for Nea Paphos: D. Michaelides, *Cypriot Mosaics* (Cyprus: Department of Antiquities, Cyprus, 1987), 16, 28–29; for the T-shaped *triclinia* mosaics from the cities in North Africa, see I. Lavin, "The Hunting Mosaics of Antioch and Their Sources," *DOP* 17 (1963), 215, 225–29.

[44]   See for example: Y. Rapuano, "Ein Yael," *IEJ* 39 (1989), 112–15; G. Edelstein, "What's a Roman Villa Doing Outside Jerusalem?" *BAR* 16 (1990), 32–42. An analysis of the relationship between the acanthus border in the mosaic pavement from Neapolis (Shechem, Nablus), which is surrounded by white tesserae, and the two partly preserved panels to its south leads to the conclusion that the room in which they were found was a *triclinium* with a T-shaped mosaic. For details on the mosaic, see C. M. Dauphin, "A Roman Mosaic Pavement from Nablus," *IEJ* 29 (1979), 11–33.

[45]   In her discussion of the Dionysiac mosaic floors found in North Africa, K. Dunbabin claims that these were suitable and popular themes for the decoration of Roman dining rooms (Dunbabin, *Mosaics of Roman North Africa*, 173). According to David Parish, this custom evolved in several ways from the fourth to seventh centuries C.E. (D. Parish, "A Mythological Theme in the Decoration of Late Roman Dining Rooms: Dionysos and His Circle," *Revue Archéologique* [1995], 307–32).

[46]   L. A. Roussin, "A New Mosaic from Sepphoris in the Galilee," in *IV Coloquio Internacional Sobre Mosaico Antiguo*, 221–30; *idem*, "The Birds and Fishes Mosaic at Sepphoris," in R. Nagy, *et al.*, eds., *Sepphoris*, 123–25.

rooms of the Roman bathhouse located to the west of the cardo. Lavish
and varied mosaics have been found in the Nile Festival building, dated
to the early Byzantine period. In addition to the geometric mosaics
found in this building, there are also figurative mosaics whose style and
design differ from the earlier examples revealed in the city. In the fifth
century C.E., the layout of mosaic floors in the East underwent a significant change. The floor surface was no longer divided into separate
panels, as in the Dionysiac and Orpheus mosaics, but rather was
rendered as a single unit.[47] The scenes now cover the entire floor and
the images sometimes face all directions. This technique was employed
in the Nile Festival mosaic as well as in the one featuring dancing
Amazons, both of which are located in the Nile Festival building.[48] The
Nile Festival mosaic, which was preserved intact and is the more important of the two, contains depictions of a Nilotic landscape within which
are incorporated various hunting scenes. Also meriting mention are the
figurative motifs that were uncovered in the other rooms of the building, such as the centaur, the pair of hunters shown in frontal view, and
the two figures (one of them an Amazon) riding horses and taking part
in the hunting of animals. Several parallels to these scenes are to be
found in Palestine, but the mosaics of the Nile Festival building apparently represent a new iconographic and stylistic tradition that was
previously unknown in the region.[49]

---

[47]   E. Kitzinger, "Stylistic Developments in the Pavement Mosaics in the Greek
East from the Age of Constantine to the Age of Justinian," in *La Mosaïque Gréco-
Romaine* (Paris: CNRS, 1965) 1, 341–51; Lavin, "Hunting Mosaics of Antioch,"
181–286.

[48]   E. Netzer, Z. Weiss, "Byzantine Mosaics at Sepphoris: New Finds," *Israel
Museum Journal* 10 (1992), 75–80; Netzer, Weiss, *Zippori*, 46–54; Z. Weiss, E.
Netzer, "The Mosaics of the House of the Nile Festival," in R. Nagy, *et al.*, eds.,
Sepphoris, 127–31.

[49]   Nilotic scenes similar to those found at Sepphoris have parallels in private as
well as public buildings excavated in the region; see A. M. Schneider, *The Church of
Multiplying of the Loaves and Fishes*, tran. E. Graf (London: Coldwell, 1937), 52–80;
M. Avi-Yonah, "The Haditha Mosaic Pavement," *IEJ* 22 (1972), 118–22; N. Tzori,

Equally splendid mosaics were found in the synagogues that have been excavated in the Jewish cities.[50] The depictions in the Tiberias and Sepphoris mosaics, as well as those discovered in other Palestinian synagogues, mainly reflect the iconographic tradition characteristic of Jewish art in antiquity. This art met the needs of the Jewish community, but was clearly not created independently. It absorbed several motifs borrowed from pagan art of that time, which were incorporated within a new framework and given a different significance.[51] Moreover, one

---

"The House of Kyrios Leontis at Beth Shean" [Hebrew], *EI* 11 (1973), 229–47. Parallels of the two riders hunting wild animals appear in a mosaic pavement at Apamea for example; see C. Dulière, *La mosaïque des amazones* (Brussels: Centre belge de recherches archeologiques a Apamée de Syrie, 1968), 1–15. This theme also appears on Coptic tapestry from Egypt, dated to the fifth century C.E.; see A. Stauffer, *Textile of Late Antiquity* (New York: Metropolitan Museum of Art, 1995), 10, 22.

[50]   Synagogues decorated with colorful mosaics were found both at Tiberias and Hammath Tiberias: M. Dothan, *Hammath Tiberias* (Jerusalem: Israel Exploration Society, 1983), 33–52; A. Berman, "First Discovery of a Synagogue in Tiberias," in Hirschfeld, ed., *Tiberias from its Foundation*, 49–52. To date, two synagogues from the Byzantine period decorated with mosaics have been found at Sepphoris, and there is some evidence of a third one: R. P. Viaud, *Nazareth* (Paris: A. Picard *et fils*, 1910), 179–84; Netzer, Weiss, *Zippori*, 55. One of the structures, located on the eastern side of the city and almost completely exposed, contains a colorful mosaic with unusual depictions, some of which make their first appearance in ancient Jewish art: Z. Weiss, E. Netzer, *Promise and Redemption, A Synagogue Mosaic from Sepphoris* (Jerusalem: Israel Museum, 1996), 14–40; *idem*, "The Synagogue Mosaic," Nagy, *et al.*, eds., *Sepphoris*, 133–39.

[51]   The zodiacs found to date in several Palestinian synagogues clearly show the nature of this process; see G. Foerster, "Representations of the Zodiac in Ancient Synagogues and Their Iconographic Sources" [Hebrew], *EI* 18 (1985), 380–91. Other examples illustrate the relationship between Jewish and Christian art during the Byzantine period and clarify this process; see M. Avi-Yonah, "The Mosaic Pavement of the Maon (Nirim) Synagogue" [Hebrew], *EI* 6 (1960), 90–93; *idem*, "La Mosaïque juive dans ses relations avec la mosaïque classique," in *La Mosaïque gréco-romaine* 1, 325–29; G. Foerster, "Christian Allegories and Symbols in the Mosaic Designs of Sixth Century Eretz Israel Synagogues" [Hebrew], in D. Jacoby, Y. Tsafrir, eds., *Jews, Samaritans and Christians in Byzantine Palestine* (Jerusalem:

can draw stylistic parallels between the mosaics of the synagogues in the Jewish cities and the other mosaics in the Syro-Palestine region.[52]

The unearthing in both cities, but especially at Sepphoris, of such an assemblage of mosaic pavements varying in their iconography, composition, style, and chronology, together with others featuring numerous geometric designs has made a significant contribution to our understanding of mosaic art and its development in ancient Palestine. Such a rich and colorful selection is almost unknown at any other site in the region and ranks Sepphoris among the important mosaic centers of the Roman and Byzantine East. The presence of such mosaics in Sepphoris and Tiberias may indicate that these cities, like others throughout the ancient world, had their own mosaic industry and mosaicists. One can assume that these artists came into contact with, or were influenced by, the other important mosaic centers of ancient Palestine and were involved in creating mosaics not only in their own cities but also in nearby villages.[53]

Yad Izhak Ben Zvi, 1988), 198–206. For broad study analyzing the relationship between Jewish and non-Jewish art, see B. Narkiss, "Pagan, Christian and Jewish Elements in the Art of Ancient Synagogues," in L. I. Levine, ed., *The Synagogues in Late Antiquity* (Philadelphia: ASOR, 1987), 183–88.

[52]   See, for example, the stylistic discussion by M. Dothan, who points out several similarities between the synagogue mosaic from Hammath Tiberias and the mosaics from Antioch in Syria (Dothan, *Hammath Tiberias*, 42–45). R. Talgam, on the other hand, thinks that these depictions have their origin in Palestinian mosaics (Talgam, "Mosaic Floors in Tiberias," 125).

[53]   Two of the rooms of the Byzantine domicile excavated in Beth Shearim near Sepphoris contained geometric mosaics. In a similar fashion the same designs decorate one of the domiciles discovered in Sepphoris and dated to the same period; see Netzer, Weiss, *Zippori*, 42–43, and cf. F. Vitto, "Byzantine Mosaics at Beth She'arim: New Evidence for the History of the Site," ʿ*Atiqot* 28 (1996), 116–27. Although such geometric designs were widespread in the region, the proximity of the two sites and the fact that they had economic, social, and cultural links with one another allow for the assumption that in this case, too, a single mosaicist created both mosaics. It can only be conjectured that artisans resident in Sepphoris were invited to make the mosaics in Beth Shearim, since it is known that in the Roman

A survey of the finds indicates that Jewish cities did not differ architecturally and artistically from other cities in Roman Palestine. The plans of Tiberias and Sepphoris, including the public buildings constructed throughout these cities, reflect the general urbanization of Roman Palestine during the first centuries of the common era.[54] Although we lack any conclusive proof that the construction was initiated, planned, and executed by the Jews, its seems quite evident that these buildings served the Jewish population—the dominant demographic element in these cities.[55] This conclusion may seem farfetched, but one must ask, why Jews would refrain from using a colonnaded street, a forum, a bath-

---

and Byzantine periods mosaicists worked not only in their own cities but also met the needs of nearby settlements. See, for example, the case of Gaza: M. Avi-Yonah, "The Gaza School of Mosaicists in the Fifth-Sixth Centuries C.E." [Hebrew], *EI* 12 (1975), 191–93; N. Stone, "Notes on the Shellal Mosaic (Ein ha-Besor) and the Mosaic Workshops at Gaza" [Hebrew], in Jacoby, Tsafrir, eds., *Jews, Samaritans and Christians in Byzantine Palestine*, 207–14. R. Hachlili rejects Avi-Yonah's view and thinks that the similarity between the mosaics listed by him is due to the fact that artisans in those places used design books (Hachlili, "On the Mosaicists of the 'School of Gaza,'" [Hebrew], *EI* 19 [1987], 46–58).

[54]   A. H. M. Jones, "The Urbanization of Palestine," *JRS* 21 (1931), 78–85; M. Avi-Yonah, *Historical Geography of Palestine from the Babylonian Exile up to the Arab Conquest* [Hebrew] (Jerusalem: Bialik, 1984), 67–73. For a clarification of the place of the Jewish community in the processes of urbanization in Roman Palestine see A. Oppenheimer, "Urbanization and the City Territories in Roman Palestine" [Hebrew], in I. M. Gafni *et al.*, eds., *The Jews in the Hellenistic-Roman World: Studies in Memory of Menahem Stern* (Jerusalem: Merkaz Zalman Shazar, 1996), 209–26. The founding of cities in ancient Palestine was followed by the massive construction of various public buildings that were meant to give them a striking and monumental appearance; see Y. Tsafrir, *Eretz Israel from the Destruction of the Second Temple to the Muslim Conquest: Archaeology and Art* [Hebrew] (Jerusalem: Yad Izhak ben Zvi, 1984), 59–88; A. Segal, "City Landscapes in Roman Palestine and Provincia Arabia" [Hebrew], *EI* 25 (1996), 456–62.

[55]   S. Safrai, "The Jewish Community in the Galilee and Golan in the Third and Fourth Centuries" [Hebrew], in Z. Baras, *et al.*, eds., *Eretz Israel*, 144–79; M. Goodman, *State and Society in Roman Galilee, A.D. 132–212* (Totowa: Rowman and Allanheld, 1983), 129.

house, or a basilica, built for the benefit of the citizens of the Roman city? The life-style of the Jews differed from that of their non-Jewish neighbors, but the actual erection of Roman-style structures was harmless. This is echoed in the homily of rabbis of the Ushan generation:

> R. Judah commenced the discussion: How fine are the works of this nation [referring to the Romans]. They have made streets, they have built bridges, they have erected baths .... R. Simeon b. Yohai answered and said: All that they made, they made for themselves: they built marketplaces to set harlots in them; baths to rejuvenate themselves; bridges to levy tolls for them ....[56]

Rabbi Judah bar Ilai praises Roman building that benefits not only society, but each and every individual. Rabbi Simeon bar Yohai perhaps does not deny the utility of Roman buildings, but rather objects to them in fear of "the ways of Rome," which uses these buildings for its own needs, in a negative way.

The similarity between Jewish and pagan cities in ancient Palestine was not limited to urban planning, art, architecture, and building techniques. Roman urban leisure habits were also generally adopted in the Jewish cities. The buildings for entertainment, especially the theater that, as mentioned earlier, was a common feature in the Jewish cities of the Galilee, symbolized for the rabbis the essential difference between Greco-Roman and Jewish culture. This is expressed in a statement of one of the sages:

> The nations of the world when You give them holidays, they eat and drink and carouse and go into their theaters and circuses, and they anger You, but it is the way of Israel that when You give them holidays, they eat and drink and are merry and go to their synagogues and academies and pray ....[57]

It can be assumed that entertainment buildings constructed in Sepphoris and Tiberias, mentioned before, were meant to serve at least their gentile residents. Nevertheless, Tiberias and Sepphoris both had a clear

---

[56] *b. Šabb.* 33b.

[57] *Pesiq. Rab.*, additions 4 (ed. Ish-Shalom, 200).

Jewish majority, as indicated in Jewish and certain Christian sources of the fourth century C.E., although it is difficult to determine what fraction of the population of the Jewish cities in the Galilee was made up of gentiles.[58] The non-Jewish population did frequent the entertainment buildings, but it is doubtful whether such institutions served this sector alone. The establishment and operation of entertainment buildings was a municipal endeavor. Municipal institutions, and often the affluent residents of a city motivated by local patriotism, initiated, built, and maintained places of entertainment for the enjoyment of their fellow citizens.[59] The municipal leadership of both Tiberias and Sepphoris was in Jewish hands throughout most of the period under discussion.[60] It is likely, therefore, that it was affluent Jewish administrators, as well as affluent Jewish citizens, who financed both the construction of buildings for entertainment and the actual performances held in them. It is also very conceivable that these buildings were frequented not only by the gentile population of Tiberias and Sepphoris, but also by the Jews who were, as mentioned above, the dominant demographic element in these cities. The Jews attended the games and spectacles and enjoyed what they saw.

[58] See above, n. 55. On the demography of Roman Palestine and the ratio between the Jewish and the pagan population, see R. Yankelevitch, "The Relative Size of the Jewish and Gentile Populations in Eretz Israel in the Roman Period" [Hebrew], *Cathedra* 61 (1991), 156–75; Y. Tsafrir, "Some Notes on the Settlement and Demography of Palestine in the Byzantine Period: The Archaeological Evidence," in J. D. Seger, ed., *Retrieving the Past: Essays on Archaeological Research and Methodology in Honor of Gus W. Van Beck* (Winona Lake: Eisenbrauns, 1996), 269–83.

[59] A. H. M. Jones, *The Roman Economy*, ed. P. A. Brunt (Oxford: Blackwell, 1974), 25–29; P. Garnsey, R. Saller, *The Roman Empire: Economy, Society and Culture* (Berkeley: University of California, 1987), 37–38; J. Reynolds, "Cities," in D. C. Braund, ed., *The Administration of the Roman Empire, 241 BC–AD 193* (Exeter: University of Exeter, 1988), 34–38.

[60] A. Oppenheimer, "Roman Rule and the Cities of the Galilee in Talmudic Literature," in L. I. Levine, ed., *The Galilee in Late Antiquity* (New York: Jewish Theological Seminary, 1992), 115–25.

A close study of rabbinic literature lends support to this conclusion.[61] Talmudic sources do not state explicitly that Jews attended games and spectacles. The injunctions of the rabbis against such attendance demonstrate the reality in which they lived: Jews residing in both the Jewish and non-Jewish cities of Roman Palestine did frequent the games, despite the rabbinic prohibition.[62] The rabbis, both *tannā’îm* and *’amôrā’îm*, based their objection to games and spectacles on moral and religious grounds. For example, R. Meir, who lived in Roman Palestine during the second century C.E., stated: "... One should not go to theaters or circuses because entertainments are arranged there in honor of the idols ...."[63] Later, R. Simeon b. Pazzi, a third-century *amora*, expressed his objection in a different tone, but still very clearly: "Happy is the man who has not walked to theaters and circuses of idolaters nor stood in the way of sinners—that is, he who does not attend contests of wild beasts ...."[64] R. Simeon b. Pazzi does not explicitly forbid visits to the buildings of entertainment and does not even reprimand those Jews who were wont to frequent them. He simply praises those who abstain from such practices, but at the same time sends a clear message to the others, that they would do well to follow suit. A similar tone reflecting the new reality is to be found in the words of other Palestinian amoraim of that period. R. Abba bar Kahana, for example, cites the words of Israel before God: "Almighty, I have never entered the theaters and circuses of the Gentiles, played with them, or enjoyed their shows."[65]

---

[61] Weiss, "Roman Leisure Culture," 16–19; *idem*, "*Lĕ-śimḥâ mâ zo’t ʿôśâ*—The Jews of Ancient Palestine and the Roman Games" [Hebrew], in *Jews and Gentiles in the Time of Second Temple Period and the Mishnah and Talmud Periods* (in press).

[62] See, for example, the case of Roman Caesarea, Z. Weiss, "The Jews and the Games in Roman Caesarea," in A. Raban and K. G. Holum, eds. *Caesarea Maritima: A Retrospective after Two Millennia* (DMOA 21: Leiden, 1996), 443–53.

[63] *t. ʿAbod. Zar.* 2:5 (ed. Zuckermandel, 462).

[64] *b. ʿAbod. Zar.* 18b.

[65] *Pesiq. Rab Kah.* 15:2 (ed. Mandelbaum, 250); *Lam. Rab., Proem* 3 (ed. Buber, 3a).

These statements and others like them clearly demonstrate an established social phenomenon—the regular attendance of Jews, like their non-Jewish neighbors, at games and spectacles. One cannot assume that the above-cited quotations merely expressed the opinion of the rabbis with regard to the entertainment culture, and were not reacting to and resulting from prevalent social realities. If the Jewish population had had no contact whatsoever with these places of entertainment, why would the rabbis have felt compelled to discuss a topic that would then have been irrelevant? It is well known that expressions of opposition voiced by the rabbis often reflected social realities that were unacceptable to them. They criticized such practices, often very strongly, while stressing what was, in their opinion, desirable behavior. This is clearly the case here. Jews frequented games and spectacles, despite rabbinic objections. The presence of buildings for entertainment in the Jewish cities, as well as the other finds revealed there, reflects the danger that the sages saw in Greco-Roman culture, with which they were compelled to deal daily.

In what way, then, did Jewish Tiberias and Sepphoris differ from other cities in Roman Palestine? It seems that two elements that significantly characterized the other cities were not very prominent in the Jewish cities, thus giving them a unique character. In contrast to the richness of figurative depictions in the mosaics of Tiberias and especially Sepphoris, the use of three-dimensional sculpture was possibly less common than at Bet Shean and Caesarea, for example.[66] In the

---

[66]   See, for example, G. Foerster, Y. Tsafrir, "A Statue of Dionysos as a Youth Recently Discovered at Beth Shean" [Hebrew], *Qadmoniot* 23 (1990), 52–54; *idem*, "Nysa-Scythopolis in the Roman Period: A Greek City of Coele Syria—Evidence from the Excavations at Bet Shean," *ARAM* 4 (1992), 121–24; R. Gersht, "Seven New Sculpture Pieces from Caesarea," in J. H. Humphrey, ed., *The Roman and Byzantine Near East* (Ann Arbor: *Journal of Roman Archaeology* Supplementary Series 14, 1995), 109–20; *idem*, "Representations of Deities and Cults of Caesarea," in A. Raban and K. G. Holum, eds., *Caesarea Maritima: A Retrospective after Two Millennia* (DMOA 21: Leiden, 1996), 305–24. For a general discussion of the sculpture in Palestine, see Tsafrir, *Eretz Israel*, 193–99.

extensive excavations conducted at Sepphoris to date, only two sculpture fragments have been found. With reference to Tiberias, the Palestinian Talmud relates of a statue placed at the entrance to the *boulē* and
certain images that decorated the bathhouse for example, but no three-
dimensional sculpture has yet been found there.[67] It is not by chance
that three-dimensional sculpture lacked prominence in the Jewish
cities. Despite the Jews' openness to figurative art during this period,
sculpture must have brought to mind the prohibition in the second
commandment "Thou shall not make unto thee any graven image or
any manner of anything that is in heaven above ..." (Exodus 20:4), thus
leading to the neglect of this art medium by the Jewish population.[68]

Another sphere in which Jewish cities differed from their pagan
counterparts was in the number of pagan temples. Although we have
evidence that there was at least one such temple in both Tiberias and
Sepphoris, it is clear that in these cities, synagogues and study halls
largely took the place of the temples found in the other cities.[69] One can
assume that the synagogues in both Tiberias and Sepphoris were scat-

---

[67]   *Boulē: y. ᶜAbod. Zar.* 3:13 (43b); bathhouses: *y. ᶜAbod. Zar.* 4:4 (43d). For the
debates between Palestinian rabbis of the second to fourth centuries C.E. on whether
it was permissible to pass by statuary or use a public building adorned with idols,
see R. Blidstein, "R. Jonathan, Idolatry and Public Privilege," *JSJ* 5 (1974), 154–61.

[68]   Sacha Stern reached the same conclusion, although his arguments regarding
the role of the rabbis and their attitude to figurative representations are questionable; see S. Stern, "Figurative Art and Halakhah in the Mishnaic-Talmudic Period"
[Hebrew], *Zion* 61 (1996), 397–419. From the Talmudic literature it is clear that
certain Jewish craftsmen and artisans earned their living even by making statues
and images and by constructing various public buildings in the Roman city; see E.
E. Urbach, "The Rabbinical Laws of Idolatry in the Second and Third Centuries in
the Light of Archaeological and Historical Facts," *IEJ* 9 (1959), 149–65, 229–45.

[69]   Evidence of the existence of pagan temples in Tiberias and Sepphoris was
presented above, n. 24. A wall built of dressed stones that was discovered within the
Arab village of Saffuriyeh was identified by N. Makhouly as a podium of a temple.
But this is questionable since the location of these remains is unknown; see Tz. Zuk,
Zippori and its Sites [Hebrew] (Jerusalem: Society for the Preservation of Nature,
1987), 50–52.

tered throughout the urban area, as befitted a city populated largely by Jews, just as temples were dispersed throughout the pagan cities of Roman Palestine.[70]

In summary, the outlook that exposure to Greco-Roman culture was not harmful to the Jewish religion paved the way for the integration of gentile influences in all realms of life, including urban planning and construction. Among certain sectors of the Jewish population in Palestine, frustration and anger following the destruction of the Temple and the suppression of the Bar Kokhba revolt gave way to a positive approach and a certain amount of openness to Rome and its culture. These changes did not occur overnight or throughout all strata of Jewish society. Rather, this was a long and continuous process, which intensified throughout the Mishnaic and Talmudic periods, reaching a peak during the fifth and sixth centuries C.E. If the finds at Beth Shearim, for example, have opened a window to this multifaceted world, the complete urban picture emerging from the key Jewish cities in the Galilee, in which the rabbinic literature was partially created, sheds further light on this subject. Jewish cities in Roman Palestine, as well as their public institutions and administration, were not very different from their pagan counterparts.

---

[70] In Sepphoris, for example, the remains of two synagogues have been discovered, one on the western side of the city and the other on the northeastern. The latter is well integrated into the street grid revealed on the east of the city; see Weiss, Netzer, *Promise and Redemption*, 11–12, 43.

IV.
PALESTINIAN CONTROVERSIES
AND
THEIR LITERARY CONTEXT

DISPLACED SELF-PERCEPTIONS:
THE DEPLOYMENT OF *MÎNÎM* AND ROMANS
IN *B. SANHEDRIN* 90b–91a*

Christine E. Hayes

Yale University

IN THIS ESSAY, I analyze an aggadic passage from the Babylonian Talmud (*b. Sanh.* 90b–91a) in order to argue the claim that rabbis of late antiquity felt a deep ambivalence about non-contextual or midrashic methods of exegesis. This claim, however, depends upon the establishment of a prior claim, namely, that the rabbinic authors of our passage saw a distinction between two modes of exegesis: contextual and non-contextual exegesis.[1] Thus my analysis of *b. Sanhedrin* 90b–91a will involve the following

* This paper emerged from my seminar on Sources of Jewish Law and Rabbinic Authority taught at Princeton University in 1995. I have benefited from conversations with my students Naomi Lubarr—whose senior project explored in depth many of the texts and themes studied in the seminar and discussed here—and Chaya Halberstam whose senior project on *Cant. Rab.* sparked my interest in applying Bakhtinian and psychoanalytic models of literary analysis to rabbinic texts. I would like to thank Daniel Boyarin, Yaakov Elman and Jeffrey Rubenstein for their extremely helpful comments and criticisms.

[1] A note on the terminology employed in this paper is in order. The terms contextual and non-contextual exegesis are not identical to, nor are they intended as substitutes for, *pĕšāṭ* and *dĕrāš* exegesis, though there is certainly some overlap between the pairs of terms. In general, I wish to avoid the terms *pĕšāṭ* and *dĕrāš* because of their considerable baggage. In particular, the term *pĕšāṭ* has a long and somewhat contested history. There has been much debate over the meaning of the term *pĕšāṭ* in rabbinic literature (the views of Loewe, Kamin and Halivni will be discussed below). Moreover, in contemporary usage, *pĕšāṭ* can refer to the author's intended meaning, or to the plain, immediate or natural sense of the text regardless of authorial intent (on this see for example David Weiss Halivni, *Peshat and Derash:*

two steps. First, drawing upon Bakhtin's notion of dialogue, I will show that our passage does indeed attest to a rabbinic awareness of two distinct exegetical approaches. The contextual approach, as defined here, is a clarification of Scripture according to context, which thus considers such features as syntax, normal usage, literary characteristics, and structure. The non-contextual approach is defined here as an exposition of Scripture that ignores or violates the context and that assumes that the slightest details of the biblical text are independently meaningful.[2] Second, after establishing that the rabbinic authors of our passage perceived a distinction between contextual and non-contextual interpretation, I will turn to the question of ambivalence. Drawing upon psychoanalytic methods of literary interpretation, I will argue that our rabbinic authors introduce or exploit the presence of *mînîm* (i.e., heretics or sectarians) and Romans in our passage in order to voice and thus grapple with their own ambivalence and radical doubt concerning non-contextual methods of exegesis. I will argue that the reactions to non-

---

Plain and Applied Meaning in Rabbinic Exegesis [New York: Oxford University Press, 1991], 49–50, 175, n. 6). The instability of the terms *pĕšāṭ* and *dĕrāš* compromises their ability to capture the distinction I wish to discuss in this paper—the distinction between contextual and non-contextual (or simply less contextual) exegesis. Thus, to say that one interpretation is more contextual than another is not necessarily to say that it more closely approaches the *pĕšāṭ* of the text (whether we take the term *pĕšāṭ* to mean the author's intended meaning or the immediate or natural sense of the text), though often that is the case. It is simply to say that it is bound more closely to the text in accord with rules of normal usage. Below we will see examples of non-contextual interpretations that are rejected in favor of contextual interpretations. However, the latter are not necessarily the *pĕšāṭ* of the text according, again, to any of the major modern definitions of that term.

[2]   Standards of contextual and non-contextual exegesis will vary somewhat as there is inevitably much subjectivity involved in assessing the nature of a particular interpretation. However, precision on this matter is not necessary here, since I am interested only in determining that the talmudic rabbis do distinguish between what *they* judge to be contextual and non-contextual interpretations—whatever our assessment of those interpretations might be—and that at times they express anxiety over and discomfort with interpretations they judge to be non-contextual.

contextual exegesis attributed to these non-rabbis are displaced expressions of radical doubt and anxiety on the part of the rabbis themselves.[3]

There have been many attempts to explain how the rabbis could
have conceived of certain extreme midrashic expositions as exegetically
possible. Some assume a radical discontinuity between the interpretive
mindset of the rabbis of the Talmud and the interpretive mindset of

---

[3]   As will become clear below, the talmudic passage in question lends itself nicely
to analysis in Bakhtinian and psychoanalytic terms, and thus I draw upon these
systems for the insights they afford in this specific case. In addition, I have chosen
the psychoanalytic mode of literary criticism because it belongs to the class of
expressive criticism. (See M. H. Abrams, *A Glossary of Literary Terms*, 5th ed. [New
York: Holt, Rinehart and Winston, 1988], 38–41 for an explication of various types
of criticism. The following discussion of expressive criticism is indebted to the
article in Abrams.) Expressive criticism is any form of criticism that regards a
literary work as the expression of, and consequently an entrée into, the author's
perceptions, thoughts, and feelings. Expressive criticism was dominant among
romantic critics of the last century, and although it has come under fire by New
Critics and others, in modern times it retains some usefulness in the work of
psychological and psychoanalytical critics and critics of consciousness. Psychoanalytic criticism treats literary texts as an expression in fictional form of the desires
and mental processes of the author, and assumes that reading a literary work
enables one to experience the distinctive consciousness of the author. It is precisely
because I view the talmudic passage examined here as an expression of a deep
tension within the rabbinic culture that produced the passage that I have selected a
mode of literary analysis whose critical premises do not preclude reference to the
intentions and mental processes of the author. In short, various forms of objective
criticism, i.e., forms of criticism that view the literary text as a self-sufficient and
autonomous object free of any reference to the world outside the text and to the
mind or intention of the author, are based on theoretical premises that are anti-
pathetical to the project of cultural-historical reconstruction herein essayed.
Consequently, the primary forms of objective criticism—the New Criticism,
Structuralism, and Post-Structuralism or Deconstruction—are not adopted here.
This is not to say that there are not some useful ideas in these forms of criticism, e.g.,
few contemporary readers of text can forgo the New Critical emphasis on close
reading for inner tensions, ambiguities, and paradox. Nevertheless, the fundamentally ahistorical tendency of New Criticism, Structuralism and Deconstruction
(a common thread uniting these quite different and often opposed approaches to
text) which denies the expressive intention or design of a work's author (the so-

contemporary readers of the Bible:[4] the rabbis felt none of our discomfort or anxiety at the notion that extreme midrashic techniques can
convey the intention of the author, because they operated on an entirely

---

called genetic fallacy), renders them unsuited to the work undertaken in this essay.

It should be stated at the outset that my adoption of Bakhtinian and psychoanalytic models is scandalously eclectic and entirely pragmatic—they help me to
uncover and describe some interesting ideas in the talmudic text. This study should
not be construed as a wholesale commitment to the larger theoretical framework of
either model as the framework of choice in the general explication of talmudic
texts.

[4]   For such a view see Halivni, *Peshat*, 20–22. The hermeneutical assumptions
regarding the nature of the biblical text upon which midrashic interpretation
depends have been discussed by many scholars (for a recent example, see Jay M.
Harris, *How Do We Know This? Midrash and the Fragmentation of Modern Judaism*
(Albany: SUNY Press, 1995), 252. James Kugel's term "omnisignificance" is
intended to capture the fundamental hermeneutical assumption of rabbinic
exegesis of Scripture. Omnisignificance is "the basic assumption underlying all of
rabbinic exegesis that the slightest details of the biblical text have a meaning that is
both comprehensible and significant. Nothing in the Bible ... ought to be explained
as the product of chance, or, for that matter, as an emphatic or rhetorical form, or
anything similar, nor ought its reasons to be assigned to the realm of Divine
unknowables. Every detail is put there to reach something new and important, and
it is capable of being discovered by careful analysis" (J. Kugel, *The Idea of Biblical
Poetry: Parallelism and Its History* [New Haven: Yale University Press, 1981], 103–
4. See the discussion of this idea in Yaakov Elman, "It is No Empty Thing:
Nahmanides and the Search for Omnisignificance," *The Torah U-Madda Journal*,
5 (1993), esp. 1–14. As Elman points out (p. 4) "the omnisignificant imperative
proceeds directly from the view of Torah as divine revelation and serves to justify
midrashic approaches to Torah." For Elman, the omnisignificant imperative is the
obligation to uncover the aggadic or halakhic meaning conveyed by minute details
of the biblical text. Elman states that "the history of 'normative' Jewish biblical
exegesis may be seen from the perspective of the rise of omnisignificance in the
tannaitic era and its transmutation through both an increasing use of certain
methods and a dropping off of others during the succeeding centuries" (p. 4).
Elman's work on the career of the omnisignificant imperative and the rise and fall
of particular midrashic methods has important implications for my claim that
certain midrashic techniques were never fully accepted among, and were a source
of anxiety for, rabbis in late antiquity (see n. 68 below, and Conclusion).

different interpretive wavelength.[5] On such a view, self-consciousness about certain midrashic practices occurred only in the post-talmudic period with the emergence of new textual assumptions, a new interpretive mindset.[6] In his masterful study of Jewish historiographical debates over the legitimacy of classical rabbinic exegesis, Jay Harris describes the problematic nature of rabbinic exegesis for some post-talmudic Jews.

> With the emergence of new textual assumptions in the tenth through thirteenth centuries in the Islamic lands, many Jewish intellectuals could no longer find in talmudic exegesis a reliable rendering of the meaning of the biblical text.
>
> ... the intellectual standards of the world in which they lived led to discomfort with their rabbinic exegetical heritage ... (*How Do We Know*, 252).

Harris demonstrates that debates over the intelligibility of rabbinic exegesis of Scripture were the result of a shift in textual assumptions[7] and in the development of new standards of textual meaning and linguistic significance (p. 6). This is certainly true. However, I will argue here that self-consciousness about, and discomfort with, extreme midrashic techniques can be found already in the talmudic period, indicat-

---

[5] So Halivni describes the rabbis' lack of discomfort over what he terms "reading in" (*Peshat*, 20). Halivni argues that the tension that "arises between what is perceived by the contemporary reader of the Bible to be the straightforward, austere sense of a Scriptural text and the more creative, seemingly artificial interpretation that the rabbinic tradition has affixed to it" (*Peshat*, vi) did not trouble the rabbis, because the rabbis do not share our exegetical sensibility, specifically our allegiance to pĕšāṭ. The rabbis' interpretive state of mind did not dictate to them that the simple literal meaning was inherently superior to the applied meaning.

[6] Halivni, *Peshat*, 34.

[7] So, for example, some leading Jewish scholars in the Babylonian/Spanish orbit of the early Middle Ages trivialized and even repudiated halakhic midrash in order to "combat Karaism and to accommodate their developing sense that rabbinic midrash stood at a great distance from the real significance of the biblical text" (Harris, *How Do We Know*, 85). Harris argues as well for a shift in the perception of religious authority (p. 6), with which I am less concerned here.

ing that a radical shift in textual assumptions is only a sufficient but not a necessary condition for exegetical self-consciousness and anxiety. Persons can feel self-conscious and anxious about their cultural practices even as they engage in and enshrine them, particularly if opportunities exist for them to view themselves as others outside their cultural system might view them. Such opportunities existed throughout the talmudic period in Palestine and Babylonia. The rabbis were clearly aware of the existence of non-rabbis and non-Jews of various stripes—apostates, Christians, pagans, philosophers, Samaritans, and more. The rabbis were also aware that these non-rabbis and non-Jews held views of the biblical text and the proper way to read it that differed from, and were often critical of, their own. It is no accident that some of the texts that evidence a rabbinic anxiety about midrashic techniques feature non-rabbis and non-Jews unsympathetic to the interpretive mindset and methods of the rabbis. In creating such texts, in fairly representing the views of their opponents and critics, the rabbis show themselves to be capable of understanding the perspective of those opponents and critics. Indeed it would appear, I will argue, that to some degree the rabbis internalized that perspective. Viewing themselves as others viewed them, the rabbis are, at times, uncomfortable with what they see.

To be sure, Harris does note that reservations regarding rabbinic exegesis are expressed already in the Talmud, but he deems this to have possessed little cultural significance:

> Of course, one finds occasional reservations regarding the authority of the exegetical enterprise, and one finds a few remarks suggesting that most of the extrabiblical norms originate in oral tradition, not exegesis. Further, one finds many aggadic statements insisting that the entire oral Torah originates at Sinai. For all of that, when it comes time for the Talmud to answer the question, "How do we know this?" it almost always cites a verse, and always feels free to engage in … discussions … which presuppose that the law or laws in question are generated exegetically. Against the thousands of exegeses offered in the Talmud to identify the source of law, neither the few expressions of reservation nor the aggadic statements measure up. To the people responsible for shaping the halakhic discussions of the Bavli, there was little doubt that law generally emerged by

means of the application of exegetical techniques ... (*How Do We Know*, 48).[8]

Without wishing to overemphasize the significance of the rabbis' reservations (Harris' term),[9] I submit that the anxiety and discomfort we will find in rabbinic texts of all periods were more culturally productive than Harris' statements would indicate.[10] The self-consciousness and discomfort experienced by rabbis deeply engaged in the creation and/or enshrinement of midrashic exegesis played an important role in the production of certain cultural constructs. Specifically, I will argue that rabbinic anxiety over the legitimacy of extreme midrashic techniques generated key articulations of the nature and source of the rabbinic authority to interpret Scripture.

Contextual and Non-Contextual Exegesis: A Rabbinic Distinction

Our first task is to establish that the rabbinic authors of our passage did distinguish between contextual and non-contextual interpretations. We can begin by reviewing the scholarly debate over a related (though not identical) question: does talmudic literature in general evince something akin to the medieval distinction between *pĕšāṭ* and *dĕrāš* interpretation of the Bible?[11] Does the exegetical terminology and con-

---

[8] Likewise, Halivni states that the late talmudic rabbis accepted the *dĕrāšôt* of the past as valid because "the authority of the past overcame their *internal opposition*" (*Peshat*, 19, emphasis mine). However, it appears that by this passing reference to "internal opposition" Halivni refers to the simple avoidance of "reading in" on the part of later talmudic rabbis rather than actual expressions of hostility, discomfort, or resistance.

[9] Or internal opposition to use Halivni's term.

[10] Harris is scarcely to be faulted for this. His book is devoted to a study of the post-talmudic period and his statements regarding the talmudic period are of a general nature and serve as a preface to the main body of his work.

[11] As noted above, the terms *pĕšāṭ* and *dĕrāš* do not coincide with my terms contextual and non-contextual. However, there is a large degree of overlap between the pairs of terms since midrashic interpretations are often non-contextual and *pĕšāṭ* interpretations are often contextual. Thus, the scholarly debate over the existence of a *pĕšāṭ/dĕrāš* distinction in rabbinic literature is relevant to our study.

sciousness of the ancient rabbis reflect such a distinction? Until recently it was assumed that the sages used various forms of the roots *pšṭ* and *drš* in order to make a distinction between *pĕšāṭ* and *dĕrāš* exegesis of Scripture respectively.[12] However, the late Sarah Kamin argued that an examination of the relevant rabbinic passages does not bear out the assumption that *pšṭ* terms refer to the contextual or plain meaning of the text as against a non-contextual *dĕrāš*.[13] The only place where the two roots appear side by side is *b. Sanhedrin* 100b. Although Abbaye advances two interpretations here—one labelled *mi-pĕšāṭēh* and the other *midrašēh* —these do not refer to *pĕšāṭ* or *dĕrāš* interpretations, as these terms came to be defined.[14] According to Kamin, evidence from parallel passages indicates that the verbal forms of the two roots are interchangeable and both mean "study," "teach," or "explain."[15]

---

[12]   I. Heinemann, "*Lĕ-hitpathût ha-munnāḥîm ha-miqṣôʿiyyîm lĕ-pērûš ha-miqrāʾ*," *Leš.* 14 (1945–46), 188, attributed to the *ʾamôrāʾîm* a counterpositing of the two terms which led over time to the clear distinction of the two methodologies. Bacher and Dobschuetz both held versions of the view that the two methods were distinguished already in the 4th century (see *EJ s.v.* "*Peshaṭ*"). One of the clearest exponents of the view that the sages recognized the difference between *pĕšāṭ* and *dĕrāš* is Israel Frankel who states "While Rabbinic exegesis as recorded in Rabbinic literature frequently deviates from *peshat*, with their extraordinary knowledge of the Bible the Rabbis had a clear appreciation of the plain meaning as distinct from the Midrash superimposed upon it" (Peshat *in Talmudic and Midrashic Literature* [Toronto: La Salle Press, 1956], 40). Frankel's work was criticized by Raphael Loewe in his review "Israel Frankel: Peshat *in Talmudic and Midrashic Literature*," *JJS* 10 (1959), 188–89.

[13]   S. Kamin, *Rashi's Exegetical Categorization with Respect to the Distinction Between Peshat and Derash* [Hebrew] (Jerusalem: Magnes Press, 1980). A similar conclusion is reached by Halivni.

[14]   The passage concerns a verse in Ben Sira on roasting a fish with the skin. Abbaye says *mi-pĕšāṭēh* the verse teaches one not to destroy or waste anything useful (in this case, the skin of the fish) while *mi-drāšēh* the verse warns against unnatural intercourse. This is a moralistic versus a metaphorical interpretation, and not a *pĕšāṭ* versus a *dĕrāš* exegesis. Compare the discussion of this passage in Halivni, *Peshat*, 73–74.

[15]   So for example, while *Num. Rab.* 18:22 reads "*R. Yannai hāyâ yôšēb u-pôšēṭ*"

The root *pšṭ* appears as a noun in two forms: the Hebrew *pĕšûṭ* in the phrase *ʾên miqrāʾ yôṣēʾ mi-yĕdê pĕšûṭô* (four times only in the Babli)[16] and the Aramaic *pĕšāṭ* in the related expression *pĕšāṭēh dĕ-qĕrāʾ* (six times only in the Babli)[17] and in *ki-pĕšāṭēh* (two times)[18] or *mi-pĕšāṭēh* (three times).[19] However, these phrases accompany *pērûšîm* that are far removed from the contextual or the plain meaning of the text[20] and therefore cannot indicate a *pērûš* by means of the *pĕšāṭ* method as defined in the medieval period.[21] Kamin argues (*Rashi*, 47–48) that *pĕšûṭô [šel miqrāʾ]* and *pĕšāṭēh dĕ-qĕrāʾ* are equivalent to *kātûb* or *pāsûq*—"scriptural text" or "verse"—in usage, and thus usually refer to a specific verse of Scripture under discussion.[22] Halivni prefers to

---

the parallel passage in *Gen. Rab.* 10:7 (ed. Theodor–Albeck, 81) reads "*R. Yannai hāyâ yôšēb wĕ-dôrēš.*" Kamin points out (p. 27) that there is no common denominator to *pērûšîm* that are introduced by the root *pšṭ*, and the term often accompanies a *pērûš* that conforms to our definition of *dĕrāš* (e.g., one achieved by a *gĕzērâ šāwâ*).

[16]   These passages are discussed below.

[17]   *b. Ketub.* 111b; *b. ʿErub.* 23b; *b. Qidd.* 80b; *b. Ḥul.* 6a, 133a; and *b. ʿArak.* 8b. The equivalent *pĕšûṭēh dĕ-qaryāʾ* occurs once in the Yerushalmi, *y. Sanh.* 1:1 (18a). For purposes of comparison, the reader is referred to Halivni's discussion of the passages listed in this and the next two notes (Halivni, *Peshat*, 54–79).

[18]   *b. Zebaḥ.* 113a and *b. ʿArak.* 32a.

[19]   *b. Yebam.* 24a; *b. Ketub.* 38b; *b. Sanh.* 100b.

[20]   See for example, *b. Ketub.* 111b; *b. Qidd.* 80b; *b. ʿErub.* 23b; *b. ʿArak.* 8b. Also, for the Hebrew phrase, see *b. Šabb.* 63a, *b. Yebam.* 11b, 24a.

[21]   Hence, Loewe, Gelles, and others agree that the sages have no concept of *pĕšāṭ*. For the view of B.J. Gelles as presented in his "*Peshat and Derash* in the Exegesis of Rashi," see the review by S. Kamin in *JJS* 36 (1985), 126–30; for Loewe see R. Loewe, "The 'Plain' Meaning of Scripture in Early Jewish Exegesis" *Papers of the Institute of Jewish Studies London*, ed. J. G. Weiss (Jerusalem: Magnes Press, 1964) 1, 140–56. Other views are summarized in *EJ, s.v.* "Peshat." (Compare Halivni, *Peshat*, ch. 2, esp. 76–79.) It appears that the rabbis had two main exegetical methods—that of *halākâ* and that of *ʾaggādâ*—neither of which is equal to our conception of *pĕšāṭ*.

[22]   The phrase *pĕšāṭēh dĕ-qĕrāʾ* occurs *only* in the question *pĕšāṭēh dĕ-qĕrāʾ bĕ-māy kĕtîb?*, which clearly means no more than "What is the [original] context of the

translate these expressions as "context" (based on the root meaning of *pšṭ* as "extension"). However, it is not clear that *pĕšûṭô/pĕšāṭēh* can be consistently translated as context, as Halivni argues, and where such a translation is possible it is likely a derivative or secondary, rather than a primary, meaning.[23]

As noted, the term *pĕšûṭ* appears in the Talmud only in the phrase *ᵓên miqrāᵓ yôṣēᵓ mi-yĕdê pĕšûṭô*.[24] Kamin points out the meaning of this

---

verse?" In each of the six sugyot in which this question appears it follows an attempt to apply a verse to an entirely unrelated issue. Our question is asked, in order to point out that in its original context the verse (i.e., *pĕšāṭēh dĕ-qĕrāᵓ*) speaks about a different matter entirely. But the *pērûš* that is brought in answer to the question is generally no more of a *pĕšāṭ* interpretation than the one to which it is opposed. In *b. Ḥul.* 6a, a verse from Prov. 23:6 "put a knife in your gullet if you have a large appetite" is used to teach about the prohibition of the wine of idolators. Subsequently the question is asked: *pĕšāṭēh dĕ-qĕrāᵓ bĕ-māy kĕtîb?* The response is equally non-contextual: the verse speaks of a student's restraint before his teacher. The question therefore is not inquiring as to the interpretation of the verse according to the *pĕšāṭ* method of exegesis. See Kamin, *Rashi* 36.

23   Thus, Kamin's exposition of the six occurrences of *pĕšāṭēh dĕ-qĕrāᵓ* is more persuasive than the interesting alternative exposition of Halivni. Kamin's translation of the phrase *pĕšāṭēh dĕ-qĕrāᵓ bĕ-māy kĕtîb?* as "what is the original context of the verse?" (lit: "the [text of the] verse [*pĕšāṭēh dĕ-qĕrāᵓ*], in regard to what [*bĕ-māy*] is it written [*kĕtîb*]?") is based on standard talmudic usage of *b-* as a technical term denoting the field or range of application of a text or statement (e.g., *ba-meh dĕbārîm ᵓamûrîm* "in regard to what circumstances were these words said?" or *bĕ-māy qā-mîpalgî* "in regard to what case or circumstances do they differ?"). Her translation is thus to be preferred over Halivni's "how is the *pĕšāṭēh dĕ-qĕrāᵓ* written?" (p. 64ff.)—which relies on a much less standard rendering of *bĕ-māy*—or "what is the *pĕšāṭēh dĕ-qĕrāᵓ*?" (p. 65ff.), an even less precise translation. Kamin's translation makes it clear that *pĕšāṭēh dĕ-qĕrāᵓ* and "context" must be two distinct things at least in the phrase *pĕšāṭēh dĕ-qĕrāᵓ bĕ-māy kĕtîb?* since the question concerns the *context* (*bĕ-māy*) of the *pĕšāṭēh dĕ-qĕrāᵓ*. *Pĕšāṭēh dĕ-qĕrāᵓ* must therefore be something other than context. Kamin's conclusion that *pĕšāṭēh dĕ-qĕrāᵓ* in this phrase means no more than the text or verse itself appears to be ineluctable. Note also Raphael Loewe's translation "authoritative meaning" ("The 'Plain' Meaning," 158) but this translation is not adopted here.

24   *b. Šabb.* 63a; *b. Yebam.* 11b, and 24a. In *b. Ketub.* 38b we have an Aramaic form of the rule: *lāᵓ ᵓātyā … u-mapqāᵓ lēh li-qĕrāᵓ mi-pĕšāṭēh lĕ-gamrē.*

phrase (Kamin, *Rashi*, 37–38): the *"pěšûṭ"* of the text is not cancelled by the existence of certain kinds of interpretations of the text (e.g., allegorical, homiletical, halakhic, etc.).[25] Further, the association of this phrase with the verbal root ʿ*qr*—"to uproot" (e.g., in *b. Yebam.* 11a)—plus direct objects such as *dibrê tôrâ* or *miqrā*ʾ or *qěrā*ʾ conveys the notion that no interpretation, no matter how fanciful or distant, can be permitted to "uproot" a verse—that is, make the verse as good as non-existent—by ignoring its details, or rendering it superfluous in its present location. The verse is assumed to have some validity and function in its own context.[26]

---

[25]   It is clear from the contexts in which the rule is invoked, that the term *pěšûṭô šel miqrā*ʾ does not refer to a *pěšāṭ* interpretation. In *b. Šabb.* 63a we read that although the latter part of Ps. 45:4, "And your sword upon your thighs, O most Mighty, with your glory and your majesty," is generally expounded so as to refer allegorically to words of Torah, the *pěšûṭô šel miqrā*ʾ is not thereby cancelled and can be used by R. Eliezer to support his view that swords, bows, shields, and spears are to be classed as ornaments (and not "burdens") and are thus not subject to the Sabbath law prohibiting carrying. R. Eliezer's interpretation is no more a plain (*pěšāṭ*) reading of the text than is the allegorization brought above. The verse is *not* talking about what items may or may not be carried out on the Sabbath any more than it is speaking about words of Torah. However, the text explicitly speaks of swords and not words of Torah. Consequently, what is reflected in the principle ʾ*ên miqrā*ʾ *yôṣē*ʾ *mi-yědê pěšûṭô* is the idea that a non-contextual interpretation (i.e., the words of Torah are God's glory and majesty) does not cause the passage in question to lose its function in its actual context. Although the terms "glory and majesty" have been applied to Torah, this does not mean that they cease to function as descriptions of God's sword. Thus, R. Eliezer's midrashic interpretation which relies on the verse's juxtaposition of "sword" with "glory" and "majesty" remains possible. For an alternative exposition of this passage see Halivni, *Peshat*, 58–60. See B. Schwartz, "On *Peshat* and *Derash*, Bible Criticism, and Theology," *Prooftexts* 14 (1994), 74–75.

[26]   Halivni, *Peshat*, 54–61, offers an alternative interpretation of the phrase ʾ*ên miqrā*ʾ *yôṣē*ʾ *mi-yědê pěšûṭô* in line with his translation of *pěšûṭô* as "context": no text can be deprived of its context. However, B. Schwartz points out in his review of Halivni's book that the sense of *yôṣē*ʾ *mi-yědê* in the statement ʾ*ên miqrā*ʾ *yôṣē*ʾ *mi-yědê pěšûṭô* "is not so much 'be deprived of' as 'leave behind, abandon,' literally 'exit the clutches of'" (p. 74) and probably means that "no midrashic interpretation can

Kamin also considers the root *drš* and notes that it appears in rabbinic texts as a verb synonymous with *prš* "to explain" or *bᵓr* "to clarify,"
and does not refer to a method of exegesis.[27] Hence, she concludes that
there is no evidence that the talmudic sages' use of the roots *pšṭ* and *drš*
in various formulations indicates a distinction between *pěšāṭ* and *děrāš*
as exegetical methods.[28]

While scholars disagree on the precise meaning of the terms *pěšāṭ*
and *děrāš*, Kamin has established beyond a doubt that the rabbis did not
use these terms or related forms as labels for two types of exegesis.
Nevertheless, it does not follow from the absence of appropriate terminology that rabbinic texts do not on occasion, and in other ways, indicate an awareness of the distinction between contextual and non-contextual modes of interpretation. I submit that an awareness of this distinction is indeed a part of rabbinic exegetical consciousness and finds
expression in, for example, *b. Sanhedrin* 90b–91a.

The text in question features early rabbis of Roman Palestine (*tan-
nāᵓîm*) in conversation with Romans and *mînîm*.[29] This passage is one

---

invalidate one based on obvious, contextual exegesis" (p. 75). In other words, non-
contextual interpretations of a passage do not mean that the passage is released
from its actual location or context, so as to have no function or signification there.

[27]   See Heinemann, "*Lě-hitpatḥût*," 185. Also, Kamin, *Rashi*, 23.

[28]   Kamin and Halivni differ over the significance of other talmudic terms such as
waddāy, *mammāš*, *kě-mašmāʿô* or *kě-šimʿô*. Halivni argues that these terms (the
term *waddāy* especially and most consistently) can connote the type of meaning
one obtains upon initial reading, akin to what we might call plain meaning (*Peshat*,
76), and are thus evidence of a rabbinic awareness of the difference between plain
and applied meaning of a text (though this awareness is not to be confused with a
valuation of *pěšāṭ* as superior). Kamin argues that these terms do not refer to
interpretations of the *pěšāṭ* type, but rather to the narrow and precise literal sense
of a term. A literal reading is not to be equated with a *pěšāṭ* reading: literalism is
often a tool of midrash. Clearly, an examination of terminology alone cannot
answer all our questions regarding the rabbis' exegetical sensibility.

[29]   Most scholars agree that *mînîm* is an indeterminate term for all those who
questioned rabbinic Judaism. It serves as a catch-all word that denotes heretics and

of many talmudic and midrashic passages that feature conversations in which rabbis and non-rabbis adopt different exegetical approaches. In such passages, it is generally the rabbi who adopts the more contextual approach, in the face of a non-contextual application of Scripture asserted for an anti-Jewish purpose[30] or in order to locate some point of (sectarian) doctrine in the biblical text.[31]

I have chosen to examine b. Sanhedrin 90b–91a because this passage reverses the usual exegetical orientation assigned to rabbis and non-rabbis. Here, the rabbis engage in non-contextual exegesis in an effort to provide a biblical foundation for a point of doctrine not explicitly

---

sectarians of various types: Jewish Christians, Gentile Christians, gnostics, pagans, apostates, Samaritans, and even Sadducees depending on context. See S. Miller, "The mînîm of Sepphoris Reconsidered" HTR 86:4 (1993), 377–402 and S. J. D. Cohen, "A Virgin Defiled: Some Rabbinic and Christian Views on the Origin of Heresy" USQR 36 (1980), 3, cited in Miller, 402 n. 93. For a useful collation (albeit with dated analysis) of all sources in rabbinic literature dealing with mînîm see R. Travers Herford, Christianity in Talmud and Midrash (London: Williams and Norgate, 1903).

[30] For example, in b. Yebam. 102b, a mîn interprets Hos. 5:6 as indicating God's rejection of Israel. R. Gamaliel's rebuttal that God has departed from but not rejected Israel is based on a fine point of grammar. In b. Sanh. 48b a mîn's non-contextual interpretation of Isa. 12:3 is countered by R. Abbahu who points out that the preposition involved does not support the construction the mîn would place upon it. (Of course, R. Abbahu's response is in the same clever and insulting spirit, but it involves no violation of grammar.) In b. ʿErub. 101a a mîn interprets the metaphor in Mic. 7:4 to the detriment of Israel, but R. Joshua b. Hananyah decodes the metaphor in light of the larger context.

[31] For example, b. Sanh. 38b depicts a mîn seeking to prove a plurality of deities from certain locutions in various biblical texts, but his efforts are defeated by R. Ishmael b. R. Yose, who demonstrates that each locution is normal, idiomatic usage that conveys no special meaning. b. Sanh. 38b also contains a long list of verses that are misinterpreted by mînîm but whose context is said to refute these misreadings (e.g., the mînîm take a plural lexeme as indicating plural deities, but a singular form in the immediate context will refute this view). Cf. Mek. Ba-ḥôdeš 5 (ed. Horovitz, 219–20) and Pesiq. R. 21. In b. Ḥul. 87a a mîn's hyperliteralism is refuted by an examination of context.

taught in the Bible—the doctrine of resurrection.[32] Against the rabbis'
creative readings, the *mînîm* and Romans assert a plain or a contextual
meaning of the text. I examine three units of this text below.[33]

UNIT I

1. *Mînîm*[34] asked Rabban Gamaliel: Whence do we know that the Holy
   One, blessed be He, will resurrect the dead? He answered them from
   the Torah, the Prophets, and the Writings yet they did not accept it
   [his proofs].

2a. From the Torah [he proved it] as it is written, "And the Lord said to
    Moses, 'Behold you will lie with your fathers and will rise up ...'"
    (Deut. 31:16).

2b. But perhaps—they said to him—[the verse means: Behold you will
    lie with your fathers] and will [thereupon] rise up *this people and go
    astray*.[35]

3a. From the prophets [he proved it] as it is written, "Your dead men
    shall live, together with my dead body shall they arise. Awake and
    sing, you that dwell in the dust: for your dew is as the dew of herbs,
    and the earth shall cast out its dead" (Isa. 26:19).

3b. But perhaps this refers to the dead whom Ezekiel resurrected [see
    Ezek. 37].

---

[32] The significance of the fact that our passage is attached to the halakhic pre-
scription of belief in resurrection will be discussed below.

[33] *b. Sanh.* 90b–91a, based upon the translation in I. Epstein, ed., *The Babylonian
Talmud* (London: Soncino, 1935–52), with some modification. The passage can be
divided into eight units that feature *tannāʾîm* engaged in debates with *mînîm* or
Romans. (The subsequent units feature amoraic derivations of resurrection from
the Torah and do not employ a debate format.) Units I, III, VII, and VIII involve
mînîm. Units II, IV, and V involve Romans, while unit 6 is a purely rabbinic
exposition. We will examine the first three units only, as these feature the divergent
exegetical approaches that concern us.

[34] The Genizah fragment reproduced by Katsch reads "Sadducees" as do some
medieval parallels (Katsch, *Ginze Talmud Bavli* [Jerusalem: Rubin Mass, 1975] 2
104, l. 20).

[35] The translation is inelegant but retains the Hebrew word order upon which the
rabbinic exegesis depends (see explanation below).

4a. From the Writings [he proved it] as it is written, "And the roof of your mouth, like the best wine of my beloved, that goes down sweetly, causing the lips of those that are asleep to speak" (Cant. 7:9).

4b. But[36] perhaps it means merely that their lips will move, even as R. Yohanan said: If a *halākâ* is said in any person's name in this world, his lips speak in the grave, as it is written, "causing the lips of those that are asleep to speak" (Cant. 7:9).

5. [They were not satisfied] until he quoted this verse: "which the Lord swore unto your fathers to give to *them*" (Deut. 11:21)—not to you, but to them is said. Hence, resurrection is derived from the Torah.

It was Mikhail Bakhtin who first used the term "dialogic" to refer to an unusual literary phenomenon: the creation within a single text of "a plurality of independent and unmerged voices or consciousnesses, a genuine polyphony of fully valid voices."[37] A text in which several voices, i.e., independent points of view or consciousnesses, are heard on equal terms, and *in which one consciousness does not dominate*, is a dialogical text.[38] Our passage is dialogic in that an exegetical consciousness other than that assumed to be the consciousness of the text's authorship is affirmed. In one and the same text we find two conflicting voices: a voice that espouses midrashic exegesis and a voice that rejects midrashic exegesis in favor of a more contextual interpretation.[39]

---

[36] The Munich ms. and several medieval witnesses insert before this word "They said to him, 'But perhaps …'"

[37] Citation taken from J. Hawthorn, *A Glossary of Contemporary Literary Theory*, 2nd ed. (London: Edward Arnold, 1994), *s.v.* "polyphonic."

[38] Dialogue does not necessarily involve two characters, but can be interior to a single character. In Bakhtinian terms, an interior dialogue is one that features two well-defined voices within the single consciousness of a literary character. These two voices will represent different personified beliefs or aspects of the character's personality.

[39] The dialogic model is superior to conventional terms of literary analysis such as "perspective," "voice" and "point of view" since dialogism conveys the additional idea that the various voices of the text are heard on equal terms, without one (usually the author's or the hero's) voice predominating.

In Unit I, *mînîm* (a variant reading is Sadducees) are said to question the first century *tannā* R. Gamaliel concerning the doctrine of resurrection—how does he know God will resurrect the dead? R. Gamaliel offers three biblical proofs, which are rejected.[40] In each case the rejection takes the form of a counter-exegesis by the *mînîm*, one that is more constrained and contextual than the exegesis offered by the rabbi.[41]

R. Gamaliel's first proof from Deuteronomy 31:16 is based upon a violation of normal language usage and syntax. The verse reads: "And the Lord said to Moses: 'Behold you will lie with your fathers and *this people* will [thereupon] rise up and go astray after other gods...'" (literally: "Behold you will lie with your fathers and will [thereupon] rise up *this people* and go astray after other gods ..."). R. Gamaliel's midrashic interpretation attaches the verb "will rise up" to the first clause so that Moses is its subject, rather than "this people." He reads: "you will lie with your fathers and will rise up"—understood to be God's prediction of Moses' resurrection. This reading not only ignores common Hebrew usage ($q\bar{a}m$ + verb of action denotes the commencement of an activity), it also creates an asyndeton between the two parts of the verse.[42]

---

[40] Statements in this article that take forms such as "R. X said..." do not imply a belief that the tradition attributed to R. X was necessarily stated by that rabbi and in precisely the words appearing in the text. They mean simply that in the world of the text, R. X is represented as having spoken in a particular way. I defer discussion of the historical value of the texts examined here, to the final section.

[41] Only in the first of the three cases can the counter-exegesis be said to be a rendering of the immediate and natural sense of the text. Nevertheless, the interpretations of the *mînîm* in the other two cases, if not completely contextual are at least more contextual or constrained than the interpretation of the rabbi. See n. 2 above.

[42] According to an early rabbinic tradition, this verse is one of five verses with uncertain syntax, such that a particular word in the verse can be construed as belonging to that which precedes it or that which follows it—Gen. 4:7; 49:7; Exod. 17:9; 25:34; and Deut. 31:16 (see *Mekilta de-Rabbi Ishmael*, ed. Jacob Z. Lauterbach [Philadelphia: Jewish Publication Society of America, 1933], 2, 142–43; parallels

The response of R. Gamaliel's interlocutors is a deflationary reassertion of the contextual reading of the verse. Perhaps the verse doesn't say that Moses will rise up; perhaps it simply says what it appears to say when the ordinary rules of usage and syntax are considered, that Moses will sleep with his fathers and *this people* will rise up for acts of idolatry! R. Gamaliel's next two proofs are similarly deflected. Although the alternative exegesis offered by the *mînîm* in these cases is not itself completely contextual, in each case it is either more contextual or more constrained than the exegesis offered by R. Gamaliel. The *mînîm* suggest that Isaiah's prophecy concerning the dead men who shall live is to be understood in its own larger context, i.e., the prophetic books of the Bible. It might therefore simply refer to the dead men resurrected by Ezekiel in Ezekiel 37. Likewise, regarding the verse from Song of Songs in which it is said that the lips of those that were asleep will speak, the *mînîm* suggest a more limited literalization of the metaphor (although admittedly it is not the immediate or natural sense of the verse). The verse might simply mean that the dead person's lips move in the grave, just as R. Yohanan taught that the recitation of a *halākâ* in a person's name causes that person's lips to move in the grave.

Note that the proof said to convince the *mînîm* of resurrection does not rely on a non-contextual reading. Deuteronomy 11:21 recounts God's oath to give the land "to them" (i.e., to Israel's patriarchs). A literal fulfillment of this oath depends upon resurrection. While this proof is not what we might call the natural sense of the text, it does not entail any non-contextual exegesis, any application of the text to an unrelated topic, that would be objectionable to non-rabbis. Unit I as a whole therefore attests to the ability of its rabbinic authors to perceive and represent the exegetical perspective of those who do not accept

---

occur in *Gen. Rab.* 80:6 [ed. Theodor-Albeck, 957–58]; *y. ᶜAbod. Zar.* 2:7 [41c–d]; *b. Yoma* 52b; and *Cant. Rab.* 1:2). This is, however, a midrashic claim and not a grammatical observation, since in most of these cases one of the suggested readings creates a syntactical problem (e.g., an asyndeton or a sentence fragment). In any event this tradition appears to have no bearing on the current discussion.

their non-contextual methods of interpretation and to do so in a dialogic manner. In other words, it is not clear that the rabbinic viewpoint is here privileged by any means other than its being assigned to rabbis rather than non-rabbis.[43] Indeed, it is not clear that any privilege attaches to the voice of the rabbis at all. In rabbinic literature, Jews in general and rabbis in particular are not always depicted favorably in comparison to the non-Jews with whom they interact. Rabbinic authors are capable of self-criticism and on occasion it is precisely a non-Jew whose meritorious behavior or speech casts the rabbis in a poor light.[44]

The question posed by the *mînîm* returns in expanded form in Unit II, this time in the mouth of a Roman (step 1) and then, in the mouth of a rabbi (step 4).

UNIT II

1.   The Romans asked R. Joshua b. Hananyah: Whence do we know that the Holy One, Blessed be He, will resurrect the dead and knows the future?

2a. He replied: Both are deduced from this verse. "And the Lord said to Moses, Behold you will lie with your fathers and will rise up. This people will go astray after other gods" (Deut. 31:16).

2b. But perhaps [the text means]: this people will rise up and will go astray after other gods etc.

3.   He replied: then at least you have the answer to half, i.e., that He knows the future.

---

[43]   Here the heuristic value of dialogism as opposed to more conventional terms of literary analysis (point of view, perspective and so on) becomes clear (see n. 39 above).

[44]   One example is *b. Giṭ.* 55b–56b in which the cowardly paralysis of the rabbis stands in stark contrast to the courageous actions of the pagan emperor Nero. On this see Jeffrey Rubenstein, "Bavli Gittin 55b–56b: An Aggada and its Halakhic Context," unpublished paper, 1996. Likewise, here we cannot assume that the rabbinic position is superior to that ascribed to the heretics and Romans simply by virtue of its being ascribed to rabbis—particularly in light of the fact that rabbinic and non-rabbinic viewpoints prove to be somewhat interchangeable in our passage, as we shall soon see. However, an alternative interpretation will also be considered here.

4. It has been stated likewise: R. Yohanan said on the authority of R. Simeon b. Yohai, whence do we know that the Holy One, blessed be He, will resurrect the dead and knows the future? From, "behold you will lie with your fathers and will rise up..."

Unit I's question is expanded in Unit II: whence do we know that God will resurrect the dead and that he knows the future? The prooftext provided and its midrashic interpretation are the same (Deut. 31:16). The Romans respond as did the *minîm* above—this just isn't what the verse says. R. Joshua ben Hananyah (step 3) concedes without further ado, as if acknowledging that one must buy into a whole set of hermeneutical assumptions and practices in order to accept a midrashic exegesis. But at least, he states, the Romans can derive God's knowledge of the future from this verse since that is independent of any non-contextual exegesis.

The unit ends with our question repeated for a third time—but this time as a rhetorical question in the mouth of a rabbi: "R. Yohanan said on the authority of R. Simeon b. Yohai: 'Whence do we know that the Holy One, Blessed be He, will resurrect the dead (and knows the future)?'" From Deuteronomy 31:16. This is accepted, without objection or qualification. For a rabbi, within the system of midrashic exegesis, this verse works as a proof. By juxtaposing the reactions of the *minîm*, Romans, and a rabbi, to the midrashic derivation of resurrection from Deuteronomy 31:16, the authors of our passage demonstrate their awareness of diverse exegetical approaches and of the resistance that non-contextual methods of exegesis engender in persons of a contextual sensibility. They know that those outside their system view their use of text as misuse, their readings as misreadings.

The third unit opens with a debate between R. Eleazar b. R. Yose and some hypothetical *minîm*[45] followed by a like debate among the rabbis.

---

[45]   Or, more likely, "Cutheans" (i.e., Samaritans) which is the reading in Munich ms., the parallels in *Sipre Num.* and *Yalqut Šimʿoni*, and appears to be the reading in the genizah fragment reproduced in Katsch, *Ginze*, 235 (Hebrew pagination), l

UNIT III

1. It has been taught: R. Eleazar b. R. Yose[46] said: In this matter I refuted
    the books of the *mînîm* who maintained that resurrection is not
    deducible from the Torah.

2. I said to them: You have falsified your Torah, yet it has availed you
    nothing. For you maintain that resurrection is not a biblical doctrine,
    but it is written, "[Because he has despised the word of the Lord, and
    has broken his commandment] that person shall be utterly cut off
    [Heb. = *hikkārēt tikkārēt*]; his iniquity[47] shall be upon him" (Num.
    15:31). Now seeing that he shall be utterly cut off in this world, when
    shall his iniquity be upon him? Surely in the next world.

3. R. Pappa said to Abbaye: Could he not have deduced both [this and
    the next world] from *hikkārēt tikkārēt*?

4. [They would have replied:] The Torah employed human language.

5. This is disputed by *tannāʾîm*. *Hikkārēt*, he shall be cut off in this world
    and *tikkārēt*, in the next—this is the view of R. Aqiba. R. Ishmael said:
    But the text has already stated (v. 30) "he reproaches the Lord and
    that person shall be cut off (*nikrĕtâ*)." Are there then three worlds?
    Rather, *nikrĕtâ*, in this world, *hikkārēt*, in the next. As for *tikkārēt*, that
    is because the Torah uses human language.

---

33. Some early printed editions read "books of Sadducees" here. See R. Rabbino-
vicz, *Variae Lectiones in Mischnam et in Talmud Babylonicum* [*Diqdûqê sôprîm*]
(Munich: Huber, 1867–86) 11, 249, n. *tāw*. See also the discussion in David Zvi
Hoffman, *Mēlammēd lĕ-hôʿîl* (Frankfurt am Main, 1926–32) 3, 79, 125.

[46]   Following the emendation suggested by Rabbinovicz, *Diqdûqê sôprîm*, 249, n.
šin.

[47]   As has long been noted, biblical terms for sin, iniquity, and transgression can
also carry the meaning of the punishment for sin, iniquity, or transgression,
depending on context (W. Zimmerli, "Die Eigenast des prophetischen Rede des
Ezechiel," *ZAW* 66 [1954], 9–19; K. Koch, "Der Spruch 'Sein Blut bleibe auf seinem
Haupt,'" *VT* 12 [1962], 396–416; G. von Rad, *Old Testament Theology*, [New York:
Harper and Row, 1962] 1, 262–72; J. Milgrom, *Cult and Conscience: The ASHAM
and the Priestly Doctrine of Repentance* [Leiden: Brill, 1976], 3–12). Here, the text
means that the punishment for his iniquity will be upon him. However, I use
"iniquity" because the final exegesis will turn on this rendering of the term.

R. Eleazar argues that resurrection can be proven from the two punishments meted out to the one who despises the word of the Lord in
Numbers 15:30–31. One punishment (*hikkārēt tikkārēt*, "he shall be
utterly cut off") will take place in this world while the other (*ʿawônāh
bāh*, "his iniquity shall be upon him") will take place in the next world.
Two late Babylonian authorities wonder why R. Eleazar did not prove
the same point from the two punishments implied by the repetition of
the root *krt* in the phrase *hikkārēt tikkārēt*—(infinitive absolute plus
finite verb). The response, that the Torah employs human language,
indicates that the use of an infinitive absolute plus finite verb is standard emphatic form in biblical Hebrew with the result that no special
meaning is to be expounded from the reduplication of the verbal root.
By placing the tradition of R. Pappa and Abbaye immediately after the
story of R. Eleazar b. R. Yose we are left with the impression that the
mînîm themselves would have responded to the exposition of the verbal
construction with the claim that the Torah employs ordinary idiomatic
language, the peculiarities of which are not always subject to midrashic
exposition.[48] (Note that the text explicitly identifies the debate between

---

[48]   The version of the text in the current printed edition as emended by the papal
censor reflects this implied meaning explicitly: "*they [the sectarians] would have
replied that* the Torah employs human language." Harris studies the nineteen
appearances of the phrase "the Torah employs human language" in the Babylonian
Talmud, and points out that it is used in objecting to only one form of midrash—
reduplication of the verbal root in constructions that feature the infinitive absolute
and finite form of a verb (Harris, *How Do We Know*, 34). His study leads him to the
following conclusions. In all but two cases the phrase is used by the anonymous
redactors of the passage to reconstruct either the putative exegetical foundations of
a legal dispute or to explain why only one side provides an exegesis of the repetition
in an exegetical dispute (p. 35). It is attributed to perhaps a dozen different
tannāʾîm, of various generations. Further, the same *tannāʾ* will in one place refrain
from interpreting repeated phrases and in another interpret them (p. 72). That a
certain sage would say that the Torah speaks in human language is the judgment of
the redactors and is an *ad hoc* statement indicating that in a specific case a certain
sage adopts this principle (p. 37ff.). In short, the Babli's redactors do not conclude
that the human language position is consistently adhered to by anybody, including
R. Ishmael. The phrase developed as a stock response in order to explain why a

R. Eleazar and the *mînîm/Kûtîm* with the debate between R. Aqiba and R. Ishmael. This suggests that the former is an externalization of what is in reality an internal rabbinic tension. We shall return to this point below.)

Thus we can see that in all three units a clear distinction is made between a contextual exegetical approach and a non-contextual exegetical approach. We also see that those authoring our passage imagine that a chasm exists between the two, such that no genuine communication between the parties who adopt these approaches—beyond each merely asserting his interpretation—is possible.[49]

---

particular sage would "abstain" from interpreting a repetition. Such abstention requires explanation since the assumption is that all sages see repetition as a potential bearer of meaning. Whether that potential becomes actual depends on certain other factors that may supersede the exegetical imperative to interpret the superfluous repetition (p. 43).

Harris also notes that our passage, *b. Sanh.* 90b, is a possible exception to the pattern that the human language position is imputed to earlier authorities by later ones because in *b. Sanh.* 90b the phrase appears to be a quotation of a *tannāʾ* (cf. the parallels at *b. Sanh.* 64b and *Sipre Num.* 112). But, Harris points to strong circumstantial evidence that suggests that the phrase "the Torah employs human language" is not an authentic part of the *bāraytāʾ* but an interpolation. However we date this phrase, it does not here, as elsewhere, constitute a general principle of exegesis ascribed to R. Ishmael. It is an *ad hoc* explanation of his refusal in this instance to expound the reduplication of the verbal root—apparently because of the appearance of yet a third form of the root in the immediate context. See Harris, *How Do We Know*, 41–43.

[49]   Although the Yerushalmi is not our focus in this paper, it is interesting to note that a similar case can be made for the Palestinian rabbinic community. *y. Ber.* 9 (12d–13a) is a lengthy passage that demonstrates the awareness of Palestinian rabbis that others do not share their hermeneutical presuppositions regarding the biblical text; nor are these others troubled by certain questions generated by the acceptance of those presuppositions. In this passage *mînîm* ask R. Simlai how many gods created the earth? The *mînîm* are armed with several biblical passages that contain a plural lexeme in connection with God (e.g., the plural form of the name *ʾElôhîm*, God's use of the cohortative ["let us …"], etc.), thus suggesting a plurality of divine powers. In each case, R. Simlai points to a singular verb or pronoun in the same verse proving that a single entity is meant after all, despite the plural lexeme seized upon by the *mînîm*. In each case, R. Simlai's disciples say to him "you have driven away these *mînîm* with a mere reed; but what will you answer us?" R. Simlai

We have established therefore our first claim—that the rabbis recognized a distinction between contextual and non-contextual interpretations. To establish the further claim that the rabbis felt ambivalence, anxiety, and radical doubt in regard to their own non-contextual methods of exegesis, we shall examine our passage with the aid of psychoanalytic methods of literary interpretation.

Non-Contextual Exegesis and Rabbinic Anxiety

Psychoanalytic theory provides a model for explaining how a literary work might contain elements at odds with the author's expressed views. In psychoanalytic interpretations of literature, texts are viewed as a reflection of psychic processes—specifically, the negotiation between the author's unconscious desires and the agency of repression.[50] Like dreams, literary works may contain repressed material that finds expres-

---

then provides a non-contextual interpretation that accounts for the presence of the plural lexeme. This passage reveals several things. First, it reveals the rabbis' awareness of two incommensurate exegetical perspectives. The *mînîm* are concerned with the contextual meaning of the verse. They are bothered by a plural lexeme because it would appear to connote a plural divinity. A contextual reading indicates that it does not and the *mîn* is satisfied. However, for those who accept the hermeneutical assumption of omnisignificance (see n. 4 above) a burning question remains. Granted the text refers to a single divinity—but why should it employ a plural lexeme in places and so risk leading the reader astray? Since no detail of this perfect text is arbitrary a meaning must be found for the use of a locution that *implies* plurality. And it is to this meta-exegetical problem that R. Simlai addresses himself in the latter part of each scene. By dividing R. Simlai's attention between the *mînîm* on the one hand and the disciples on the other, the passage underscores the chasm that separates those who do and those who do not maintain the hermeneutical assumption of omnisignificance. R. Simlai handles himself in both of these two radically divorced worlds. He addresses the *mînîm*'s question as to the verse's basic meaning. Turning from the *mînîm* to his disciples, he enters equally sympathetically into their mindset and addresses their question as to the meaning of employing an odd locution in the verse in question.

50   For a summary of psychoanalytic interpretation of literature, see Abrams, *Glossary*, 227–31, and Fowler, *A Dictionary of Modern Critical Terms* (London and New York: Routledge and Kegan Paul, 1987), 192–96.

sion in disguised form. The Freudian concepts of condensation and displacement—mechanisms for the transformation of the repressed—are employed in the study of literary symbolism, and the interplay of characters in a literary work can be read as an interplay between elements in the psyche.[51]

Applying these insights to our passage, I submit that the interplay of characters here can be read as an interplay between elements within the collective rabbinic psyche. A particular and unusual feature of our passage supports this claim. I refer to the fusion and confusion of the *dramatis personae*. In this short passage there are no clear-cut boundaries drawn between rabbi and heretic, or rabbi and Roman.[52] As we

---

[51]   For the application of psychoanalytic methods of hermeneutics to the study of rabbinic literature see M. Niehoff, "Associative Thinking in the Midrash Exemplified by the Rabbinic Interpretation of the Journey of Abraham and Sarah to Egypt" [Hebrew], *Tarbiẓ* 62 (1993), 339–59 and Boyarin, *Intertextuality and the Reading of Midrash* (Bloomington: Indiana University Press, 1990), ch. 6. Niehoff employs Freudian techniques of dream interpretation in her analysis of *Gen. Rab.* on Gen. 12:10–20, thereby exposing the contradictions that emerge from the rabbis' repression or displacement of negative aspects of Abraham's character. Boyarin employs the psycho-dynamic metaphor in his analysis of a passage from the *Mekilta*. He describes the *Mekilta*'s text as bringing to consciousness some of the repressed elements of Israelite cultural history that are scattered throughout the Bible—specifically, mythic material from Israel's pagan past.

[52]   I am not here referring to the phenomenon well known in rabbinic literature whereby non-rabbis, including non-Jews, are depicted arguing with rabbis and employing rabbinic terminology, methods of argumentation and so on (e.g., *b. Bek.* 5a and *b. ʿAbod. Zar.* 54b). In such cases, the "rabbinization" of the non-rabbi's speech does not interfere with the preservation of his distinct and non-rabbinic voice or point of view. In other words, non-Jews may speak "Rabbinese" but they maintain their own consistent point of view diametrically opposed to that of the rabbis. Thus, the Roman general questioning R. Yohanan b. Zakkai in *b. Bek.* 5a, for all his citation of Scripture, has a consistently maintained persona and point of view that stands over against that of the rabbi. He ridicules the rabbis and their biblical text by pointing out arithmetical inconsistencies. Likewise, the philosopher who tries to stump the rabbis in *b. ʿAbod. Zar.* 54b is no less a distinct and non-rabbinic character for his citation of Scripture, and there is no danger of confusing him with the rabbis despite the rabbinic elements in his speech. By contrast our passage fails

have seen, words placed in the mouth of a heretic or Roman are attributed to a rabbi elsewhere in the passage, with the result that it is difficult to assign the text's duelling exegetical voices to particular characters with any consistency. Heretics sound like rabbis and rabbis sound like heretics. For example, in Unit I step 4b, the *mînîm* state that the verse cited by R. Gamaliel might simply mean that the dead person's lips move in the grave. But this counter-exegesis is itself a rabbinic dictum attributed to R. Yohanan.[53]

Unit II reinforces the fusion and confusion of voices in our passage since the question asked by sectarians in Unit I (whence do we know that God will resurrect the dead) is now asked by Romans and then, rhetorically at least, by a rabbi (see step 4). Similarly, in unit III distinctions between *mînîm* and rabbis are blurred. The hypothetical debate between R. Eleazar b. R. Yose and his adversaries over the interpretation of the absolute infinitive is an entirely rabbinic one. It parallels the debate between R. Aqiba and R. Ishmael.[54] As regards exegetical orien-

---

to maintain the integrity of its characters so that there is no clear rabbinic point of view as opposed to a non-rabbinic point of view. Points of view blend into one another so that the point of view espoused by—indeed almost definitive of—a heretic is in the self-same passage espoused by a rabbi.

[53] Our printed editions do not clearly attribute this very rabbinic counter-exegesis to the sectarians, but it is quite explicit in the Munich ms. and in several parallel texts which read "*They [the sectarians] said to him*: perhaps it means merely that their lips will move, as R. Yohanan said..." (see Rabbinovicz, *Diqdûqê sôprîm*, 249, n. *nun*). Even if the sectarian response ends with the statement that the verse means merely that their lips will move and the subsequent tradition of R. Yohanan is to be read as a return to the anonymous voice of the Talmud, we still have a rabbinization of the sectarians. For once the sectarian reading of the verse is seen to be itself a reading promoted by a rabbinic authority (R. Yohanan) the distinction between heretic and rabbi becomes blurred. Here then is a clue that the *mîn* functions as little more than the externalization of an internal rabbinic objection to or anxiety over non-contextual exegetical methods.

[54] The tradition of R. Pappa and Abbaye serves to shuttle between the two pairs of disputants, by providing common terminological ground for comparison. In other words. R. Pappa and Abbaye suggest that R. Eleazar could not adopt a certain proof with the sectarians because they resist the notion that certain textual details

tation, R. Eleazar's position equals that of R. Aqiba while the *mînîm*'s position equals that of R. Ishmael. In short, views ascribed to heretics in these three units are subsequently and surprisingly shown to be views espoused by rabbis.

This confusion among the *dramatis personae* suggests that the dialogue found here is an interior dialogue, that the two voices are voices within a single consciousness—in this case, the collective rabbinic consciousness. Assigning the anti-midrashic position to *mînîm* and Romans might be understood as an effort by the rabbis to disown that position, to externalize what is in reality their own resistance to non-contextual exegesis. In psychoanalytic terms, heretics and Romans serve as characters onto which the rabbis can project a radical doubt unacceptable to the collective rabbinic conscious; rabbinic objections to and anxiety over midrashic methods of exegesis are displaced onto heretics and Romans. This displacement, like any displacement, is imperfect, and it is precisely this imperfection that enables us to trace its contours and recognize the degree to which it represents an externalization of internal rabbinic dialogue.[55] This hypothesis is consistent with the findings of other scholars working in related areas who have noted similar displacements from rabbinic or Jewish characters to non-rabbinic or non-Jewish characters.[56]

---

can be expounded and can thus be compared to R. Ishmael who espouses the principle—in this very case—that the Torah employs human language.

[55]   I use this phrase in two ways—internal to rabbinic culture and internal to the individual rabbinic consciousness.

[56]   Stuart Miller notes that *b. Ber.* 56b in which R. Ishmael interprets the sinful dreams of a certain *mîn*, is dependent on Palestinian stories in which the sinful dreams are attributed to a Jew; see Miller, "Reconsidered," 396–97. Tal Ilan argues in a recent work that the Roman Matron depicted in dialogue with rabbis was originally a Jewish woman named Matrona who was transformed into a pagan figure in later, especially Babylonian, material; see Tal Ilan, "Matrona and Rabbi Jose—An Alternative Interpretation," *JSJ* 25 (1994), 18–51. Miller also shows, that in later Babylonian polemics the *mîn* functions as a literary convention or Gentile foil to the rabbis; see Miller, "Reconsidered," 385, 394–99.

In the previous section I employed Bakhtinian dialogism to identify the presence of distinct voices within b. Sanhedrin 90b–91a. In the present section, I invoked psychoanalytic theory to locate these distinct voices within a single (rabbinic) consciousness and to explain their relative value and function. To this point the dialogic and psychoanalytic approaches have complemented one another. But when we turn from a description of the text itself to a description of the rabbinic redactor(s) of our text, the dialogic and psychoanalytic approaches provide incompatible models. According to the dialogic model, the rabbinic redactor(s) of our passage consciously and artfully juxtaposes two conflicting voices, neither of which is privileged and neither of which is necessarily his own. On the psychoanalytic model, the redactor(s) unconsciously gives expression to two voices at war within himself. The psychoanalytic model therefore assumes a deeply conflicted redactor, struggling to repress his underlying resistance to and anxiety over the midrashic methods he overtly endorses. In the next section, I will present evidence in support of this second model. This evidence will be drawn first from the immediate context of our passage and then from the broader context of rabbinic literature generally.

Confirmation: Rabbinic Ambivalence as a Cultural Stimulus

The immediate halakhic context of our passage supports the claim that the passage betrays a rabbinic anxiety over extreme midrashic exegesis, placed in the mouths of *mînîm* and Romans.[57] There are, of course, scores of *mišnāyôt* that contain laws for which the biblical sources

---

[57]   The joint study of *halākâ* and *ʾaggādâ* is a feature of the method of cultural poetics, whose application to rabbinic literature is set forth by Daniel Boyarin in *Carnal Israel: Reading Sex in Talmudic Culture* (Berkeley and Los Angeles: University of California Press, 1993). Boyarin assumes that both *halākâ* and *ʾaggādâ* represent attempts to work out the same cultural, political, social, ideological, and religious problems. The two genres are intimately connected; specifically, the *halākâ* can be read as a background and explanation for aggadic texts. I am indebted to Jeffrey Rubenstein for emphasizing the importance of the halakic context of our passage.

are not immediately apparent, are not provided in the Mishnah and are the subject of discussion in the *gĕmārāʾ*. Our text featuring rabbinic anxiety over midrashic methods could have been attached to any of these. Why then, does the passage occur here, at *m. Sanhedrin* 10:1?

Our passage appears here, I would argue, because the very content of this mishnah is anxiety-producing. *m. Sanhedrin* 10:1 explicitly declares belief in resurrection to be a necessary precondition for a share in the world to come: "All Israel have a portion in the world to come … but the following have no portion therein—he who maintains there is no resurrection [from/taught in the Torah] …."[58] Resurrection is a particular source of anxiety precisely because (1) the Mishnah declares it to be a fundamental belief, denial of which deprives one of life in the world to come, and (2) it is nevertheless not found in the Torah. Exegetical derivations of resurrection are difficult and tenuous as our passage and subsequent sections attest, and given what weighs in the balance, these derivations fail to inspire confidence. In short, the rabbis feel anxious about this mishnah's demand upon them, as well as feeling anxious about the ability of their exegetical methods to convince themselves and others of this all-important doctrine. This complex anxiety is then displaced into the mouth of heretics and Romans almost of necessity. After all, the mishnah's formulation makes it clear that those who doubt resurrection are those outside the community of Israel, and they are by definition *mînîm* of various types. Any internal rabbinic debate of the issue and its manner of derivation will be transposed into a debate between rabbis and non-rabbis of various kinds.

My claim of rabbinic ambivalence—i.e., a simultaneous acceptance of and resistance to the midrashic method—also finds confirmation in texts of all periods that can be divided into two groups: those that focus on the dangers inherent in a non-contextual program of exegesis, and

---

[58] The phrase "from/taught in the Torah" is missing in the parallel in Tosefta 13:5, in some medieval witnesses and earlier printed editions (see Rabbinovicz, *Diqdûqê sôprîm*, 247, n. *alep*) and in the Genizah fragment reproduced in Katsch, *Ginze* (for text see vol. 2, 235 [Hebrew pagination], l. 4; for notes, see vol. 2, p. 103).

those that focus on the creative possibilities inherent in such a program.[59] The first group, sensitive to the dangers inherent in rabbinic exegetical methods, is marked by expressions of anxiety, embarrassment, or general discomfort. The second group, alive to the possibilities inherent in rabbinic exegetical methods, is marked by expressions of exuberance and confidence that overcome this anxiety. Common to and *generating* the production of both sets of texts is the exegetical self-consciousness found in *b. Sanhedrin* 90b–91a, an ability to distinguish between contextual and non-contextual interpretations and a sensitivity to the implications—both positive and negative—of a non-contextual approach. Taken together these texts suggest that the rabbis' exegetical self-consciousness was an important stimulus contributing to the construction of central rabbinic claims regarding the source and nature of their authority to interpret Scripture.

1. EXEGETICAL ANXIETIES

Anxiety over unintuitive or non-contextual exegesis is found in texts that contain objections to specific exegetical methods on the part of some rabbis or a rabbinic generality. While the notion of a systematic distinction between two schools of exegesis (the more extreme school of R. Aqiba and the more contextual school of R. Ishmael) in second century rabbinic circles has been called into question,[60] texts dating to

---

[59]   Here I turn to the broader phenomenon of exegetical ambivalence throughout the rabbinic estate in both tannaitic and amoraic times. For that reason I draw upon various texts of all periods.

[60]   Harris has argued that the idea of two overarching systems of exegesis with different ideas regarding scriptural language and the authority of derivations represented by R. Aqiba and R. Ishmael is the invention of the redactors of the Palestinian Talmud. These redactors construct and gloss passages out of tannaitic midrashic materials in order to convey this idea. Where the Yerushalmi imposes consistency and order on the chaotic mass of inherited tannaitic materials, the Babli does not. The Babli's redactors felt free to reconstruct the putative exegetical positions of *tannāʾim* in a strictly *ad hoc, ad locum* manner (Harris, *How Do We Know*, 43–46, 51–72; see also the discussion in n. 48 above).

For our purposes, Harris' conclusion that the Yerushalmi's redactors supposed

all periods occasionally depict rabbis as rejecting or seeking to establish rules to limit the use of midrashic methods in a manner that signals a basic discomfort with non-contextual exegesis.[61] Tannaitic examples include *Sipra Ṣaw* 8:1 (ed. Weiss 33a)[62] in which R. Yose ha-Gelili expresses irritation at R. Aqiba's inclusive interpretation of *"kol,"* and *Sipra Tazrîʿa* 13:2 (ed. Weiss 68b) where R. Ishmael objects to R. Eliezer's interpretation of *wāw* with the words "it is as if you are saying to the biblical text, 'Silence, while I give an interpretation!'"[63]

---

two different tannaitic approaches to Scripture "one expanding the range of acceptable teachings, one restricting that expansion" supports the general claim made at the outset of this paper that a radical shift in textual assumptions is only a sufficient and not a necessary condition for exegetical self-consciousness and anxiety. The Yerushalmi's redactors (fourth c. Palestine) lived prior to the shift in textual assumptions noted by Harris; they shared the basic hermeneutical assumptions of classical rabbinic culture. Yet they show themselves to be capable of imagining two distinct exegetical approaches—one more constrained and contextual than the other—to the degree that they impose these distinct approaches on earlier tannaitic material that does not in itself evince such a distinction. Thus, it would appear that persons committed to and operating within a given interpretive mindset can nevertheless conceive of alternative interpretive approaches, and so possess some degree of self-consciousness.

[61]   This is not to say that the party objecting to a particular non-contextual interpretation is a proponent of a contextual alternative. It is rather a question of degree. In other words, R. X may not be immune to non-contextual exegesis but he will draw the line at some of the more extreme and artificial interpretations proposed by R. Y. What is important for our purposes is that it appears that rabbis do make distinctions between acceptable and unacceptable interpretations not merely on the basis of substance but also, if occasionally, on the basis of method. To be sure, there is no consistency—what one is willing to accept another feels compelled to reject as forced—nor do the talmudic distinctions correspond to medieval or modern notions of contextual and non-contextual exegesis. Nevertheless, and despite individual variations and inconsistencies, rabbis do make distinctions between more and less contextual interpretations.

[62]   See the discussion in Elman, "Empty Thing," 5.

[63]   Harris spells out the intent of R. Ishmael's objection as follows: "You approach Scripture as if its language had no meaning apart from that which you impose on it. You have transgressed all natural boundaries of linguistic usage; the language of

The situation in post-tannaitic texts is more complex. On the one hand, the Babli in some ways continues with the techniques and program of the *midrĕšê halākâ*. As Harris observes, the redactors of the Babli recast, adjust, and otherwise manipulate antecedent midrashic material so as to create a fully-developed talmudic discussion (*How Do We Know*, 32). Regarding most midrashic techniques (e.g., the exposition of *wāw* or *kol, gĕzērâ šāwâ*, etc.; see Harris, *How Do We Know*, 44–46) the Babli generally assumes that no *tannā²* was opposed to the use of any exegetical technique in principle[64] and refusal to employ a particular technique was in general *ad hoc* and *ad locum*. One exception may be found in *b. Yebamôt* 4a. The sugya here mentions the *tannā²* R. Judah as among those who will not base interpretations on the midrashic method of *sĕmûkîn* (juxtapositions).[65] (We should note that the rejection of this same method of interpretation is attributed to a *mîn* in *b. Ber.* 10a, an example of displacement, but this time across two separate texts rather than within one passage.[66])

Scripture is now as putty in your hands to do with what you will" (Harris, *How Do We Know*, 23). See also *Sipra Ṣaw* 5, 11:6 (ed. Weiss, 35d) (parallel in *b. Menaḥ.* 89a) and *Sipre Num., Šelaḥ,* 112 (ed. Horovitz, 123). Compare similar traditions concerning *tannā²îm* in texts of later redaction, such as *b. Sanh.* 64b; *b. Ker.* 11a; and *y. Šabb.* 19:2 (17a).

[64] An exception to this general rule may be the Babli's recognition—in agreement with other rabbinic documents—that *tannā²îm* were split on the use of *kĕlāl û-pĕrāt û-kĕlāl* vs. *ribbûy û-miyyût wĕ-ribbûy*. See Harris, *How Do We Know*, 44.

[65] The stammaitic discussion makes it clear that he does not do this as a general principle, not merely in a specific case.

[66] The text in *b. Ber.* 10a reads:

> A certain *mîn* said to R. Abbahu: It is written (Ps. 3:1) "Psalm of David when he fled before Absalom his son" and it is written (Ps. 57:1) "Of David, Michtam, when he fled before Saul in the cave." Was the incident of Absalom first? [No!]—yet since the incident of Saul was first, it should have been written first. He said to him: there is a difficulty only for you who do not interpret *sĕmûkîn*, but for us, who do interpret *sĕmûkîn*, there is no difficulty.

Two important data emerge from this passage. First, it is another example of the

On the other hand, however, post-tannaitic strata within the Talmud reveal a gradual abandonment of certain midrashic methods. In other words, some methods freely ascribed to *tannāʾîm* in the reconstructions of the Babli's redactors are not generally attributed to—and one may presume are not employed by—*ʾamôrāʾîm*. Midrashic expositions of *ʾô*, *hēh*, etc., are with rare exception featured in *bāraytôt*.[67] Elman concludes that:

> ... as has long been observed, the Amoraim were much more restrained, on the whole, than the Tannaim and their successors were still more restrained in their use of these techniques.[68]

---

rabbinic awareness of two competing and incommensurate exegetical perspectives. The rabbis represent the *mîn*'s exegetical perspective as a contextual one; the *mîn* does not accept non-contextual interpretations or the methods that produce them and thus would never accept the rabbinic explanation for the sequence of the verses in question since the latter depends upon a non-contextual exegetical method. Second, as stated above, this passage in conjunction with *b. Yebam.* 4a is another example of the phenomenon of displacement—though across texts, rather than within a single passage. In *b. Ber.* 10a the rabbinic authors place in the mouth of a *mîn* an objection to a midrashic method of exegesis that in *b. Yebam.* 4a is clearly attributed to a rabbi (R. Judah).

[67] See *b. Šabb.* 63b and *b. B. Qam.* 43a in which expositions of *ʾô* and of *ʾim* are attributed to the early Palestinian *ʾamorāʾ*, R. Yohanan. As with the Babli's treatment of tannaitic midrash, these passages contain much redactional reconstruction of the sage's teaching. I thank Yaakov Elman for pointing out these passages to me.

[68] Elman, "Empty Thing," 6. On the periodization of rabbinic legal midrash with reference to particular midrashic techniques, see the work of Y. Elman and M. Chernick, as cited in Elman, "Empty Thing," 63, n. 28. See also Y. Elman, "Lĕ-tôldôt ha-ribbuy ba-talmud ha-bablî," *Proceedings of the Eleventh World Congress of Jewish Studies* (Jerusalem: World Union of Jewish Studies, 1987). In this paper, Elman studies three techniques of rabbinic extension. Certain *dĕrāšôt* found in the Babli are attributed only to *tannāʾîm* (for example, the exposition of *hēh* or *wāw* in extensions of the *ʾên lî* type) and to Rab and Samuel among Babylonian *ʾamôrāʾîm*. Such *dĕrāšôt* are exceedingly rare among later *ʾamôrāʾîm*. In contrast to the virtual disappearance of expositions of superfluous letters, the exposition of superfluous words in *dĕrāšôt* of the *ʾim ʾênô ʿinyan* type is increasingly attributed to later

In short, the Babli incorporates and manipulates antecedent (i.e., tannaitic) midrashic material, even as it ceases to employ midrashic techniques. It is not only the case that certain midrashic techniques are employed less frequently in amoraic literature. In addition, expressions of anxiety over non-contextual interpretations continue in post-tannaitic, as in tannaitic, texts. In some passages, the rabbis are aware that their exegetical project can be exasperating or appear ridiculous to those whose exegetical orientation is contextual. They are further aware that their promulgation of laws and interpretations that stray far from a contextual reading of the biblical text undermines their authority in the eyes of some. This is the theme of several texts involving *mînîm* and *ʾapîqôrsîm*. These heretics' exasperation with and disgust for the rabbis is the basis for their rejection of the rabbis' authority to expound Torah for all Israel. In *y. Sanhedrin* 10:1 (27d) and *b. Sanhedrin* 99b–100a an *ʾapîqôrôs* is said to be one who insults a scholar or expresses exasperation with the arbitrary results of their interpretations through phrases such as "These scribes!" (*y. Sanh.* 10:1 [27d]) or "Of what use are the rabbis to us? For their own benefit they read Scripture and for their own benefit they study traditional teachings!" (*b. Sanh.* 99b). It is not surprising that *mînût* is defined as "walking after one's own heart" (see for example *Sipre Num.* 115 [ed. Horovitz, 126]), i.e., not heeding the instruction of the rabbis or accepting their authority as the teachers and expounders of Torah.[69]

That the use of non-contextual methods of exegesis was a source of anxiety to the rabbis is evidenced by texts in which a rabbi's authority is rejected because his non-contextual exegesis of Scripture is the object of ridicule and scorn. The rabbinic authors of such texts perceived themselves to be vulnerable on precisely this point. One example must suffice. In *b. Sanhedrin* 100a (= *b. B. Bat.* 75a), one of R. Yohanan's

---

ʾamôrāʾîm and the *stam*. Nevertheless, Elman's statement that on the whole the *ʾamôrāʾîm* were more restrained than the *tannāʾîm* holds true.

[69] See also *b. Sanh.* 38b where Adam is described as a *mîn* because he defies authority.

disciples derides his fantastic exegesis of Isaiah 54:12 and so challenges his authority. (It is interesting to note that a parallel version of our story in *Pesiqta de-Rab Kahana* 18 [ed. Mandelbaum, 297–98] states that it was a certain *mîn*, rather than a certain disciple, who was guilty of this disrespect. Once again, it appears that a disturbing self-perception expressed by a rabbi in one text is displaced into the mouth of a heretic in another text.[70])

2. EXEGETICAL EXUBERANCE

If midrashic methods inspired so much resistance and justified rebellion against rabbinic authority, why were they adopted? The answer is obvious. The rabbis knew that the very feature of midrashic exegesis that inspired resistance and rebellion—its generation of interpretations far removed from, if not antithetical to, the contextual meaning of a biblical passage—was at one and the same time its greatest strength and virtue. For the rabbis, midrashic exegesis was a powerful tool for the continuous unfolding of the divine will through time and—if accepted—for the establishment of the rabbis' own authority.[71] Thus, in contrast to texts that express simple anxiety, we also find texts in which the rabbis boldly assert their authority as teachers and interpreters despite the fact that their methods can result in interpretations so distant from a contextual reading of the biblical text. In these texts, anxiety gives way to exuberance as the rabbis confront the vision of their own strangeness, only to embrace it and even celebrate it.

The classic example of rabbinic self-acceptance in the face of radical doubt is the amoraic tradition of *b. Menaḥot* 29b in which Moses listens

---

[70]   Cf. *b. Ber.* 10a and *b. Yebam.* 4a discussed above.

[71]   Harris, *How Do We Know*, 3, describes what was at stake for the rabbis in the broad acceptance of the legitimacy of rabbinic exegesis: "Exegesis of the Torah was the means through which the rabbis established the authority of the extrabiblical laws and practices they inherited; it was the medium they employed to create new laws in their own times; and it was the tool they used to resolve more far-reaching problems, such as contradictions within the Torah, or between the Torah and other biblical books."

befuddled and uncomprehending to R. Aqiba's complex midrashic expositions of Torah.

> Rav Judah said in the name of Rav:
>
> When Moses ascended on high he found the Holy One, blessed be He, engaged in attaching crownlets [decorative squiggles] to the letters [of the Torah]. He said to Him, 'Lord of the Universe, why should you bother with this!?'[72] He answered, 'There is a man who is destined to arise at the end of many generations, named Aqiba b. Joseph, and to expound upon each squiggle heaps and heaps of laws.' [Moses] said to him, 'Lord of the Universe, show him to me.' He replied, 'Turn around.' Moses went and sat down behind eight rows [in R. Aqiba's schoolhouse, with the least skilled students], but he could not understand what they were saying. His strength left him.[73] But when they came to a certain topic and the disciples said to him [R. Aqiba], 'Rabbi, whence do you know it?' he replied to them, 'It is a law given to Moses at Sinai!' And Moses was comforted.[74]
>
> Thereupon he returned to the Holy one, Blessed be He and said to Him, 'Lord of the Universe, You have such a man and You are giving the Torah by me?!' He replied, 'Be silent, for such is my decree.'[75]
>
> [Moses] said to him, 'Lord of the Universe, You have shown me his Torah, now show me his reward.' He replied to him, 'Turn around.' And Moses saw them weighing out R. Aqiba's flesh in the market place.[76] Moses said to Him, 'Lord of the Universe, that was his Torah and this is his reward!?' And He replied, 'Be silent, for such is my decree.'[77]

This story—at once humorous and tragic—enables the rabbis brilliantly to voice their simultaneous admiration for and anxiety over the midrashic virtuosity of earlier greats, of whom R. Aqiba is the premier example. The opening lines sound one of the primary themes of the

---

[72] Lit. "who constrains your hand" [to do such a trivial and unnecessary task]?

[73] An expression used to indicate despair or depression.

[74] Or: "his mind was set at ease."

[75] Or: "so it has occurred to me to do."

[76] A reference to his martyrdom at the hands of the Romans.

[77] See note 75.

story:[78] the derivation of mounds of laws from the slimmest biblical details (cf. *m. Ḥag.* 1:8). God's participation in this project—by encoding the text in such a manner that the complex exegesis of the rabbis can proceed—implies his endorsement of it. God tells Moses that R. Aqiba will expound these minute orthographic details so as to yield heaps of laws. Incredulous, Moses asks God to show him R. Aqiba at work. Granted a vision of R. Aqiba's schoolhouse where the biblical text is expounded to yield these heaps of law, Moses is at a complete loss to understand. Moses, the very one to whom God entrusted his Torah and the first to teach Torah to Israel, does not recognize this Torah in the hands of a master exegete some 1500 years later. Moses' non-recognition—a figure for the rabbis' own aching suspicion that midrashic techniques have rendered them unrecognizable—depresses him, until R. Aqiba comes to a certain topic. When the students ask R. Aqiba the source of this particular law he refrains from his tortuous derivations from Scripture. This, he says, is a law given to Moses at Sinai and does not emerge from exegesis of Scripture. In other words, there are some things that even R. Aqiba would admit cannot be derived from Scripture, and at this Moses heaves a sigh of relief. It is following this *refusal* to expound that Moses praises R. Aqiba's great wisdom. The story therefore expresses great ambivalence about extreme methods of midrashic exegesis.[79] These methods may be part of a divine plan but the truly wise man knows when to refrain from them (and we can all breathe easier when he does!).

In the story, Moses never does understand the proceedings of the schoolhouse, the complex exegetical processes by which a vast structure of laws and teachings had come to rest upon "insignificant" orthographic details in the biblical text. Indeed, R. Aqiba's midrashic virtuosity makes Moses quite nervous—and in this he surely reflects the

---

[78] This rich and intriguing passage addresses several themes, not all of which are relevant to this study.

[79] Thus, in all likelihood it originates in circles opposed to the exegetical pyrotechnics traditionally associated with R. Aqiba and his school.

anxiety of the rabbinic author(s) of the story. On the other hand, the depiction of God as partner to R. Aqiba's midrashic excesses suggests that this anxiety is not absolute. Portraying God as R. Aqiba's partner betokens at least a desire on the part of the author(s) to believe that despite the yawning gulf that appears to separate the teachings of the rabbis from the divine Torah of ancient Israel, there is an organic unity between them. Midrash may engender an agonizing sense of distance and difference between the Torah and rabbinic *halākâ*, but midrash is also the bridge that connects the two, and in Moses' mouth are placed words of praise and approbation for R. Aqiba. In this story, the amoraic rabbis assert their faith in the power and creative possibilities inherent in the midrashic method despite—or, rather, because of—their equally explicit anxiety over the odd and unintuitive nature of its results.[80]

There are several aggadic texts that declare the supreme authority of the expositions and interpretations of the rabbis. God himself is bound by the rulings of the rabbis in an aggadic passage in *b. Baba᾿ Meṣi῾a᾿* 86a.[81] The famous story of the Ovens of Akhnai in *b. Baba᾿ Meṣi῾a᾿* 59b is the *locus classicus* for a statement of the authority of the rabbis to interpret Torah even if their interpretations run counter to the intention of the text's author—God himself. All these texts betray an exegetical self-consciousness, an awareness that the rabbis' own methods of interpretation involve unintuitive and non-contextual readings that can provoke ridicule, resistance, and ultimately rejection of their authority. However, in these texts the rabbis grapple with their anxiety and emerge victorious, overcoming their radical doubt with grandiose assertions of divine approval of the midrashic method and the complex of law and lore resulting from it: the Oral Torah.

---

[80]   Compare Elman, "Empty Thing," 3, for an interpretation that highlights another aspect of the conflicted nature of this passage.

[81]   In this passage, Rabbah bar Nahmani decides a controversy between God and the heavenly academy. Cf. *Pesiq. Rab Kah, Pārâ ᾿adummâ* (ed. Mandelbaum, 73) where God cites a *halākâ* in the name of R. Eliezer, to the astonishment of Moses.

Harris describes the existential struggle of post-talmudic Jews confronted with what appeared to them to be the exegetical distortions of rabbinic tradition:

> Ultimately, their sense of who they are and what they can be was linked to their ability to confidently appropriate or justifiably reject all or part of their rabbinic heritage. Addressing the question of how or whether to remain connected to this heritage was existentially urgent for these scholars. This need proved to be a major cultural stimulus for Jews in the nineteenth century (*How Do We Know*, 257).

It has been the goal of this paper to demonstrate that the same existential struggle faced the ʾamôrāʾîm and the redactors of the Talmud. How to remain connected to a heritage that rested upon techniques of reading employed less frequently (in some cases not at all) was existentially urgent for these scholars also, and this issue was a major cultural stimulus in the talmudic period also, resulting in the elaboration of central theories regarding the nature and source of the rabbinic authority to interpret Scripture.

Conclusions

The rabbis exhibit a high level of exegetical self-consciousness, an ability to see themselves and their exegetical activities as they may have been seen by outsiders (whether actual outsiders such as *mînîm* and pagans, or the rabbis in their own moments of alienation). They are surely aware of a distinction between contextual interpretations of text, which find ready acceptance, and non- (or less) contextual readings, which depend for their acceptance on the prior acceptance of a set of hermeneutical assumptions, and which provoke ridicule and resistance from any who do not share those assumptions.[82]

What are the implications of the foregoing discussion for historians of Jewish culture? We have seen that the rabbis' dual exegetical consciousness gave rise to conflicting attitudes toward the non-contextual mode of exegesis, expressed in many rabbinic texts both early and late.

---

[82]   See n. 4 above regarding the rabbis' hermeneutical assumptions.

However, there is an important literary difference between these early and late texts.[83] Earlier texts assign both pro- and anti-midrashic views to rabbis, and, with rare exceptions, rabbis mentioned in these texts are rabbis of Roman Palestine (*tannāʾîm* and early Palestinian *ʾamôrāʾîm*; see the examples cited above). Post-tannaitic texts, generally speaking, do not. In these late texts, *named* sages rarely object to midrashic methods;[84] rather, the anti-midrashic view once openly attributed to some rabbis is found increasingly in the mouths of *mînîm* and Romans. Alternatively, it is found in the anonymous voice of the *stam* (the anonymous redactional layer of the Babli).[85] This suggests that the redactor (or redactors) of our passage either introduces *mînîm* and Romans into pre-existing sources featuring debates over the doctrine of resurrection, or exploits the presence of *mînîm* in these earlier sources, for the indirect expression of an anti-midrashic sentiment.[86]

It is this literary difference between early and late texts that has significance for the cultural historian. Following the theory argued most

---

[83]   The conventional designation of tannaitic texts and *bāraytôt* as early and amoraic texts as late is adequate for our purposes. Further, insofar as most of the relevant *bāraytôt* display features that we will identify as characteristic of tannaitic and not amoraic texts generally, the conventional designation appears to be justified in this case.

[84]   With the exception of *bāraytôt* that appear in the Talmuds. *Bāraytôt* assign both pro- and anti-midrashic views to named sages and are thus consistent with tannaitic texts generally, e.g., *b. Ber.* 31b; *b. Yebam.* 4a, etc. However, it should be noted that in some cases it is likely that anti-midrashic views are retrojected to tannaitic authorities.

[85]   E.g., *b. Yebam.* 24a and *b. Sanh.* 45b, the latter containing an anonymous response to a named sage's query regarding the permissibility of hyperliteral exposition.

[86]   As noted above, since the mishnah to which this gemara attaches states that one who denies the resurrection has no portion in the world to come, the gemara's representation of a debate over the doctrine of resurrection will almost of necessity depict those doubting resurrection as outside the community of Israel—*mînîm* and Romans. The presence of *mînîm* and Romans can then be exploited by a redactor to give voice to doubts about the midrashic method itself.

persuasively by Richard Kalmin, that rhetorical, attitudinal, and other differences in the sources that constitute rabbinic texts are best explained by the view that rabbinic texts actually preserve sources from different periods and places,[87] the following cultural-historical reconstruction can be hazarded.

At all times rabbinic Jews saw a distinction between contextual and non-contextual exegesis,[88] and sources from all periods attest to that distinction. Early rabbinic sources indicate that rabbis of Roman Palestine who introduced extreme methods of non-contextual exegesis might have met with the objections and ridicule of other rabbis who favored more contextual interpretation. The rabbinic movement was not in the tannaitic period united behind or even identified with a single method of exegesis, and the direct expression of hostility toward or rejection of the midrashic techniques of one's colleagues was not perceived to be rebellious or heretical. In the course of time, some more extreme methods of non-contextual exegesis fell from favor generally and were limited or dropped. Yet because these methods had produced much of rabbinic tradition and were the *modus operandi* of earlier rabbinic luminaries, they were closely identified with the rabbinic movement and its authority. Consequently, and paradoxically, we see in the Babylonian Talmud a deep ambivalence. On the one hand, many texts in the Babli extol the exegetical virtuosity of earlier midrashic masters

---

[87]   Richard Kalmin, *Sages, Stories, Authors and Editors in Rabbinic Babylonia* (BJS 300: Atlanta: Scholars Press, 1994). In this important book, Kalmin argues forcefully and persuasively that "the Talmud preserves identifiable sources which were not fully homogenized by late editors, and contains usable historical information regarding the centuries prior to its final editing" (p. xiii). The sources that comprise the Babli can be identified "by appeal to internal contradictions and shifts of perception and terminology within the Babli, and by comparison with the Yerushalmi" (p. 143).

[88]   Or, more precisely, between more contextual and less contextual exegesis. Again, that this distinction is not consistent, that it varies from text to text and rabbi to rabbi, and that it might not correspond to our own distinction is beside the point.

and so give the appearance of united support for and celebration of non-contextual methods of exegesis. On the other hand, not only are some of the extreme methods of non-contextual exegesis no longer employed, but also residual common sense objections to midrashic methods continue to be expressed—but now either anonymously or indirectly. The anonymous and indirect expression of these objections suggests that their direct expression in this later period was perceived to be disrespectful, rebellious, perhaps even heretical. (Indeed heretics are often the mouthpieces for such views.)

The preceding analysis demonstrates that discomfort with, resistance to and anxiety over non-contextual exegesis is not a post-talmudic phenomenon only, but a thoroughly talmudic one. Further, just as the need to come to terms with rabbinic exegesis was a major cultural stimulus for the post-talmudic Jew, so was it a major cultural stimulus for the talmudic rabbis whose struggle with the midrashic heritage bequeathed them by the *tannāʾîm* issued in important articulations and celebrations of rabbinic exegetical authority.

INDEX

R. Abba 165
R. Abba bar Kahana 243
R. Abbahu 158–59, 165, 167–70
Abbaye 256, 269
Abraham 28, 152
Abrasax 15
Achilles 39, 43
Aelia Capitolina, see: Jerusalem
agora 167
agoranomos 223
Agrigento 205
Aharon b. Zohar 170
Ahinoam Cave Cemetery 87–88, 90,
    92–93, 95, 99–100, 102, 106,
    110–13
Aleppo 123
Alexander the Great 34
Alexandria 42, 52, 74, 203
al-Kindi 48
ambōn 76
Ambrose 161
ᶜammê hā-ᵓāreṣ 187
ᵓamôrāᵓîm 243, 280, 286–87
amphitheater 168
amulets 15, 54, 104, 172
Anastasius 59–60, 65–66
angels 10–11, 16, 149
Antioch 149, 231
Antoninus 37, 39
Apamea 31–32, 35
Aphek-Antipatris 102
Aphrodisias 205
Aphrodite 18
ᵓapîqôrsîm 281
Apollonius of Tyana 37
apostles 27

apse 78
R. Aqiba 146, 270, 273–74, 277–78,
    283–85
aqueduct 177
Arabia 46, 125, 133, 137–38, 141–42,
    198–200, 206
Arabs 19, 28, 47, 177
Aramaic 92
Arava 46
Arcadius 203
arcosolium, see: Cemetery
Arians 22, 209
Ark of the Covenant 82
Armenians 62
Arsenius 65–66
Artemidorus 217
Artemis 207–8, 214
Ashkelon 44, 68
Ashkenaz 82
Aste 166
Athens 37, 205
Atil 208
Augustus 162
Aurelian 35
Avdat 46
Avi-Yonah, Michael 33–35, 63, 68,
    160, 173

Baalbek 216
Baba Rabba 62
Babatha daughter of Simon 133–43,
    145, 147, 150–51
Babatha Archive 115, 133, 142, 147
Babylonian Talmud (Babli) 5, 76, 249,
    257, 279–81, 287–88
Bakhtin, Mikhail 263, 275